Matthew Wong | Vincent van Gogh
Painting as a Last Resort

Matthew Vincent

Painting

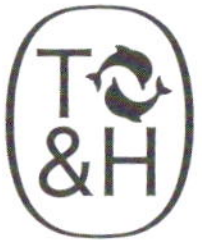

Wong van Gogh as a Last Resort

Edited by
Joost van der Hoeven

With contributions by
Kenny Schachter
Richard Shiff
Sofia Silva
John Yau

Van Gogh Museum, Amsterdam

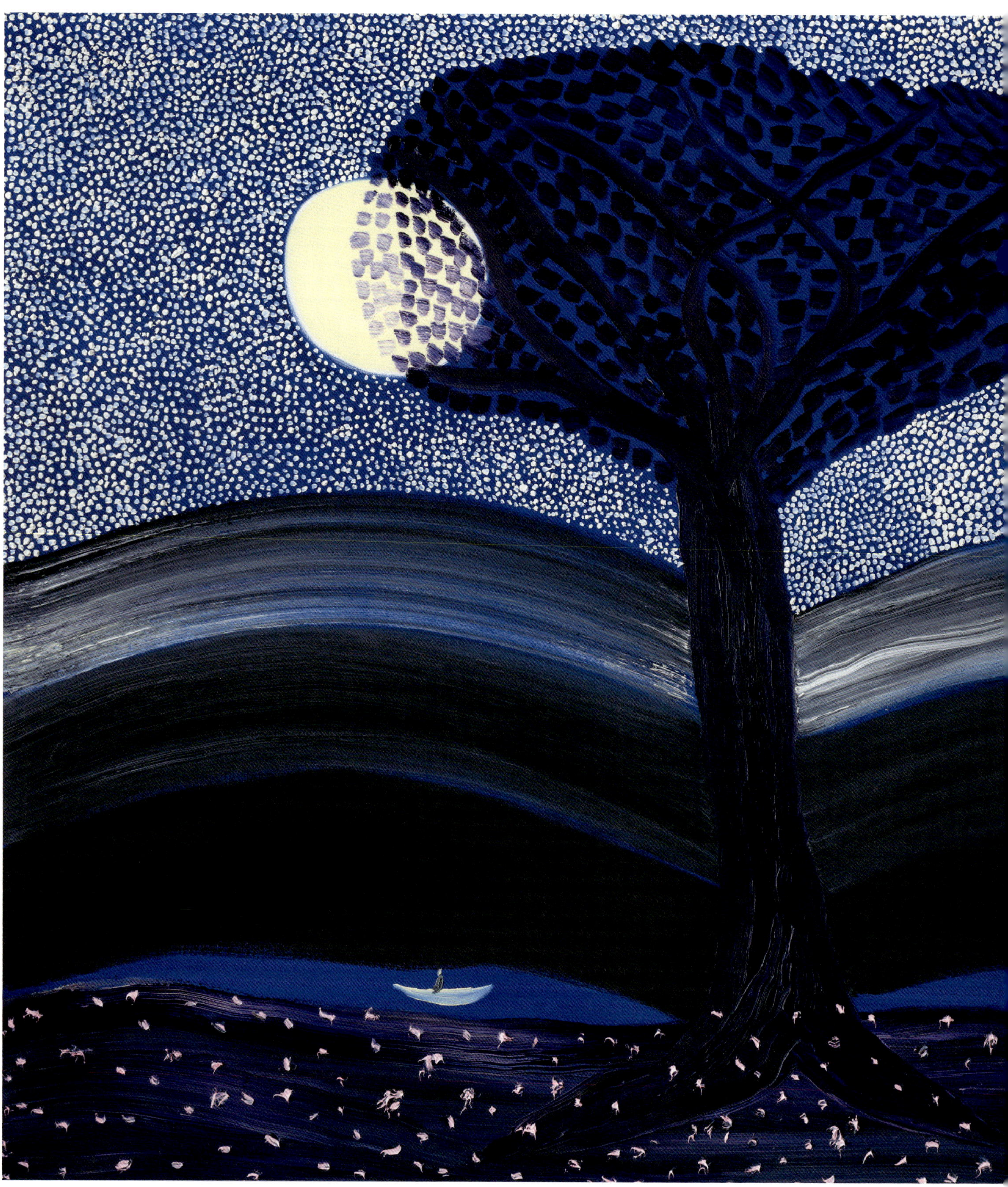

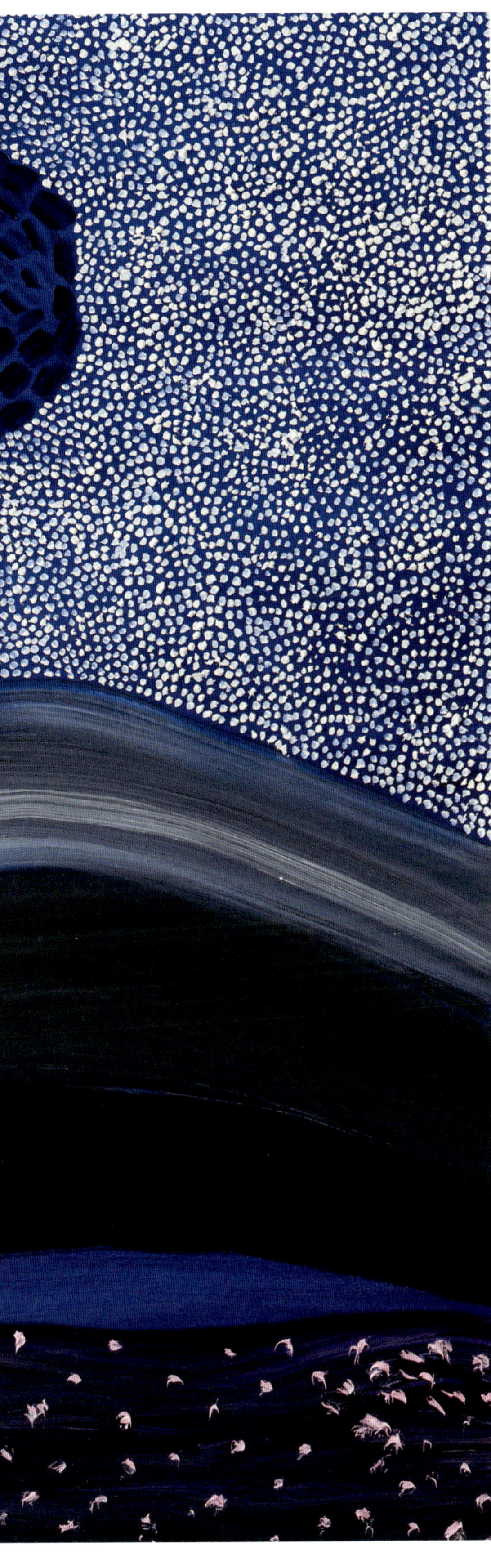

Contents

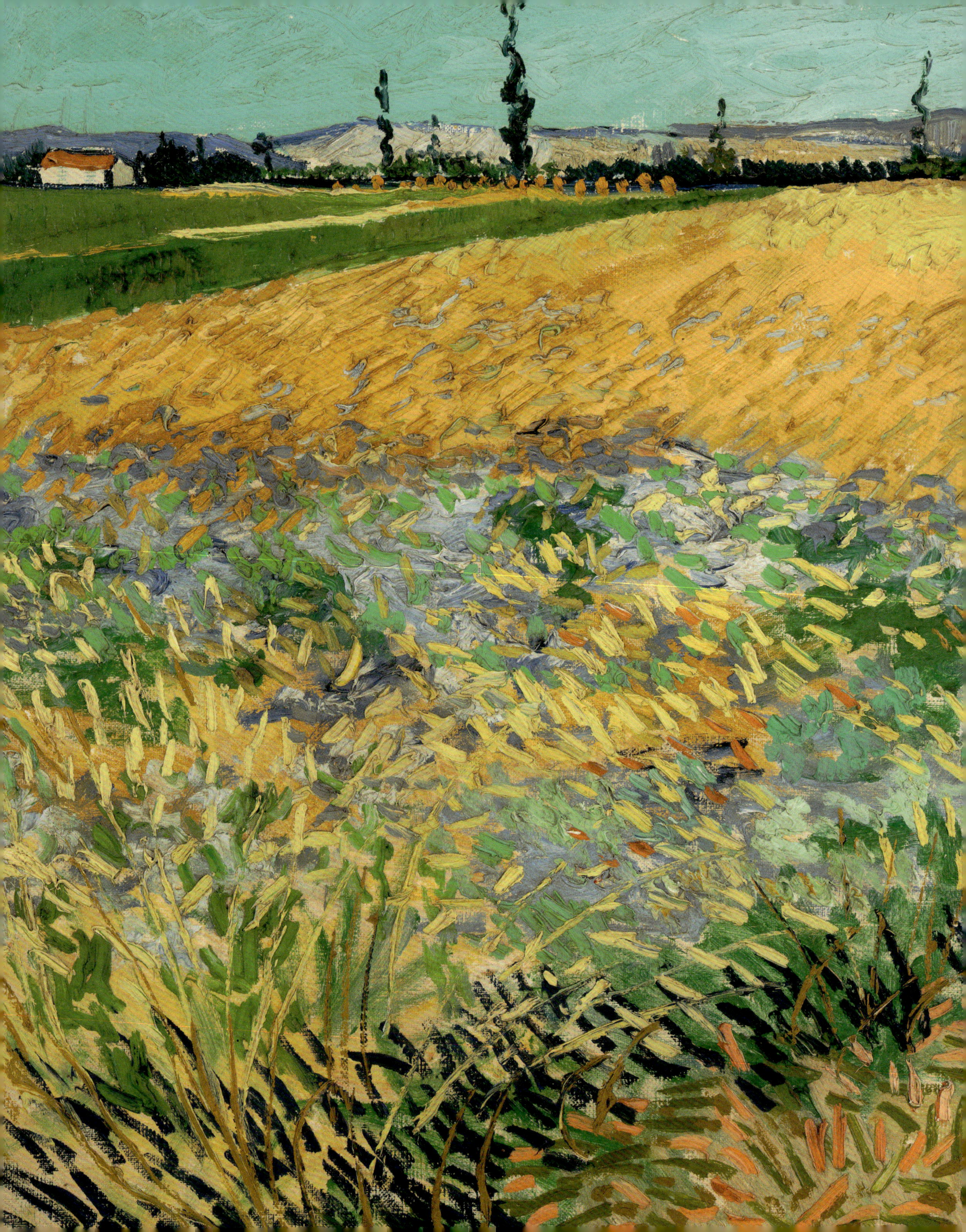

Foreword

Inspiration is at the core of so much of what we do at the Van Gogh Museum. The way we present our permanent collection underscores how Van Gogh was inspired by his predecessors and contemporaries, while our temporary exhibitions of modern and contemporary art demonstrate how he in turn inspired artists who came after him. Van Gogh remains an inexhaustible source for many, often very different artists right up to the present day. Bringing their work together with his sparks a dialogue in which entirely new ways of seeing are made possible. The museum has created two such dialogues in recent years, with ambitious exhibitions about David Hockney (2019) and Etel Adnan (2022).

For our latest contemporary art exhibition, we turn our attention to Matthew Wong (1984–2019), a Chinese-Canadian artist who achieved a luminous and impressive body of paintings in the space of just eight years. A self-taught painter and draughtsman, Wong soaked up an astonishing amount of art history in that short period, in order to discover for himself where he fitted into 'the greater dialogue between artists throughout time'. In doing so, he looked to both Euro-American and Chinese art history, with Henri Matisse, Shitao, Gustav Klimt, Yayoi Kusama, Alex Katz and Vincent van Gogh among his most important examples. He drew on them to create imaginary landscapes and interiors, which contain many stylistic references to art history, yet which remain extraordinarily personal and original. Wong's paintings are emotionally charged: both his painting style and the subjects he depicted are a reflection of his inner world.

The present exhibition and this accompanying publication were prompted by the fact that Vincent van Gogh was a major inspiration for Wong. They focus on the artistic and the personal connections between the two artists, without wishing in any way to imply that Wong was beholden to Van Gogh alone: his interests were very wide, and the Dutch painter was only one of them. Yet Van Gogh is unmistakably present in Wong's expressive use of colour and painting style. The direct, unfiltered way in which Wong communicated his state of mind through his work is found virtually nowhere else than in Van Gogh. There are also several

Vincent van Gogh, *Wheatfield*, 1888
(detail of fig. 51)

striking parallels between their lives. Wong saw a soulmate in Van Gogh, even though he lived 130 years earlier. They both immersed themselves in painting after a long quest for a mission in life – for Wong, it was even his 'last resort'. Each struggled with mental health issues – a struggle that ended in both cases in a tragic, premature death.

The wide variety of art-historical references that typify Wong's work reflect the unlimited access a twenty-first-century artist has to the internet and social media. Wherever and whenever he happened to be working, he always had centuries of art at his fingertips through his phone. In that respect, his work is truly contemporary. At the same time, however, he employed long-established methods such as oil on canvas or ink on rice paper to give shape to that work. In this way, Wong connected today's digital world with traditional art history and demonstrated that great historical examples like Van Gogh are still relevant.

This exhibition – the first survey of Wong's work to be presented in Europe – is the brainchild of researcher Joost van der Hoeven. As the curator of the exhibition and editor of this catalogue, he creates a nuanced picture of Matthew Wong's life and work and his connection with Van Gogh. Joost invited a diverse group of authors to write about Matthew Wong's art based on their wide-ranging expertise, with this rich and varied catalogue as the result. It begins with a heartfelt note by the artist, curator and critic Kenny Schachter, who knew Wong personally. This is followed by a comprehensive introduction by Joost himself, which describes Wong's artistic practice from its beginning to its end, and is shot through with an account of his creative dialogue with Van Gogh. In his inventive and intriguing essay, Professor Richard Shiff examines how typically nineteenth-century concepts such as melancholy and paradox resonate in Wong's work. The poet and art critic John Yau offers a trenchant and poignant essay on Wong's ink drawings. The publication is rounded off by an interview with the artist and essayist Sofia Silva, who presents an illuminating vision of his work through her extensive Facebook correspondence with the artist. I am deeply grateful to Joost and his fellow authors for their contributions to this magnificent catalogue.

Neither the exhibition nor this publication would have been possible without the extraordinarily generous and unwavering help of Monita and Raymond Wong, who work unceasingly at the Matthew Wong Foundation to preserve their son's artistic legacy. Their knowledge, advice, loans and financial support were indispensable at every phase of this project, for which we are exceptionally grateful. Our thanks are also due to Winnie Ip, Brian Wong and Elizabeth Donnelly of the Matthew Wong Foundation, who assisted us with great dedication. John Cheim, another driving force behind this project, supported Monita and Raymond in various ways. The team at Cheim & Read – Maria Bueno, Sara Hutchins and Howard Read – has been invaluable, for which we are indebted.

Besides this crucial support, the research underpinning the project relied substantially on the knowledge of the close-knit community of friends and acquaintances that Matthew Wong left behind. Joost spoke to many of them while preparing this publication. They took the time to share their stories, for which we are extremely grateful, particularly to Peter Shear, Sofia Silva, Brendan Dugan, Benjamin Styer, Fedor Deichmann, Jonas Wood, Nicole Wittenberg, Kenny Schachter, Jerry Saltz and Ludovica Barbieri. We are likewise beholden to the many lenders who shared their works with us. We would, as ever, like to express our gratitude to the Vincent van Gogh Foundation, which made available six outstanding works by Van Gogh, and once again to Monita and Raymond Wong, who contributed around half of the works by Matthew Wong in the exhibition.

Finally, I would like to thank our donors, who made this beautiful and valuable project possible. Our principal partners are the Ministry of Education, Culture and Science, the VriendenLoterij, ASML and DHL, to whom we are especially grateful for their generous contributions to this exhibition project. Thanks also to our exhibition partners Fonds 21, Van Lanschot Kempen and the Sunflower Circle, and to Alfred and Ellen Abraham and the Green Family Art Foundation, for whose generous contributions we are especially appreciative.

I am delighted that this exhibition will run at the Van Gogh Museum in Amsterdam for the exceptionally long period of six months and that it will also travel to the Kunsthaus Zürich. It is my hope that the exhibition and publication will underscore that art history is a huge, unceasing exchange of inspiration, in which artists like Matthew Wong keep the work of great figures such as Vincent van Gogh alive and relevant.

Emilie E.S. Gordenker
Director of the Van Gogh Museum

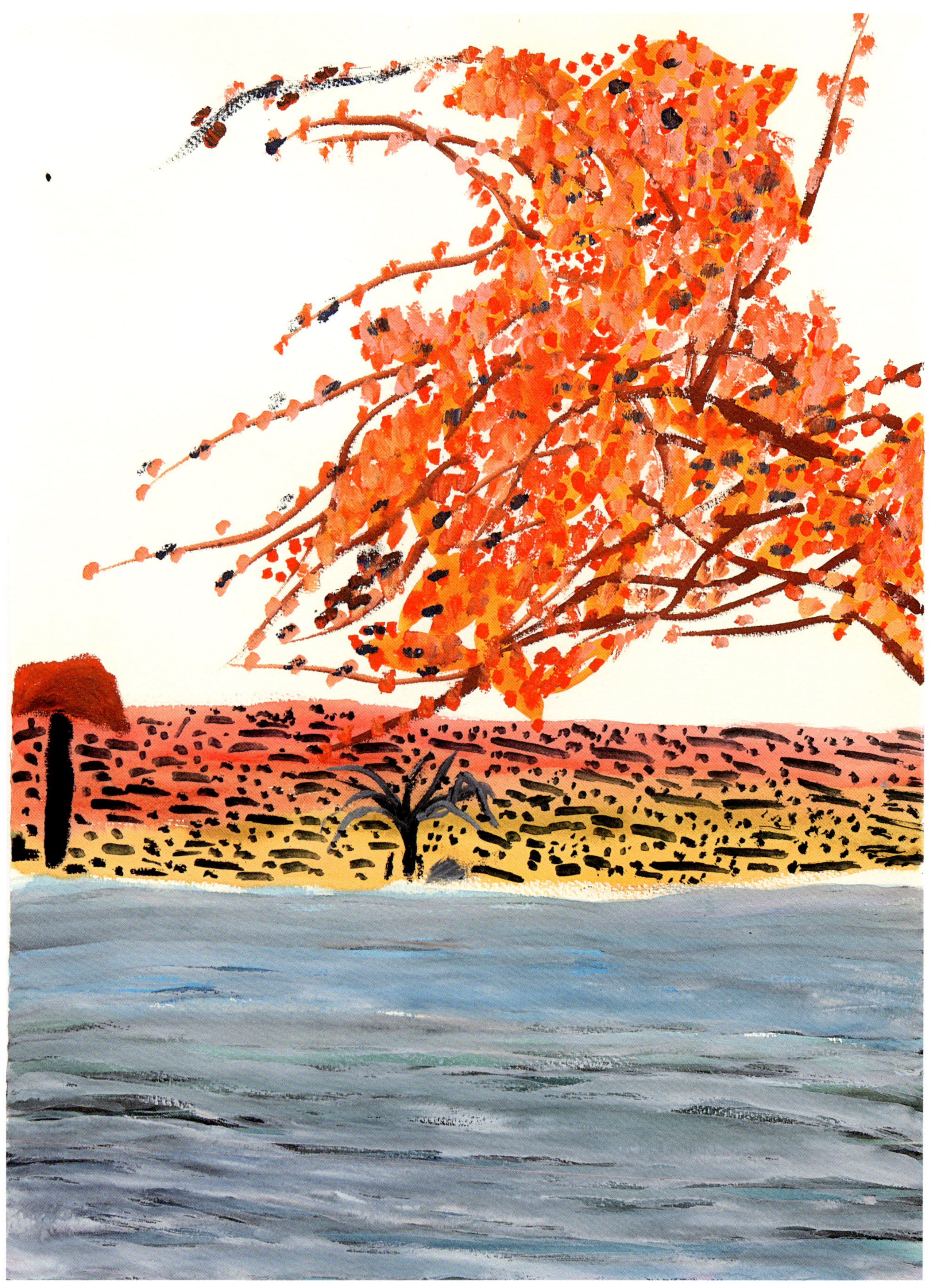

Lenders to the Exhibition

The directors and exhibition curators are extremely grateful to all museums, collectors and the anonymous lenders for their generous loans:

Josh Abraham
Brooker-Pardee Family Collection
John Cheim
Cheim & Read
Lisa and Michael Cotton
Nancy and Sean Cotton
Dallas Museum of Art
Brendan Dugan
THE EKARD COLLECTION
Green Family Art Foundation
HomeArt
Liz Lange and David Shapiro
Level & Co
Matthew Wong Foundation
The Metropolitan Museum of Art
Phillip Meyer and Xing Yu Toh
The Museum of Modern Art
Private European Collection
Cindy and Armond Schwartz
Judith and Danny Tobey
Vincent van Gogh Foundation
Wilfram AG, St. Moritz

1 / Matthew Wong, *White Sea, White Sky*, 2016
Gouache on paper, 76.2 × 55.9 cm
Private collection

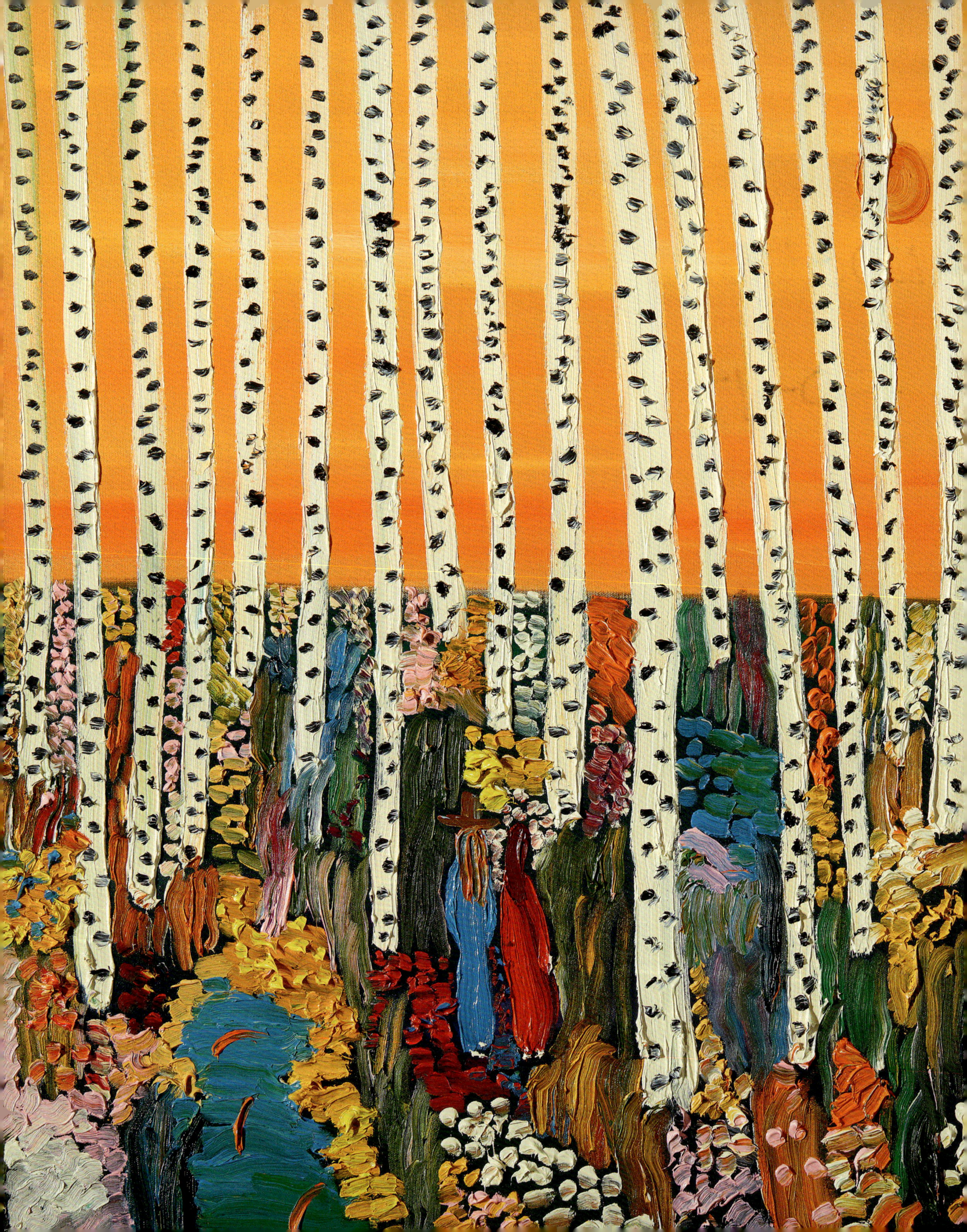

Kenny Schachter

A Finger in a Nerve
A Personal Note

Life affects people in different manners with differing degrees of ferocity. How we physically navigate our way in the world, carving individual paths through the muddle, also bears on our sensitivities and sensibilities. Pursuits take shape, some impacted by circumstances (both innate and outside our control) while others are volitionally moulded by sheer will. Matthew Wong's art life was the reflection of an agitated, obsessive curiosity that could never be sated, leaving him exposed, yet stridently in command. For Matthew – and Vincent van Gogh, with whom he is paired in this exhibition – the vibration of colour was felt (and expressed) like a finger poked into a stripped nerve.

Art is creative destruction that entails taking what's been done before, historically, and putting it through a blender to re-contextualize and recast it. Artists are not acquiescent witnesses merely mirroring the world around us, though they do that too, but critics of society and technology. Van Gogh did not solely paint sensuous sunflowers and sunsets; he simultaneously signified aspects of poverty, working-class subjugation and social issues – from the plight of peasants to conditions of prisoners. Matthew's post-mortems were introverted: confronting, prodding and mapping states of psychological actuality.

Imbued with a sense of desolation, cloaked in disaffection, you can taste the solitude in the making of Wong's paintings; still, Matthew had a light-hearted, animated social presence. Aside from the appearances of a formal language steeped in traditional drawing and painting, social media played a key role in his process, contributing to his education, development and overall mindset. I wouldn't say Wong was self-taught

Matthew Wong, *Dialogue*, 2018
(detail of fig. 37)

as a painter – he studied cultural anthropology and photography at university – but rather gleaned his applied skillset scraping knowledge and techniques from the people he admired and accessed via Facebook and Instagram. I was lucky enough to be one of them. Speaking to Matthew, you could grasp his restlessness and impatience, while he was also sponge-like, foraging for information he could suck up and harness for his own undertakings.

Matthew would go in and out of periods actively engaging with his network of contacts online, then withdrawing like a turtle in its shell. He would contact me and express concern as to whether his profile should be forward facing or inward, whether to expand or contract from the participatory nature of what is nothing less than a contact sport. Towards the end of his life, he fixated on posting disparate pairings of artists, comparing and contrasting their works like a DJ spinning staccato song fragments. Often the connections would be indecipherable, other than to Matthew himself. Conversely, they were fascinating and elucidating, providing insight into the way his mind functioned like an atom smasher, and would have made for a riveting book.

Paintings, such as *Landscape with Mother and Child* (fig. 95), *A Walk Through Primordial Garden* (fig. 40) and *Dialogue* (fig. 37) are fervidly redolent of lust and passion. You all but expect to hear an accompanying soundtrack blaring in their wake. The works are cinematically epic like mini narratives or short stories, but don't expect closure by way of a happy ending; simultaneously, you are left with incongruous sensations of elation and hope while feeling alone and lonely. In *Coming of Age Landscape* (fig. 66), *Somewhere* (fig. 126) and *Good Morning* (fig. 96), all dating from 2018, the palettes are pared down to no more than a handful of colours while managing to convey the spectrum of a rainbow. Wong was adept at manipulating paint and emotion with equal acuity.

While Van Gogh and Wong regularly couched their paintings in the genre of landscape, these are anything but prosaic backdrops for mere topographies. What you see are twitchy, voluminal swirls of treacly swathes of pigment, as sculptural as they are painterly. They are invitations to climb physically into the compositions and get lost – once adrift, perhaps we'd experience something akin to the stoic impassiveness seemingly felt by both artists. Remote characters trapped in grim circumstances, as featured in the writings of Samuel Beckett, come to mind rather than the works of other visual artists. You could try and search for narratives, but Wong's meanings are largely hermetic and unknowable – they pull you in while purposely keeping you at arm's length.

Matthew was cool in his appearance – his personal style expressed via emerging designers held deep interest – and calm in his seeming level-headedness. He couldn't be swayed by trends in art or fashion. There was never the impression of any internal torment or unrest other than as represented in the works. Like Matthew, my 21-year-old son Kai, a personable, talented artist in his own right (we all spent considerable time together), also took his life, never for an instant betraying his inner distresses or despondencies. To be with either was uplifting and fun in that they were effortlessly communicative all the while giving and inspiring. There were no clues as to their sufferings, which were clearly unendurable.

Matthew teased us with his tragically foreshortened life and works, advanced beyond the years of formation, leaving us discontented, wanting more. That so much, of such profundity, could have been painted so swiftly is mind-boggling. His beguiling, playful spirit, voracious in its capacity to absorb everything within (and without) his grasp, was also supportive and generous, considerate of others. It is futile to speculate on what might have been – undoubtedly staggering and magnificent. We are better served absorbing and contemplating what is before us: a fully-fledged body of work, adding to the canon something old and new, analogue and digital, steeped in history and ahistorical. Art is a means of self-expression and communication; with this writing and exhibition, Matthew Wong continues to do both. —

VINCENT

The waves of the sky are washing
The day off my boots. I study
My reflection in a tree, which sings
Back to me in a playful tone
The outline of a skull. All around
The shirts of children are laughing
And chasing each other's tails.
I smile. I ask a flower for her name
And she whispers ever so timidly,
"Blue." I follow a stranger's shadow
Through a long alleyway, and watch
With sorrow and longing as it goes
From red to green, to brown, to violet.
I look up at the sky and squint. The moon
Is the color of remembering.

Matthew Wong, 12 August 2015

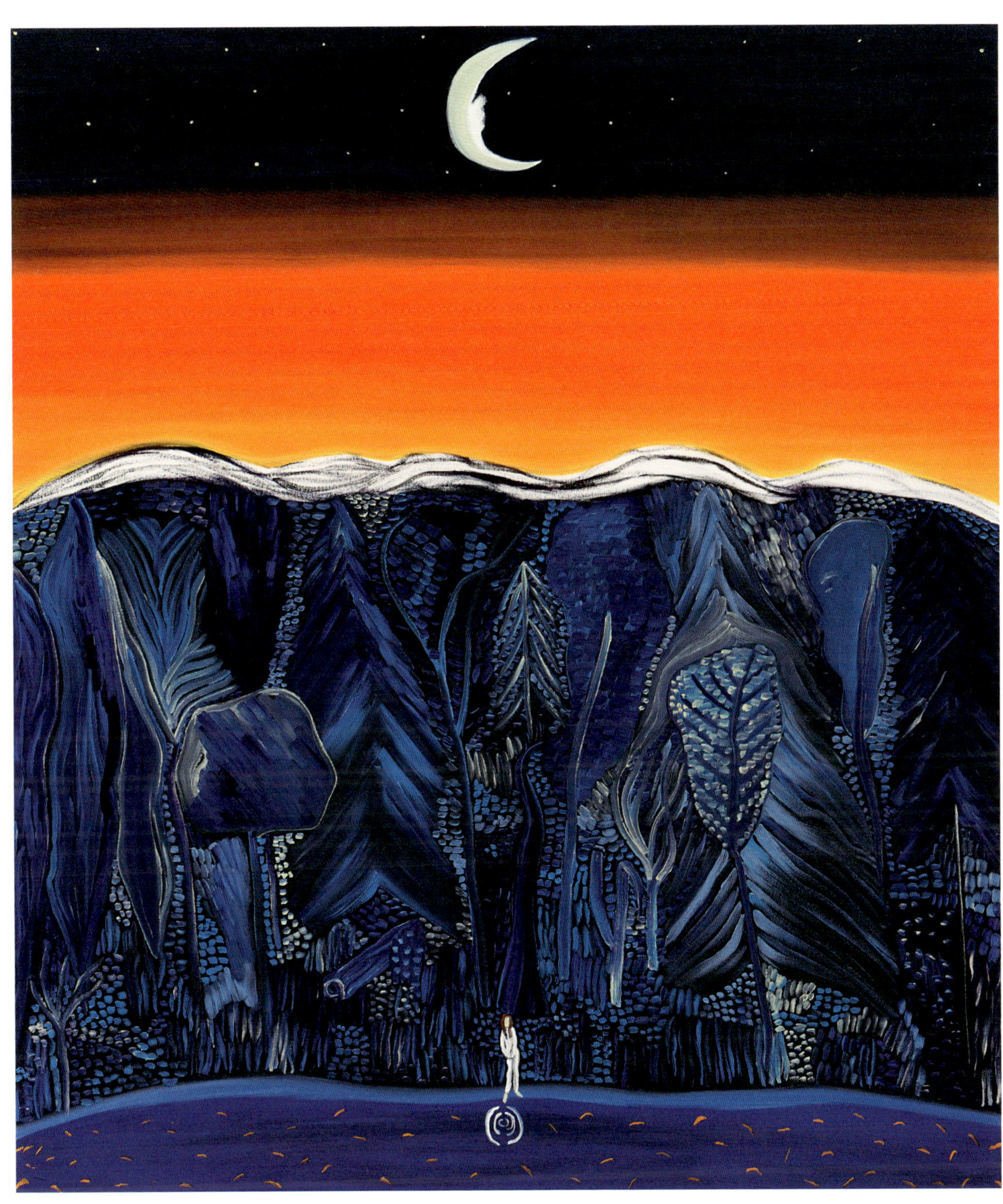

2 / Matthew Wong, *End of the Day*, 2019
Oil on canvas, 203.2 × 178.1 cm
Lent by the Metropolitan Museum of Art, New York.
Gift of Monita and Raymond Wong, in memory
of their son, Matthew Wong, 2023 (2023.235)

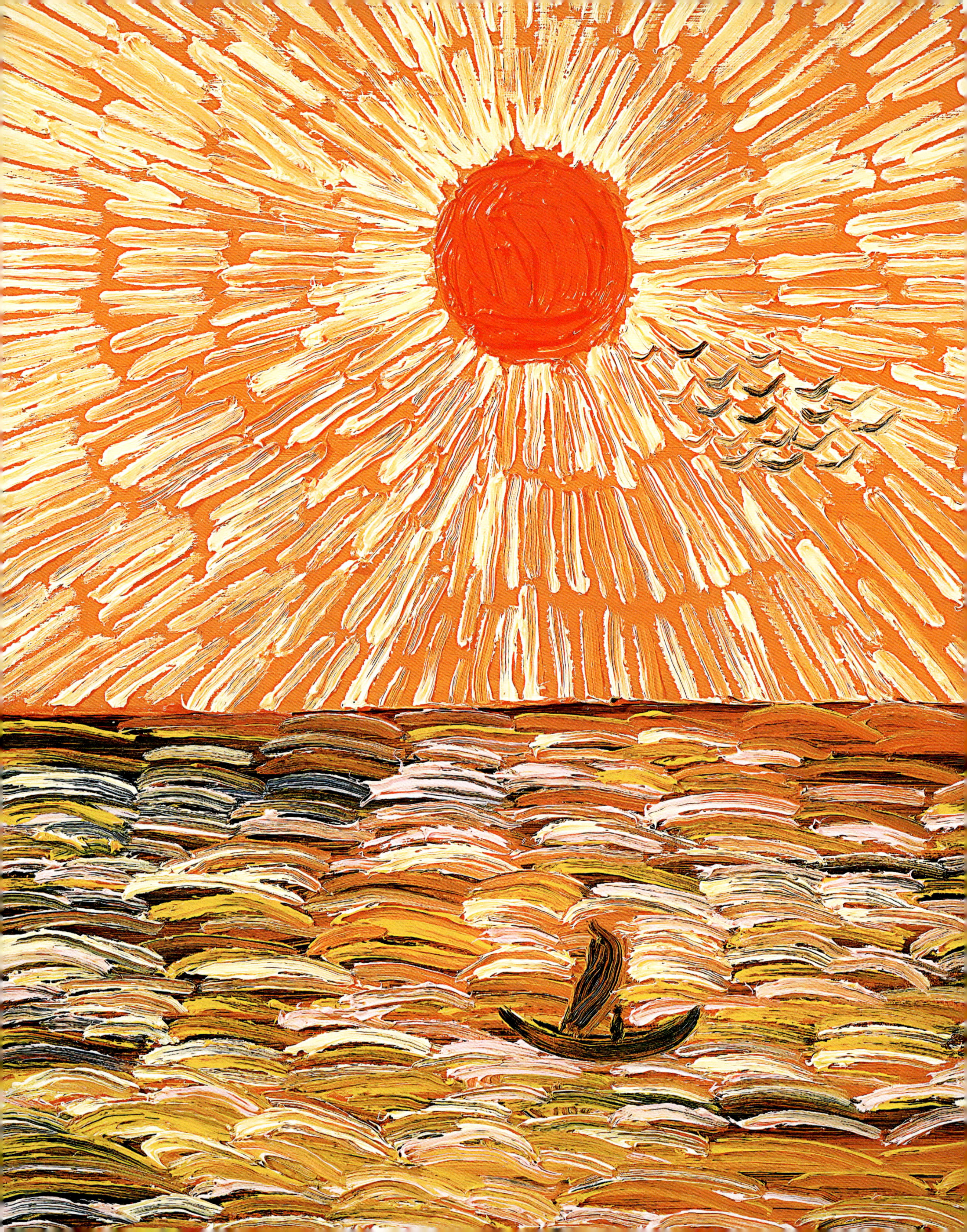

Joost van der Hoeven

Painting as a Last Resort
An Introduction

Matthew Wong, *The Journey Home*, 2017 (detail of fig. 5)

Matthew Wong (1984–2019) from Hong Kong was twenty-seven when, in November 2011, he found himself in the ballroom of the Museo Correr in Venice, surrounded by three giant canvases by the American artist and film-maker Julian Schnabel (fig. 3). The works had been installed there as part of Schnabel's *Permanently Becoming and the Architecture of Seeing* exhibition. Wong was a photography student at the time, interning at the Hong Kong pavilion for the Biennale, and he spent his spare moments exploring the art on display in the Italian city.[1] Schnabel's canvases were only partially painted, but the dynamism and movement with which he applied his paint made the compositions compelling and almost violent. The combination of pure expression and immense scale triggered something fundamental in Wong, who never imagined that paint on canvas could have such an impact. This feeling was further intensified by a visit to the exhibition of Christopher Wool, another American artist, who was showing a series of eight large abstract ink stains on canvas in the Biennale's Central Pavilion (fig. 4).[2] Just as Schnabel's work had done, these powerful abstract canvases awakened the visual artist in Wong.

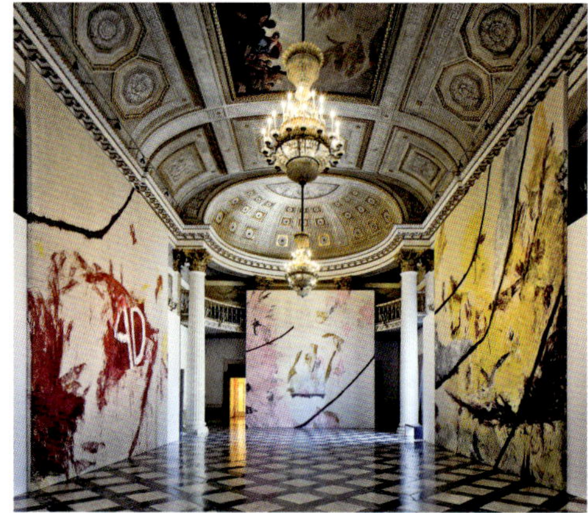

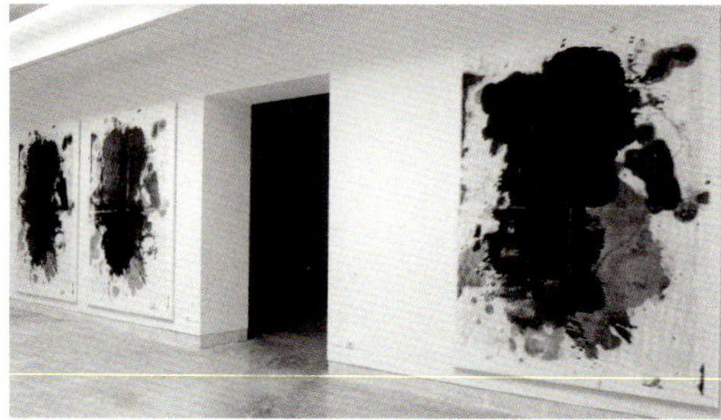

3 / Julian Schnabel's *Anno Domini, El Espontaneo (for Abelardo Martinez)* and *Catherine Marie Ange*, Museo Correr, Venice, 2011

4 / ILLUMInations by Christopher Wool at the Venice Biennale, 2011

Almost immediately after these experiences, he bought a sketchbook, charcoal and ink, and began to experiment with drawing.[3] Shortly after that he also produced his first compositions with acrylics, spray paint and Tipp-Ex.[4] This was a radically new direction for Wong, who had been working on his master's in photography at the City University of Hong Kong since 2010. His approach to photography – not without merit – was to create quick snapshots of intuitively selected moments in Hong Kong's urban life (fig. 14).[5] Having seen the work of Schnabel and Wool, however, his attraction to photography waned. Not long after graduating in 2012, he already viewed himself primarily as a draughtsman and painter rather than a photographer.

Painting to Wong was yet another new direction in what had been a prolonged quest for purpose and recognition. Before studying photography, he had obtained a bachelor's degree in cultural anthropology at the University of Michigan and held several traineeships and jobs at organizations ranging from PricewaterhouseCoopers to the Asia Art Archive in Hong Kong. However, he never stuck it out with an employer for more than a few months, as his precarious mental health invariably caused him to stumble.[6] Wong suffered from severe depression, anxiety and Tourette's syndrome, and was also diagnosed with autism in 2017. His life was scarred by his condition: he was bullied at school and found social interactions challenging. Because of his depression he had to 'live with the devil every day'.[7]

When photography likewise came to nothing, he decided 'to turn to painting as a last resort with no prior skill or experience'.[8] He fervently hoped that this new vocation would give a clear direction to his life and bring him the recognition he longed for. Wong made his art primarily for himself, but following a lifetime of rejection, he did everything he could to make this last resort a success.[9]

That success came with improbable speed. By 2017, barely six years after his epiphany in Venice, he was being represented by the New York gallery Karma, while his work was sold at major events including the Dallas Art Fair and Frieze New York. His first solo exhibition at Karma followed in 2018, drawing rave reviews from leading New York art critics such as John Yau and Jerry Saltz.[10] The latter called it 'one of the most impressive solo New York debuts I've seen in a while'.[11] In *The New York Times*, Roberta Smith declared him to be 'one of the most talented painters of his generation'.[12] Wong's work was bought by major private collectors and the Dallas Museum of Art acquired one of his paintings.[13]

The works that were received with such admiration were the result of a unique combination of talent and vision, immense drive and dedication, an insatiable interest in art history, and a willingness to give every last ounce of himself. Wong swiftly became known for his imaginary, mystical landscapes, which he brought to the canvas with a huge sense of colour and a great deal of impasto. The unabashed beauty of his paintings made them accessible and appealing to everyone, yet at the same time, his scenes possess a sense of depth and melancholy. In spite of his success, Wong took his own life in 2019, eight years after making his first drawing.

On the shoulders of giants

Matthew Wong was born in Toronto in 1984 and moved frequently between Hong Kong and Canada in the course of his life. His parents came from China and held senior positions in the Chinese and Hong Kong textile industries, but they chose to spend substantial parts of Wong's childhood in Canada because of its excellent health care and education. Wong's mother knew the country, having studied there, and made a point of travelling to Canada to give birth to what would be her only child. Numerous long-distance changes of home meant that the young Matthew frequently had to contend with entirely new physical and cultural environments. This weakened his bond with specific locations, while making that with his parents – his mother especially – all the stronger. Not long after he began to paint, she devoted her life entirely to her son's artistic practice. Work commitments regularly kept Wong's father away from home for long periods, but he too continued to be involved in his son's ventures. Aside from a short period during his years as a student in Michigan, Matthew would live with his parents for the whole of his life.[14]

Wong's bicultural upbringing meant that as an artist he felt an affinity with both the European-American and Chinese art traditions. Self-taught as a painter, he drew inspiration from a great many artists from across the centuries and made no secret of his influences. In addition to Schnabel and Wool, they included (in no particular order) Willem de Kooning, Henri Matisse, Shitao, Milton Resnick, Zhu Jinshi, Joan Mitchell, Gustav Klimt, Wu Guanzhong, Brenda Goodman, Edvard Munch, Peter Doig, Lois Dodd, Alex Katz, Katherine Bradford, Jonas Wood, Scott Kahn, Yayoi Kusama, Bada Shanren, David Milne and Vincent van Gogh.[15] In the case of many of these artists, Wong spent short periods specifically exploring their work, whereas Van Gogh would be important to him from virtually the beginning until the end of his eight-year career.

Wong had already made personal mention of Van Gogh to his friends in 2013, and he shared his affinity publicly in 2015 when he posted one of his own paintings alongside a work by Van Gogh on his Facebook page.[16] In a 2018 interview, he cited the Dutch artist as one of his principal sources of inspiration.[17] The impact of Van Gogh on Wong's

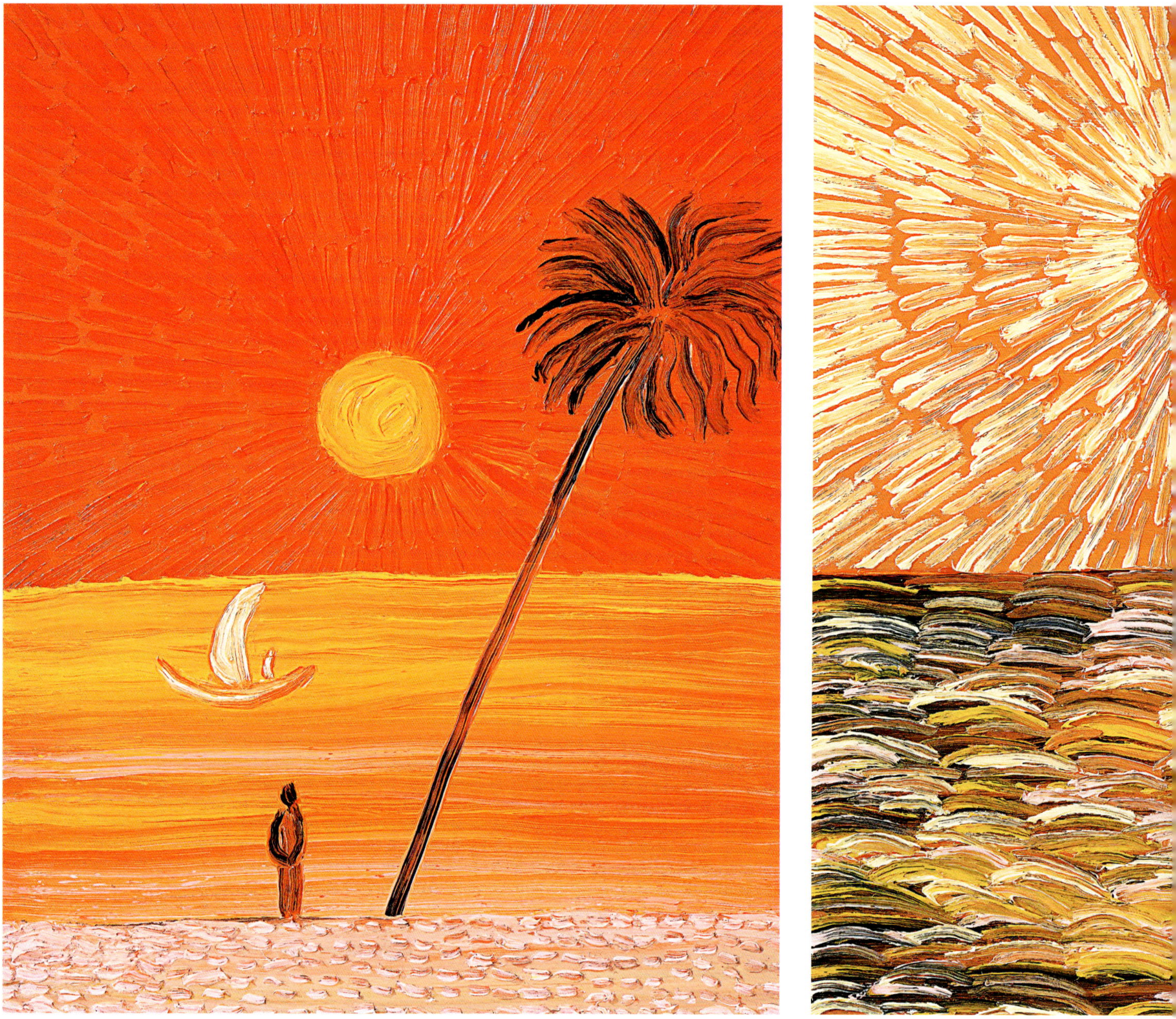

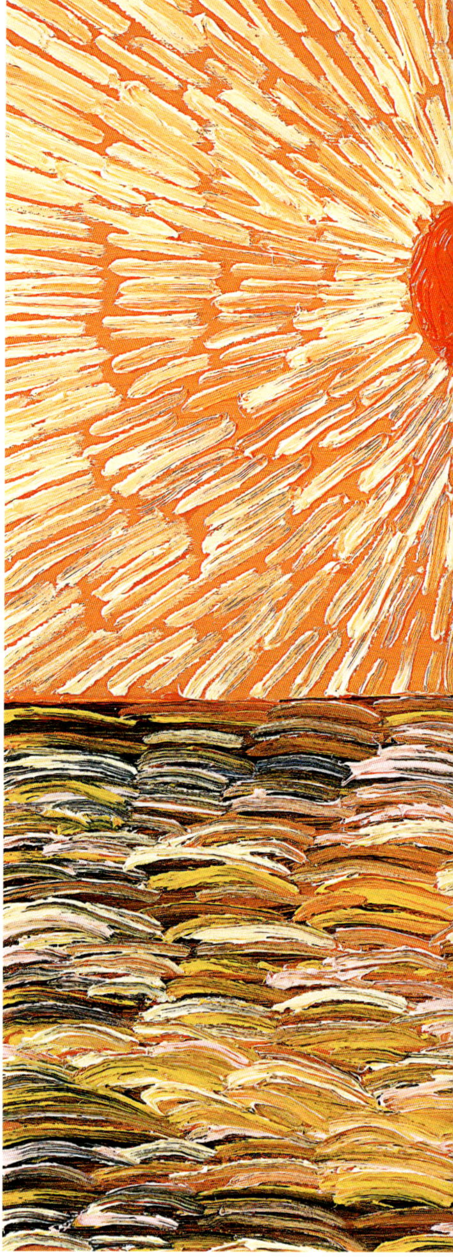

5 / Matthew Wong, *The Journey Home*, 2017
Oil on three panels, 50.5 × 40.5 cm
Private collection, courtesy of HomeArt

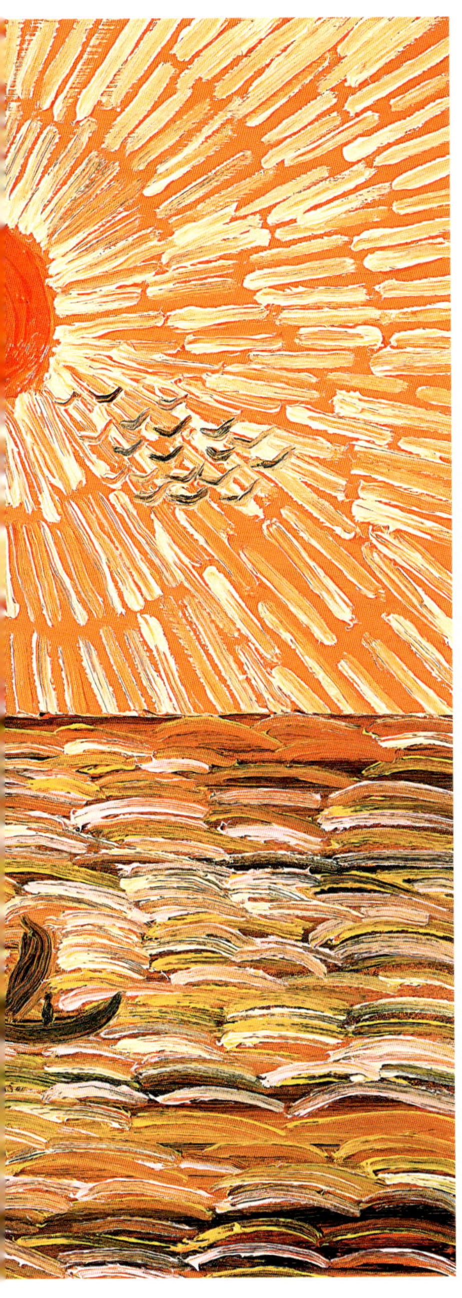

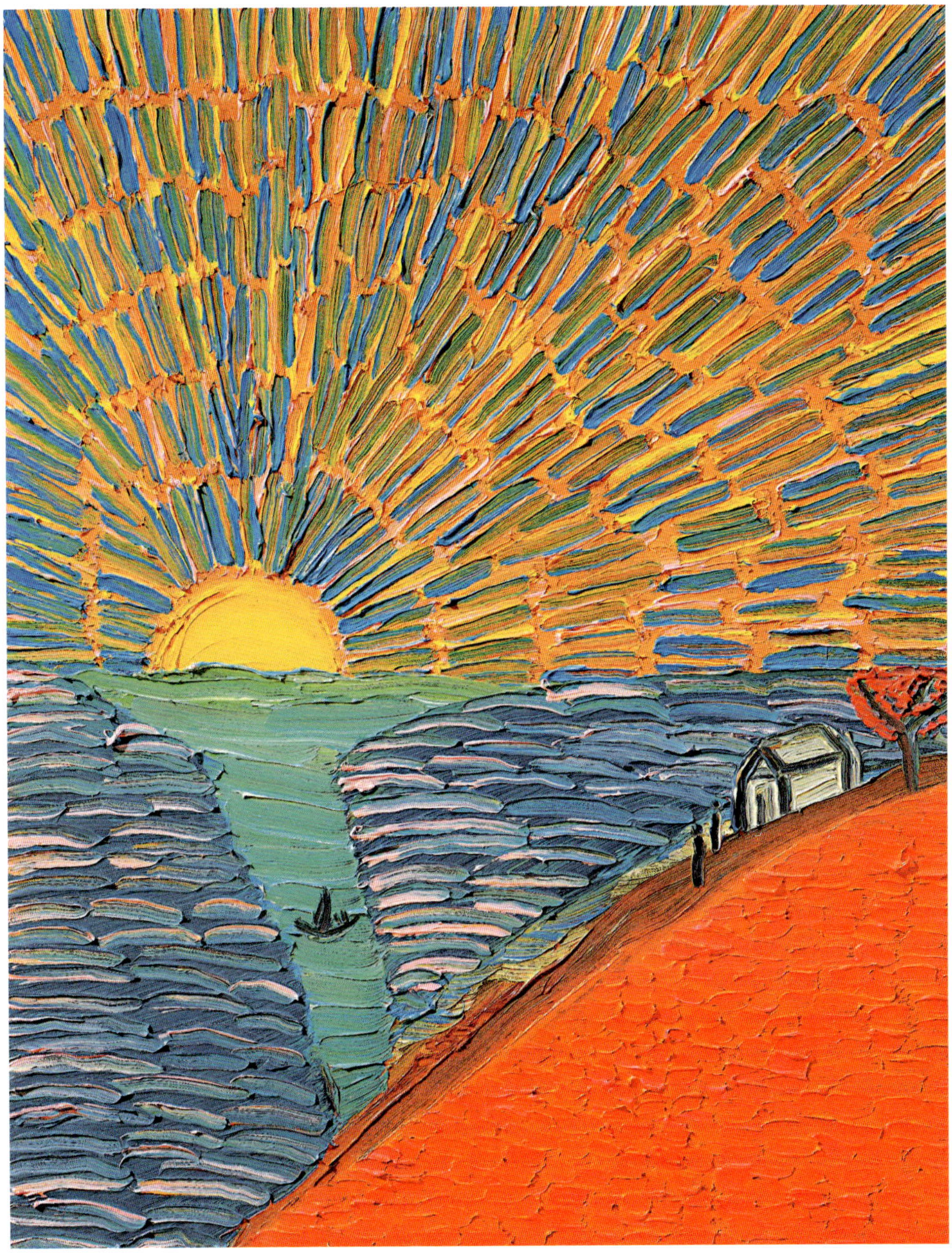

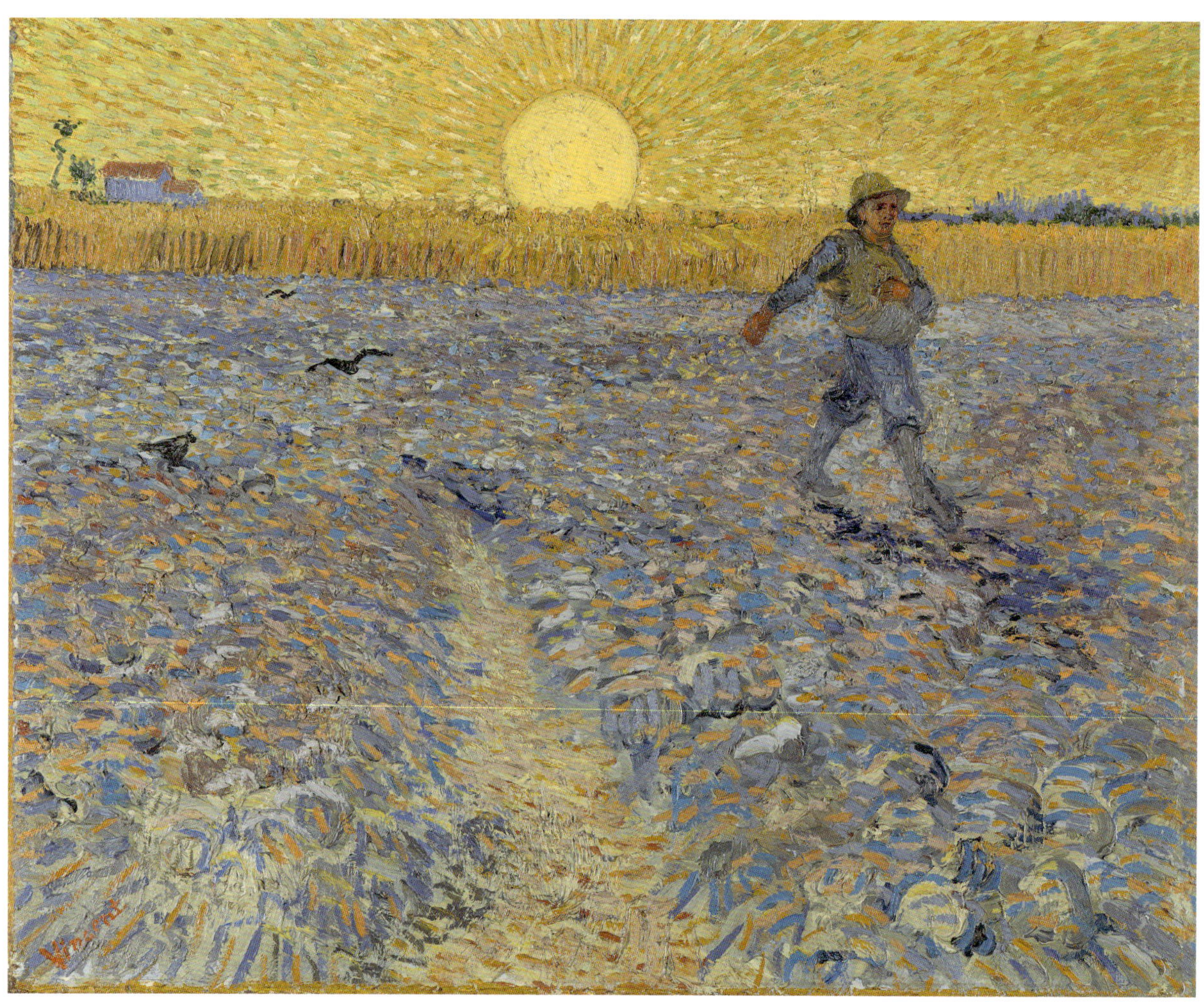

6 / Vincent van Gogh, *The Sower*, 1888
Oil on canvas, 64.2 × 80.3 cm
Kröller-Müller Museum, Otterlo

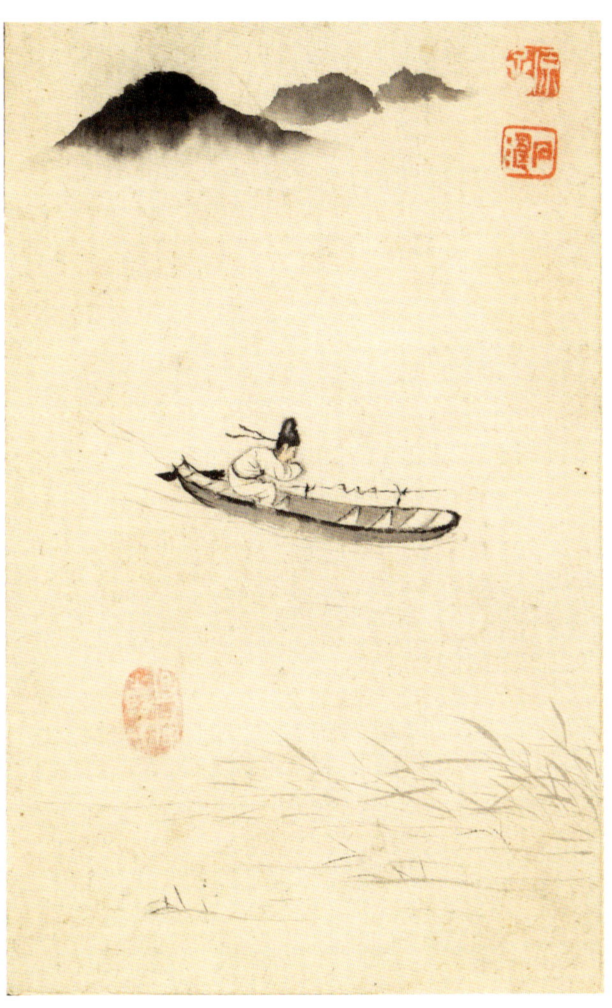

work is unmistakable, most notably in the expressive use of bright, unblended colours, impastoed paint surfaces and an emphasis on mark-making. It is easy to see in *The Journey Home* (fig. 5), for instance, how his approach to paint and colour, as well as his choice of motif, immediately evokes an association with Van Gogh. The way he painted the suns in the triptych using thick, radial beams, is especially reminiscent of how Van Gogh visualized them in *The Sower* (fig. 6). At the same time, the subject of a solitary figure in a small boat making its way home is borrowed from the Chinese Qing dynasty painter Shitao (1642–1707), as can be seen in the work *Returning Home* (fig. 7).

Wong's connection with Van Gogh went beyond the artistic: besides drawing on the Dutchman's work for inspiration, he identified with his life story. He stated in 2018 that: 'I see myself in him [Van Gogh]. The impossibility of belonging in this world.'[18] Despite his success, Wong's mental health and the tics associated with Tourette's caused him to struggle with the social aspects of life as an artist, making him feel excluded from the art world. This condition of being an outsider was reflected, he felt, in the story of Van Gogh, who had likewise struggled with his mental health. In 2019, shortly before the end of his life, Wong created three works as a homage to Van Gogh: *Untitled*, *The Space Between Trees* and *Starry Night* (figs. 9, 11 and 13), free variations on *Van Gogh's Chair*, *The Painter on the Road to Tarascon* and *Starry Night* respectively (figs. 8, 10 and 12).

It is not known to what extent Wong realized it, but there are many other striking parallels between him and Van Gogh besides 'the impossibility of belonging in this world'. Both taught themselves to paint, developed at an incredibly fast rate and created enormous bodies of work within a short space of time. Both were great admirers of the written word – as readers and writers alike – and wrote brilliantly. In the course of their careers, each of them moved to locations far away from the major centres of art, and found it difficult to cope with but also without the art world. They each struggled with their mental health, a struggle that would prove fatal to both of them. And both their painting careers, lastly, were preceded by a prolonged search for a purpose.

Like Wong, Van Gogh had made several unsuccessful attempts to make himself useful before resolving to become an artist. From the ages of sixteen to twenty-three, he was employed by the art dealers Goupil & Cie, where his conduct brought about several transfers

7 / Shitao, *Returning Home*, c. 1695
Ink and colour on paper, 21.1 × 13.5 cm
The Metropolitan Museum of Art, New York

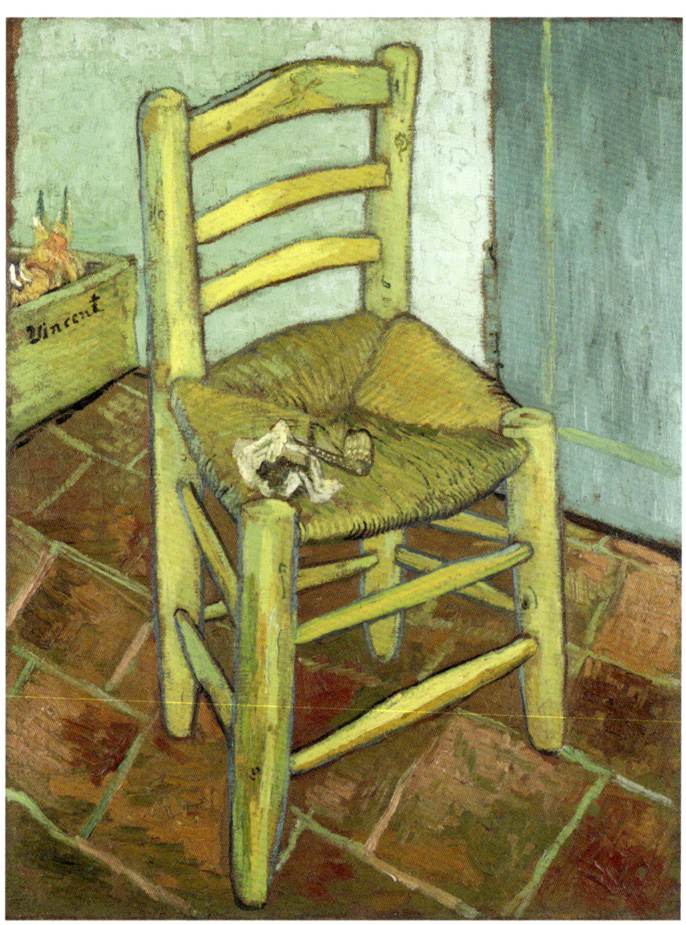

and ultimately his dismissal. This was followed by abortive attempts to become a teacher, a theology student and a preacher, which ended in an impasse. In Van Gogh's case, it was his brother Theo who, in the summer of 1880, advised him to try his hand as an artist. Vincent swiftly began to draw fanatically, writing to his brother: 'I couldn't tell you how happy I feel to have taken up drawing again. It had already been on my mind for a long time, but I always saw the thing as impossible and beyond my reach. But now, while feeling both my weakness and my painful dependence in respect of many things, I've recovered my peace of mind, and my energy is coming back day by day.'[19] He was twenty-seven at the time, the same age as Wong when he embarked on his artistic career.

It would be unfair to Wong's story to present it entirely in the shadow of Van Gogh, and that is certainly not what the present catalogue or exhibition intend. There are at least as many differences between the two artists as there are similarities: they were both highly distinctive individuals and they lived in different times and in different parts of the world. All the same, their artistic connections transcend the years that separate them. What was important to Van Gogh retained its validity for Wong in the twenty-first century, and so it is enlightening to take Van Gogh as our guide when delving deeper into the wondrous artistic journey that unfolded once Wong chose to paint. Since his trajectory was shaped by artists other than Van Gogh alone, several of Wong's other inspirations will also be discussed.

From photography to painting

Wong's experiences in Venice were followed by a period of roughly a year and a half, in which he took photographs, drew and painted. While these media differ fundamentally from one another, Wong approached everything in a similar way: 'All my creative work is improvisatory in approach. It's really about listening to your gut and going from there. I don't ever know what kind of photo I'll end up with on a given day or what a finished drawing would look like.'[20] His photography involved wandering the streets of Hong Kong without a specific purpose, 'in the manner of Baudelaire's flaneur'.[21] Along the way, he captured what subconsciously appealed to him. He often took the picture without even looking through his viewfinder, in a purely intuitive, chance process

8 / Vincent van Gogh, *Van Gogh's Chair*, 1888
Oil on canvas, 91.8 × 73 cm
The National Gallery, London.
Bought, Courtauld Fund, 1924

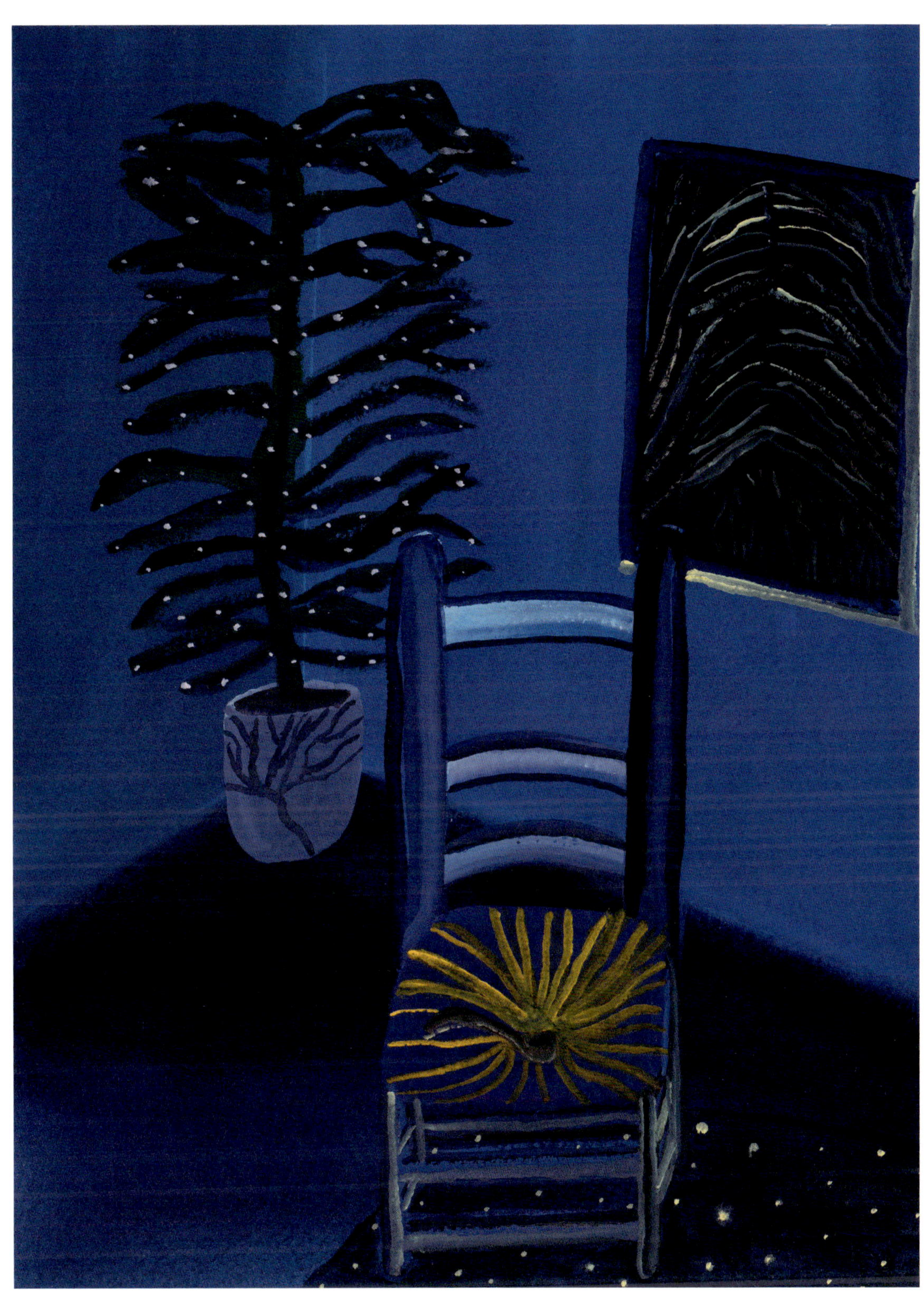

9 / Matthew Wong, *Untitled*, 2019
Gouache on paper, 30.5 × 22.9 cm
Matthew Wong Foundation

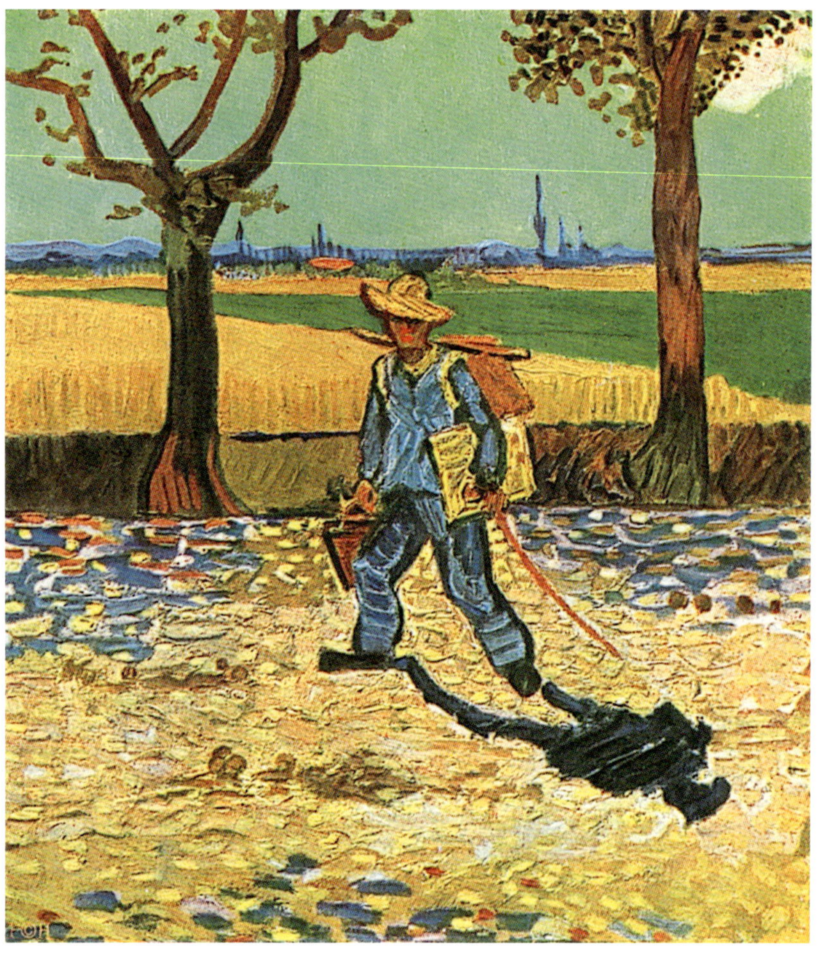

10 / Vincent van Gogh,
The Painter on the Road to Tarascon, 1888
Oil on canvas, 48 × 44 cm
Lost in the Second World War

11 / Matthew Wong,
The Space Between Trees, 2019
Oil on canvas, 61 × 50.8 cm
Collection of Judith and Danny Tobey

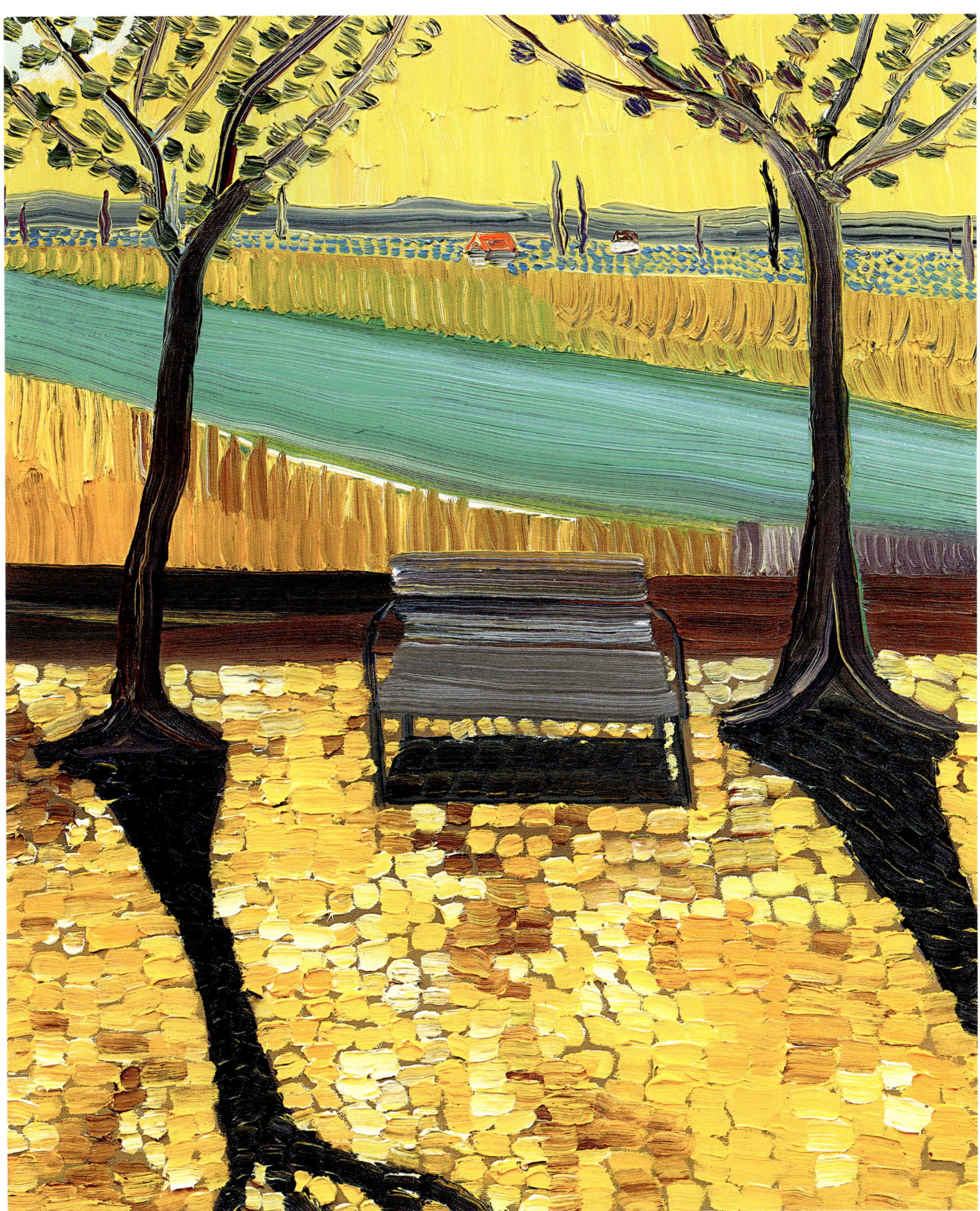

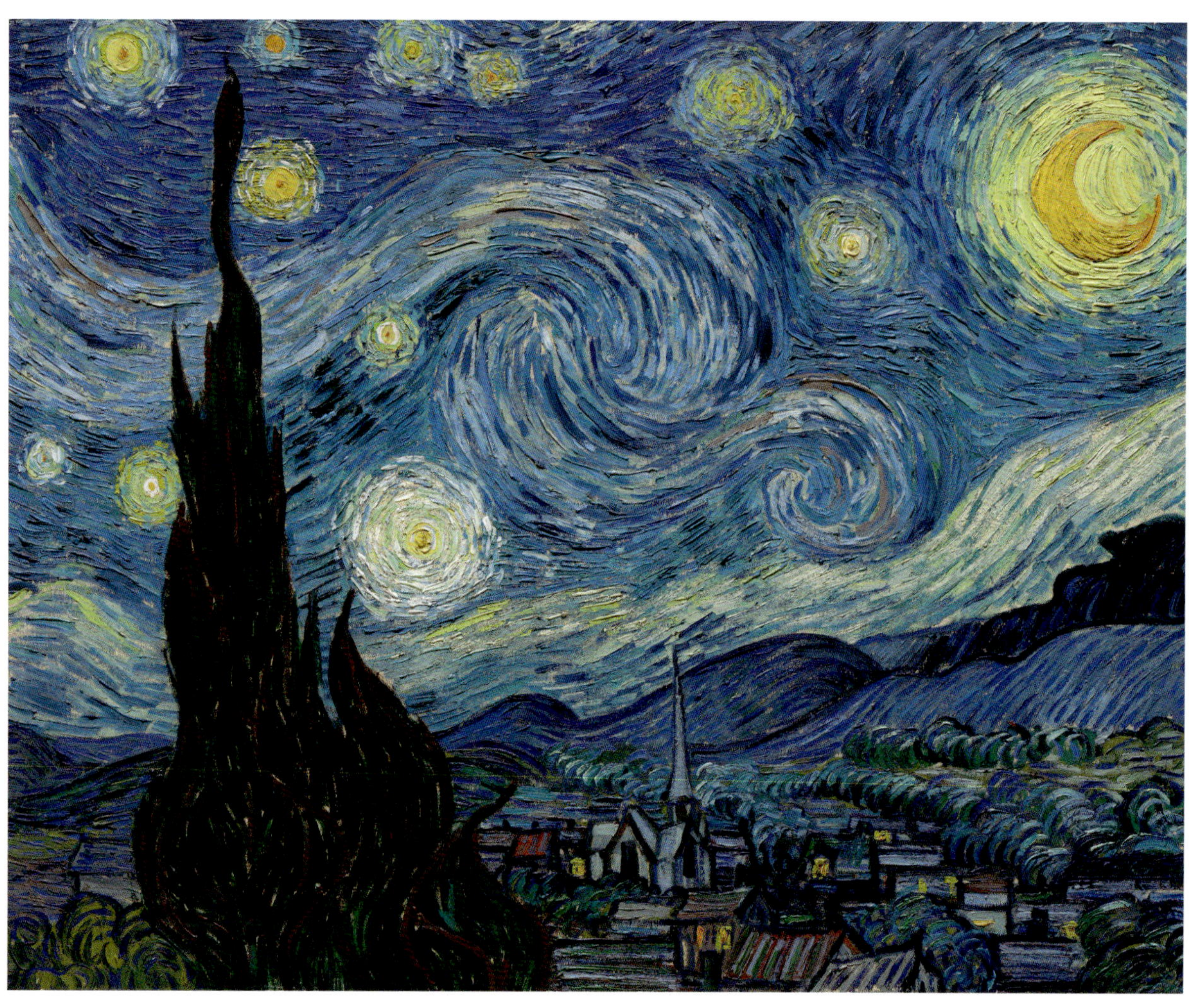

12 / Vincent van Gogh, *Starry Night*, 1889
Oil on canvas, 73.7 × 92.1 cm
The Museum of Modern Art, New York.
Acquired through the Lillie P. Bliss Bequest

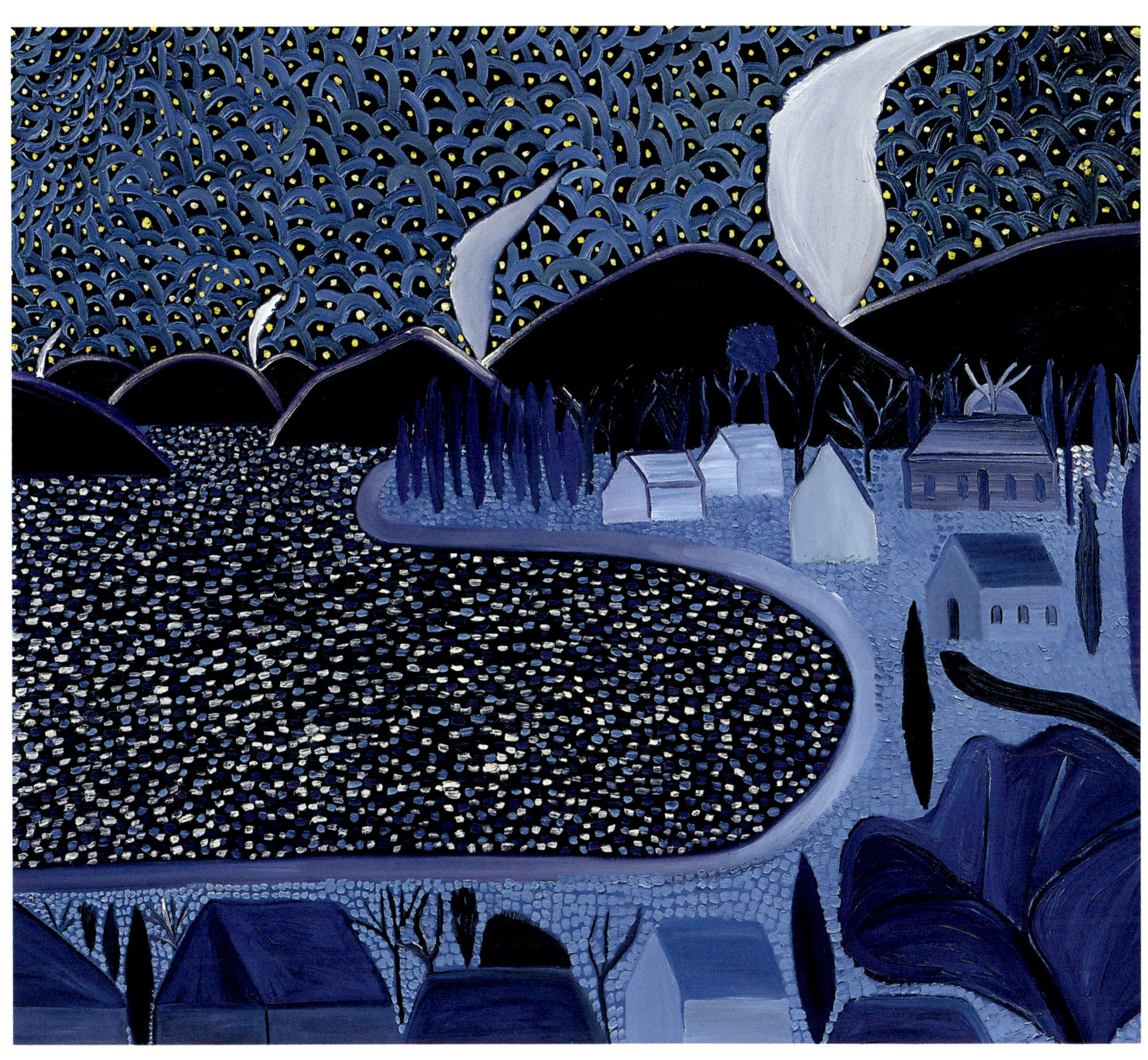

13 / Matthew Wong, *Starry Night*, 2019
Oil on canvas, 152.4 × 177.8 cm
Matthew Wong Foundation

exactly that constitutes 'good' work (and the opposite). Wong's Facebook chats essentially served as mentoring sessions for him as a painter. One of his most notable online friendships was with the American artist Peter Shear. By sharing his thorough knowledge of the history of modern American and European painting, Shear would contribute significantly to Wong's development.

Wong eagerly soaked up everything that was shared with him, displaying an almost photographic memory. At the same time, he kept up a correspondence with other people on poetry, literature, music (mostly rap), film and fashion – all subjects of which he was highly knowledgeable. Throughout his career, Wong translated the wide range of interests he discussed on Facebook into his visual work. He summed it up neatly in 2018: 'I am a bit of an omnivore for sights, sounds and ideas and am always on the lookout for perspectives I had not considered before.'[35] A song or a poem could be his prompt for a painting and he often borrowed titles for his works from music, poetry and cinema. He named a series of his earliest experimental ink works, for instance, after *Unknown Pleasures*, the influential 1979 album by British post-punk band Joy Division. A painting from 2019 alluded to the same album (fig. 125). The painting *So Much Depends...* (fig. 15), meanwhile, refers to William Carlos Williams's poem 'The Red Wheelbarrow', which begins with those words, and he named one of his first abstract paintings after Jimi Hendrix's album *Electric Ladyland*. The titles appear cryptic but were always chosen deliberately and speak to the breadth of his cultural interests.

Wong's habit of keeping up an extensive correspondence is reminiscent of Van Gogh, although the vast majority of Vincent's letters were addressed to his brother, while Wong chatted with fellow artists. Like those of Van Gogh, Wong's exchanges are full of reflections on his own work and that of others, as well as treatises on the state of the art world and candid discussions of his personal life. Contrary to the unease he experienced in real-life social situations, Wong felt comfortable online and could be smart, spontaneous and witty. In essence, he was just as much an artist-writer as Van Gogh had been. He had, moreover, been writing poetry regularly since 2009.[36]

The greater dialogue

Besides educating himself via Facebook, Wong frequently visited the central library in Hong Kong to explore the art-historical literature there or he went online to seek out art-related websites, 'figuring out where I can fit into the greater dialogue between artists throughout time'.[37] In the early stages of his career, Wong was drawn to Abstract Expressionists like Willem de Kooning, Joan Mitchell, Milton Resnick and Bill Jensen,

15 / Matthew Wong, *So Much Depends...*, 2017
Oil on canvas, 61 × 50.8 cm
Matthew Wong Foundation

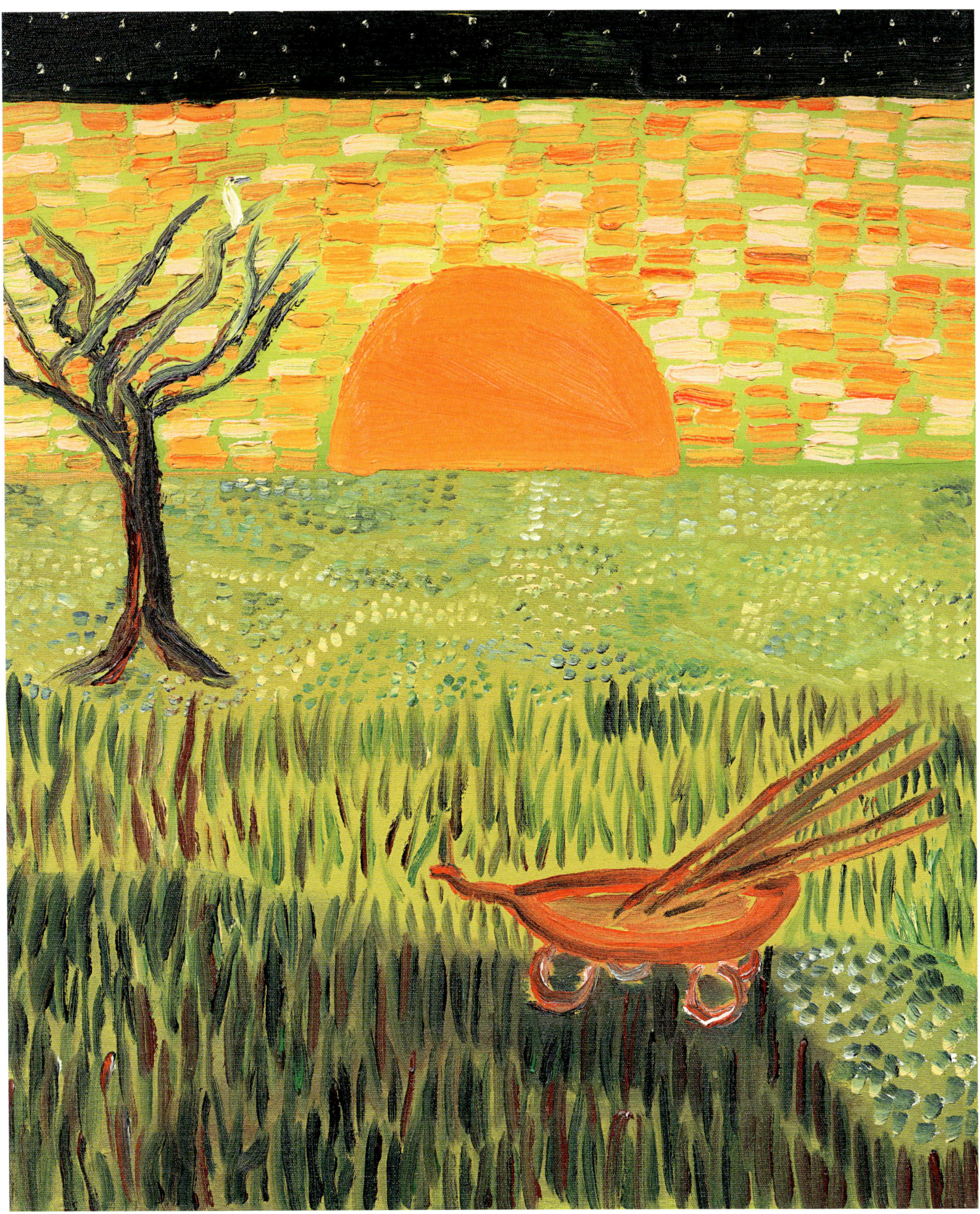

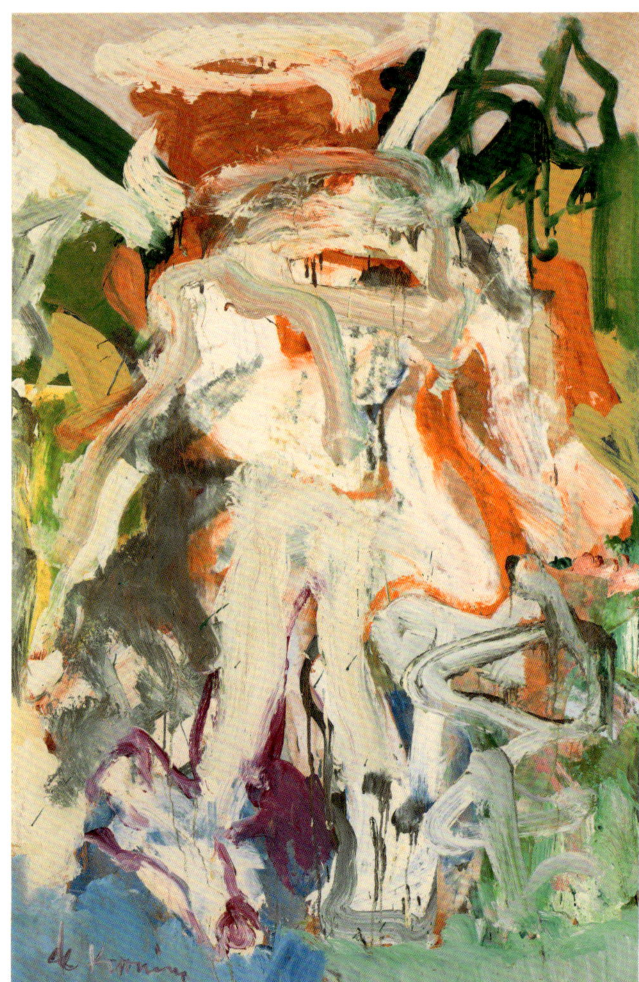

16 / Willem de Kooning,
Woman in Landscape III, 1968
Oil on paper, 161.3 × 108 cm
Whitney Museum of American Art, New York. Purchase, with funds from Mrs. Bernard F. Gimbel and the Bernard F. and Alva B. Gimbel Foundation

to whom improvisation and expression were of central importance to their art.[38] He closely studied their work online and tried to incorporate their examples in his own paintings. Wong told Shear, for instance, that he aimed to literally work his way through the oeuvres of de Kooning and Resnick to see where it would take him.[39] *Untitled* (fig. 17), for instance, is very similar to the works making up de Kooning's famous *Woman in Landscape* series, such as *Woman in Landscape III* (fig. 16). He showed his admiration for Mitchell, meanwhile, through (among other things) the painting *Valley* (fig. 90), the title of which refers to *La Grande Vallée* (the series of twenty-one monumental canvases that Mitchell painted in 1983–84) while in terms of its colour combination, the work more closely resembles Mitchell's *Two Sunflowers* (fig. 93). The painting technique and the fact that *Valley* consists of two separate, adjoining canvases are likewise references to Mitchell. Van Gogh had also caught Wong's attention in this period, as he detected a certain naivety in the Dutch painter that he found appealing.[40]

By 'the greater dialogue between artists throughout time', Wong was not only referring, incidentally, to American or European art: Chinese art was at least as important to him. During his study trips to the library, he divided his time between the two traditions.[41] Following his close study of traditional Qing dynasty painters such as the previously mentioned Shitao (fig. 114) and Bada Shanren (1626–1705) (fig. 108), and the more recent New Ink Movement (c. 1960–80), he tried 'to see where I can fit into the Chinese painting equation, the scroll format, etc. while bringing something more personal to time worn tropes'.[42] Wong stated that as an artist, it was almost impossible for him to prevent something of his Chinese roots from resonating in his art: 'China is such a hermetically sealed culture. I don't know if I relate totally to it, and yet there are parts of me that can't quite escape those roots by default.'[43]

The influence of Chinese painting was mainly expressed in the first three years of Wong's career in his choice of ink and rice paper as media. He set himself the goal of using traditional Chinese materials to create works inspired by mainly American Abstract Expressionism.[44] As such, this was not an original approach for Hong Kong artists, who face the challenge of relating to the bicultural legacy of a Chinese city that had been subject to British colonial rule between

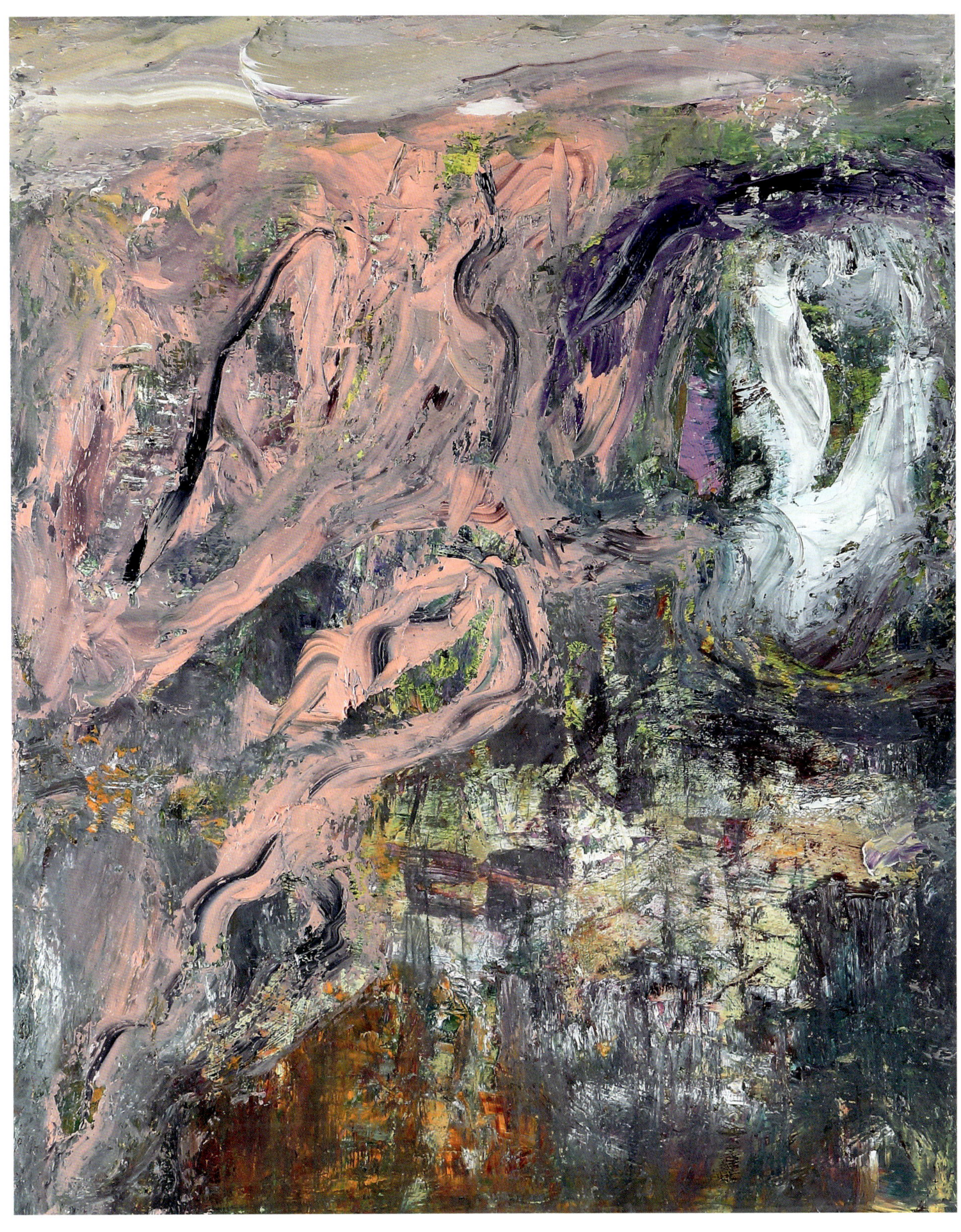

17 / Matthew Wong, *Untitled*, 2014
Oil on canvas (painted over), 99.1 × 78.1 cm

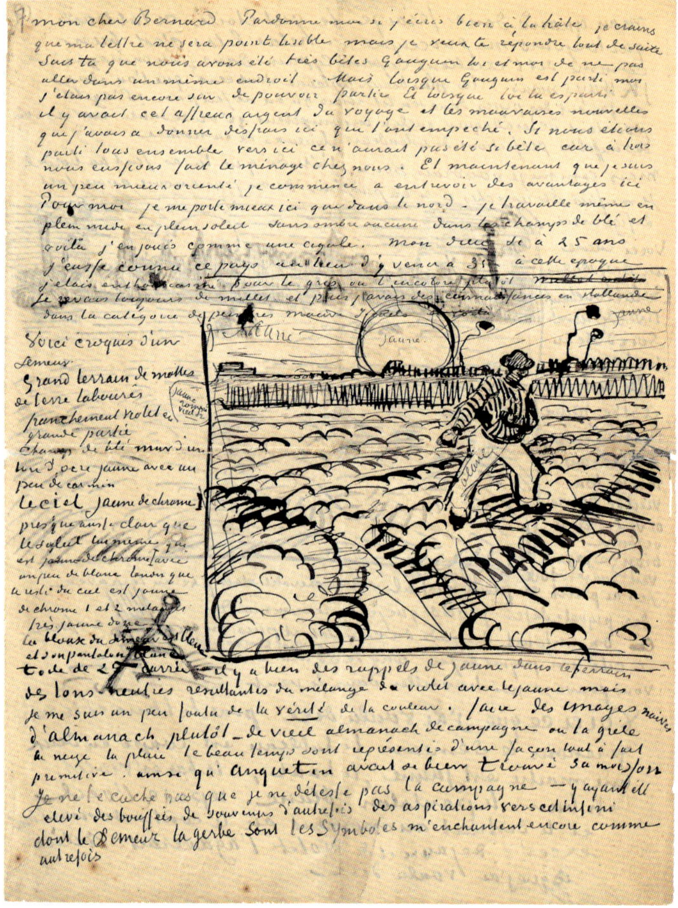
mon cher Bernard Pardonne moi si j'écris bien à la hâte je crains que ma lettre ne sera point lisible mais je veux te répondre tout de suite. Sais tu que nous avons été très bêtes Gauguin toi et moi de ne pas aller dans un même endroit. Mais lorsque Gauguin est parti moi j'étais pas encore sûr de pouvoir partir et lorsque toi tu es parti il y avait cet affreux argent du voyage et les mauvaises nouvelles que j'avais à donner des frais ici qui l'ont empeché. Si nous étions partis tous ensemble vers ici ce n'aurait pas été si bête car à trois nous eussions fait le ménage chez nous. Et maintenant que je suis un peu mieux orienté je commence à entrevoir des avantages ici. Pour moi je me porte mieux ici que dans le nord – je travaille même en plein midi en plein soleil sans ombre aucune dans les champs de blé et voilà j'en jouis comme une cigale. mon dieu si à 25 ans j'eusse connu ce pays au lieu d'y venir à 35 – à cette époque j'étais enthousiasmé pour le gris ou plutôt incolore. Je rêvais toujours de Millet et puis j'avais des connaissances en Hollande dans la catégorie de peintres comme Mauve, Israëls etc.

Voici croquis d'un semeur. Grand terrain de mottes de terre labourées franchement violet en grande partie. Champ de blé mûr d'un ton d'ocre jaune avec un peu de carmin. Le ciel jaune de chrome presque aussi clair que le soleil lui même qui est jaune de chrome 1 avec un peu de blanc tandis que le reste du ciel est jaune de chrome 1 et 2 mélangés. Très jaune donc. La blouse du semeur est bleue et son pantalon blanc. Toile de 25 carrée. Il y a bien des rappels de jaune dans le terrain, des tons neutres résultants du mélange du violet avec le jaune mais je me suis un peu foutu de la vérité de la couleur. Faire des images naïves d'almanach plutôt – de vieil almanach de campagne où la grêle la neige la pluie le beau temps sont représentés d'une façon tout à fait primitive. ainsi qu'Anquetin avait si bien trouvé sa moisson. Je ne te cache pas que je ne déteste pas la campagne – y ayant été élevé, des bouffées de souvenirs d'autrefois, des aspirations vers cet infini dont le Semeur, la gerbe sont les symboles m'enchantent encore comme autrefois

18 / Vincent van Gogh, sketch of a sower with setting sun in letter to Emile Bernard, c. 19 June 1888 [628]
The Morgan Library & Museum, New York. Thaw Collection, given in honor of Charles E. Pierce, Jr., 2007

1842 and 1997.[45] The dynamic, intuitive way in which he approached the medium nevertheless enabled Wong to add something personal to 'time worn tropes', as clearly visible in two drawings – both of which remained *Untitled* – one from 2013 and the other from 2014 (figs. 87 and 111). The near-landscape composition of the 2013 drawing is highly expressive and conveys tension and movement, whereas the grid of flowing ink in the work from 2014 exudes calm and contemplation. The drawings demonstrate Wong's ability to bend his materials to a wide range of abstract compositions.

As he embarked on his career as an artist, Wong looked for examples, context and guidance in all sorts of fields. The internet and the nearby library gave him access to an infinite amount of images and information. Art history was available everywhere, any time, and was crucially important to his work. The equivalent experience for Van Gogh lay in the large amount of art he had already been exposed to before beginning to produce his own. A huge volume had passed through his hands during his time at the art dealers Goupil & Cie, and he himself collected prints of works by artists from different generations and, later, magazine illustrations too. These examples, as well as his memories of all he had seen throughout his career, served as a database from which – like Wong after him – he could derive context, support and inspiration.[46] Where de Kooning and Mitchell had featured at the start of Wong's career, for Van Gogh it was the likes of Jean-François Millet and Charles-François Daubigny.

Ambition

Wong's desire to engage in a dialogue with the big names of Euro-American and Chinese art history reveals something not only about his artistic objectives but also the degree of his ambition. Where Van Gogh in his early years did not dare claim 'in any way' that he could rise to the level of his examples, Wong wanted nothing more than to position himself among the masters of painting and even to challenge them for their crown.[47] In a letter to his brother Theo in 1887, Van Gogh wrote: 'To succeed you have to have ambition, and ambition seems absurd to me.'[48] For Wong, the opposite was true. He was not disheartened by his slim chances of success as a self-taught painter who did not produce his first work until he was twenty-seven. Painting was his 'last resort', and he went to great lengths to become the exception to the rule.

In 2013, barely two years after his revelatory experience in Venice, Wong was already showing his work at the Song Zhuang Art Festival in Beijing. He also organized solo exhibitions on his own initiative in the two years that followed, including professionally published catalogues. The first of these – *Matthew Wong: Chapter One* – was held at the Cuiheng Art Museum, Zhongshan, part of the complex in which Wong's studio was located, and featured a series of his abstract expressionist canvases. (see p. 162, fig. C)[49] The second was titled *Pulse of the Land* and was held at the Hong Kong Visual Arts Centre, where artists could put their names on a waiting list to organize an exhibition (see p. 162, fig. B).[50] Wong would pull out his phone to show photographs of his paintings whenever the opportunity arose, and he frequently turned up unannounced at Hong Kong galleries to present his work.[51]

Wong also shared his work on Facebook on a daily basis, allowing his development to be tracked closely: he was keenly aware that he needed to be seen if he were to have any chance of breaking through. His approach was akin to Van Gogh's habit of including sketches of works in his letters to his brother Theo and artist friends such as Paul Gauguin and Emile Bernard (fig. 18). While a letter obviously has a far narrower reach than a Facebook post, the principle is essentially the same.[52]

Wong's Facebook friends bore witness to the astonishing rate at which his work was evolving. He never lingered too long over completed paintings and once wrote after a period spent working in a particular style: 'It's been on my mind lately how something can become a mannerism so quickly.'[53] He invariably expected each new work to be better than the last: 'I think that's the mindset everybody has to take otherwise why do it?'[54] Wong was ruthless with work that ceased to please him: as far as he was concerned, it no longer had any right to exist. If he found himself short of canvas – something that frequently happened, given the pace at which he worked – he had no compunction about painting over an existing piece.[55] Van Gogh was no stranger to this practice either: he often painted over earlier work too for reasons of economy.[56] In Wong's case, it also provided a means of controlling his artistic legacy: work that he no longer endorsed did not get the chance to see the light of day. The handful of paintings from his first exhibition *Chapter One* in Hong Kong that were sold to friends and family at the time are the only ones to survive from this early period. The rest were all painted over. It is easy to identify such examples as Wong always wrote the title on the back. When he painted over an existing work, he simply crossed out the old title and date and added the new ones next to them.

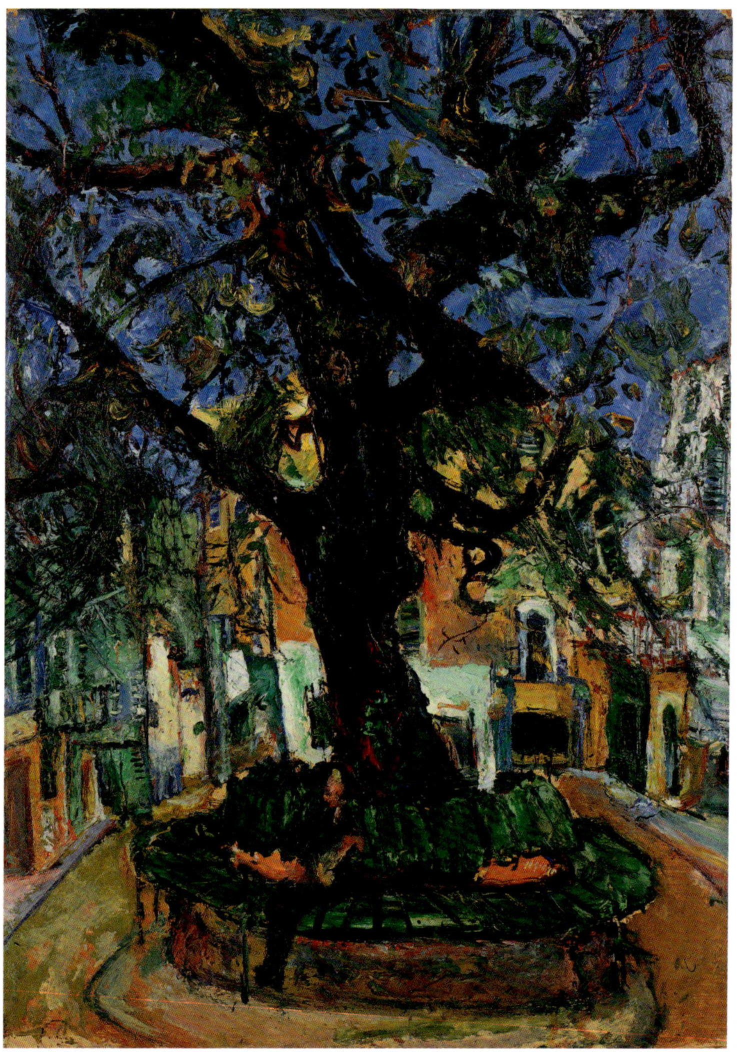

19 / Chaïm Soutine,
Great Tree of Vence
(*Le grand arbre de Vence*), c. 1929
Oil on cardboard/attached to plywood, 61 × 44.5 cm
Kunstmuseum Bern. Bequest of Georges F. Keller 1981

Towards the figurative

Not long after *Chapter One*, Wong began to question his focus on the abstract. The type of abstract expressionist paintings he had been creating made it difficult, he felt, to distinguish between good and bad work. This bothered him, 'which is why i feel i have to move out of it'.[57] The expressive power of colour and the painter's touch remained central to his practice, but now he wanted to deploy that power in figurative work. He no longer took his cue from Mitchell and de Kooning, but from artists who worked both expressively and figuratively, such as Brenda Goodman, Frank Auerbach, Chaïm Soutine (fig. 19) and Vincent van Gogh.[58] He experimented with a variety of techniques, looking for an appropriate way to introduce representation into his work. One moment he created a landscape from wildly applied brushwork, while at another he painted imposing black trees over a colourful background (*The Swing*, for example, fig. 20). A third technique he experimented with entailed applying several layers of paint on top of each other and then drawing a picture with his finger in the wet upper layer, the resulting lines exposing the paint beneath (fig. 21).

His ink paintings swiftly became figurative too, as Wong began to relate more closely to traditional Chinese painting. *Stargazing* (fig. 113), for instance, shows how he was now using his brush and ink in a more controlled and calligraphic way. Wong's depiction of mountains and use of a distorting, high perspective in *Landscape of the Longing* (fig. 115), meanwhile, showed that he had begun to follow the example of Shitao and others more precisely (fig. 114). At the same time, the title of the work refers to a central theme in Shitao's oeuvre, indicating just how close Wong had become to the Chinese master's work in this period. The drawings anticipated his paintings in terms of stylistic development: the rhythm and beauty of the brief touches and the immense influence of traditional painting would only truly manifest themselves in his painted work at a later stage. All the same, Chinese influences were already seeping into Wong's paintings by 2015, as

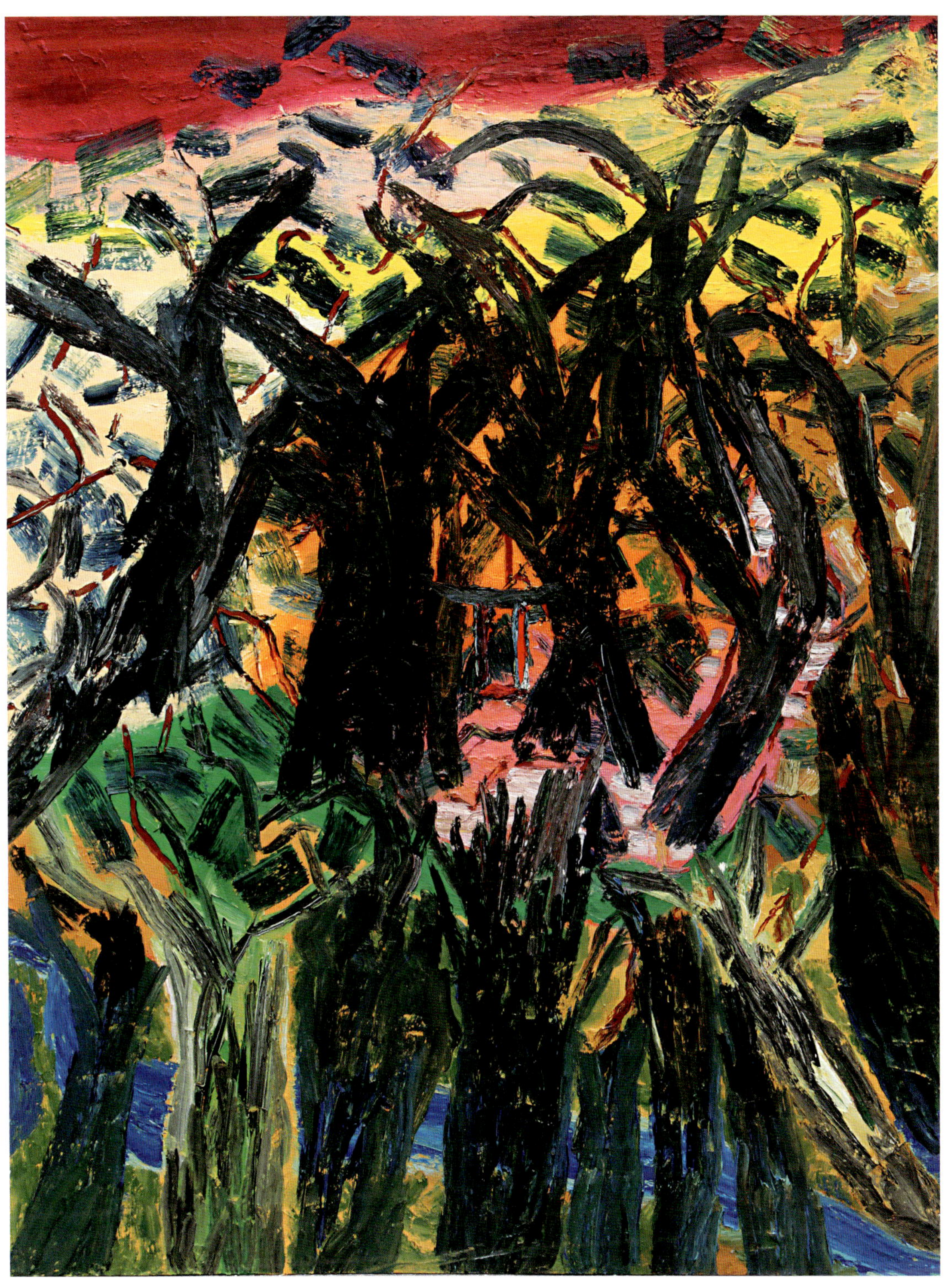

20 / Matthew Wong, *The Swing*, 2015
Oil on canvas, 220 × 170 cm
Private collection

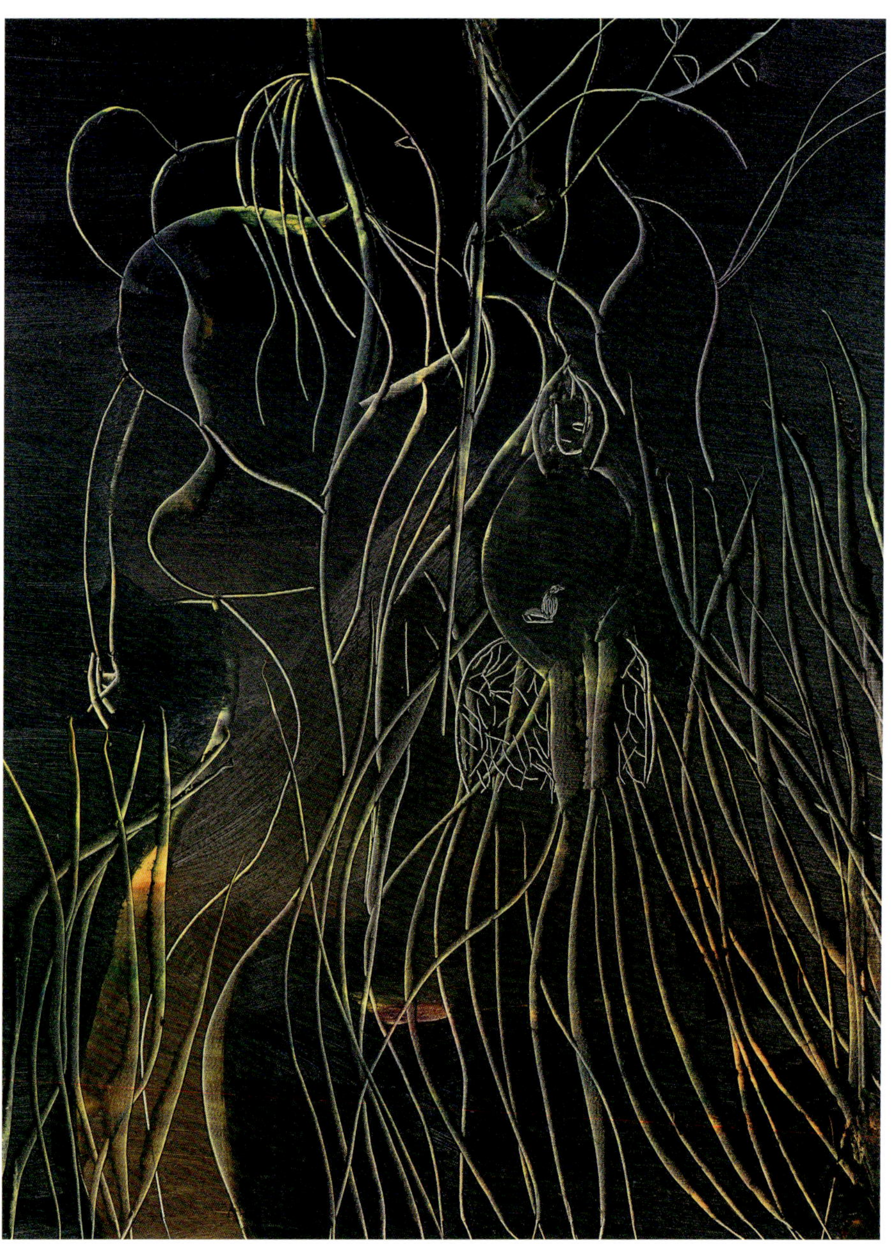

21 / Matthew Wong, *Autism*, 2015
Oil on canvas, 120 × 90 cm
Matthew Wong Foundation

22 / Matthew Wong, *Contemplating Infinity*, 2015
Oil on canvas, 144 × 114 cm
Matthew Wong Foundation

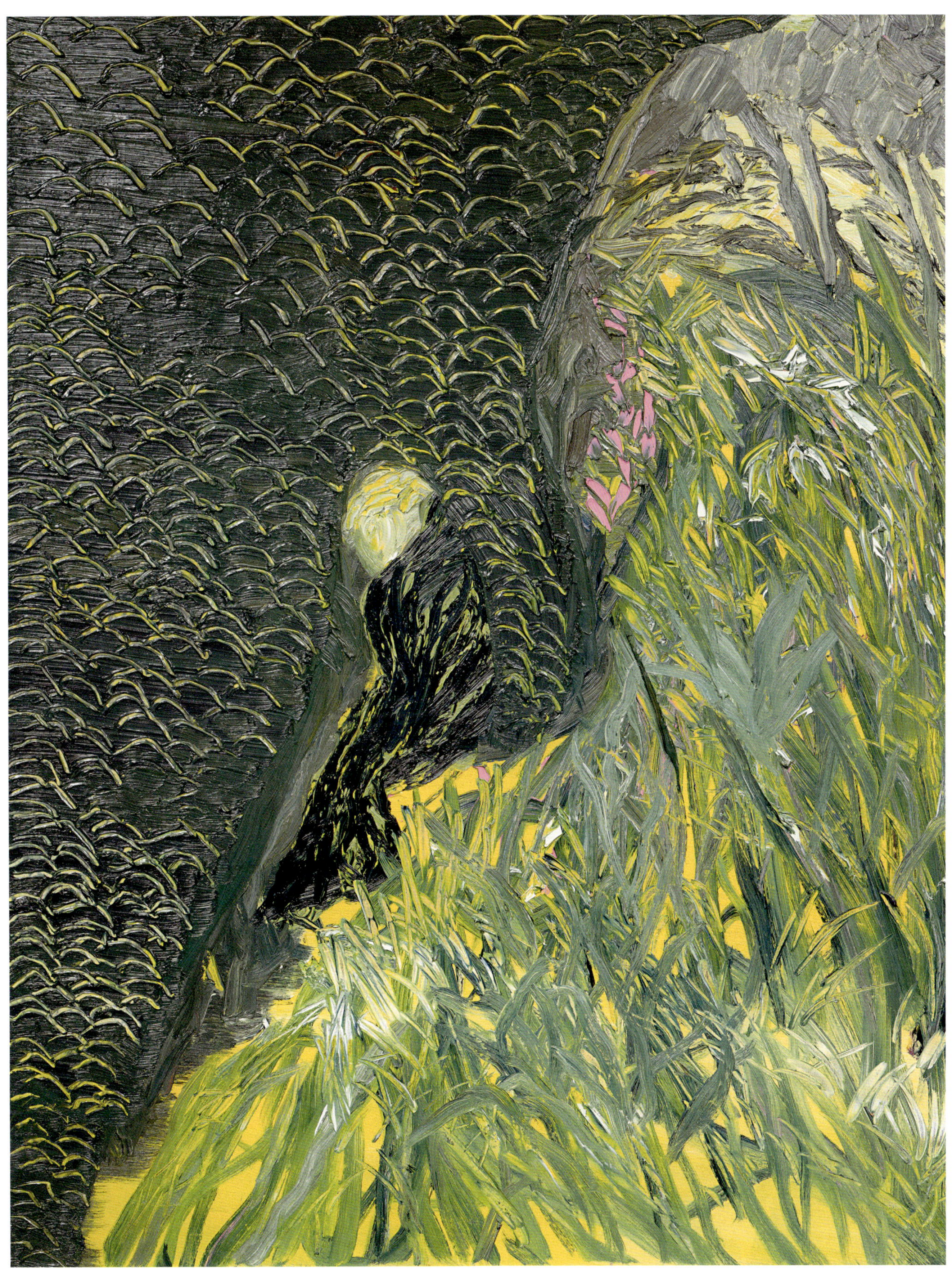

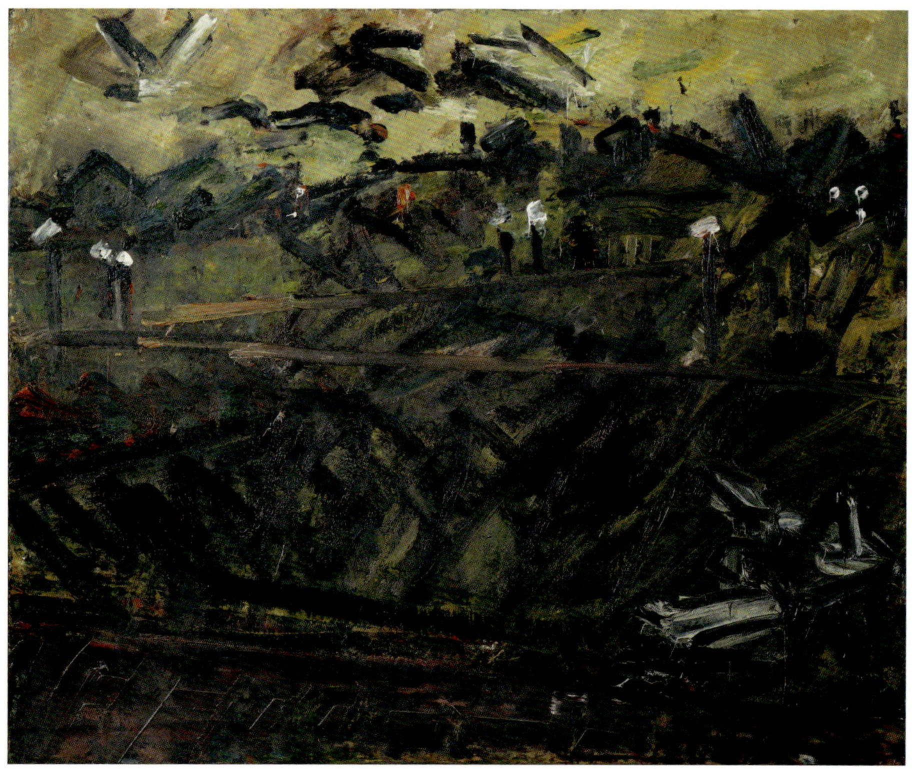

can be seen, for instance, in *Contemplating Infinity* (fig. 22), in which a figure gazes out over an infinitely unfolding Chinese mountain landscape.

In addition to its subject matter, *Contemplating Infinity* is a painting in which the various stylistic experiments of 2015 came together. Dynamic brushwork is visible in the lower right corner, while the expansive landscape in the upper left is drawn with the artist's finger in layers of wet paint. By allowing a figure to emerge between the two zones, Wong pulled the painting away from the abstract and towards the figurative. *Contemplating Infinity* was one of the works that Wong selected for his exhibition *Pulse of the Land*, which also featured a series of results of his widely varying experiments in 2015. In the introduction to the catalogue Wong had his technique compared to the brushstrokes of Soutine and Van Gogh.[59] The predominantly sombre palette of the exhibited works, including *The Swing* and *Autism* (figs. 20 and 21), likewise reflected Soutine's work, but was even closer to the dark paintings of Auerbach, such as *Primrose Hill – Winter* (fig. 23). Wong's use of colour here is a direct expression of the persistently dark mood with which he struggled in 2015.[60]

Pulse of the Land was a success and quite a few of the works were sold, yet this did little to alter Wong's state of mind. Never good at the best of times, it reached a particular low in 2015. Having been the centre of attention for a few days, he was once again the artist at the beginning of his career in a city with which he felt little connection. He was dismissive of the work of other Hong Kong artists and his attempts to get a foot in the door of the city's gallery circuit came to nothing. He felt 'spiritually defeated/exhausted'.[61] The artists with whom he sensed an affinity were almost all in the United States, and the distance that separated him from them felt insurmountable. A masked portrait in the ink painting *Untitled* (fig. 24) seems like an acute expression of his sense of being trapped.

23 / Frank Auerbach, *Primrose Hill – Winter*, 1981–82
Oil on board, 121.9 × 152.4 cm
Barber Institute of Fine Arts, University of Birmingham. The Henry Barber Trust

Wanderings in North America

In early 2016, Wong's mother took him on a long trip around the United States and Canada in an attempt to break him out of his depression. They began their journey in New York and finished in Edmonton having spent time in Michigan and Los Angeles along the way. The purpose of their stay in New York was to meet some of Wong's Facebook contacts in person, including the established art dealer John Cheim, who had assumed a kind of mentoring role for him. He had commented positively about Wong's painting *Memento* (fig. 25) on Facebook, before asking if the artist could send him a few of his works.[62] Cheim ended up buying one of them, prompting Wong and his mother to visit him in New York.[63] It turned out to be a good move: Cheim became the first link in a process that would swiftly lead to the success Wong went on to achieve in the United States. It was through his advice that the young artist ended up being represented by the Karma gallery, which took his work to the leading fairs and gave him his first New York solo exhibition in 2018.[64]

In the two years between meeting Cheim and the opening of the exhibition, Wong continued to work steadily and to develop at the same rapid pace. He was unable to do as much as usual during his stays in New York and Michigan (February–March 2016), but he got back up to speed in Los Angeles, where he worked in the apartment his mother had rented for them. There was not much space, so he restricted himself to smaller formats and avoided oil paint, working chiefly in acrylic and gouache instead. He hoped that he could use these fast-drying media to bring more colour and optimism to his work. While this was partly a tactic to connect more effectively with the American market, the cheerful colours were also intended to pull himself out of his persistent depression.[65] Van Gogh had resorted to a similar strategy 130 years previously, when he too used colours to encourage and cheer himself up at times when things were not going well.[66]

As he had done in previous periods, Wong turned to new artists for inspiration, this time including Henri Matisse, Katherine Bradford and Yayoi Kusama.[67] He began, for instance, to apply his paint in dots borrowed from Kusama (fig. 26), both with a brush and directly from the tube. At the same time, though, Van Gogh's example remained important. A work like *Trees and Undergrowth* (fig. 36), which Van Gogh built up using stipples and short brushstrokes, might also have served as a model in this period. Wong's dots brought light and an unmistakable beauty to his work, which had until recently been heavy and sombre.

Bearing in mind the examples of the previously mentioned artists, Wong reflected on the public, hedonistic and somewhat exhibitionist

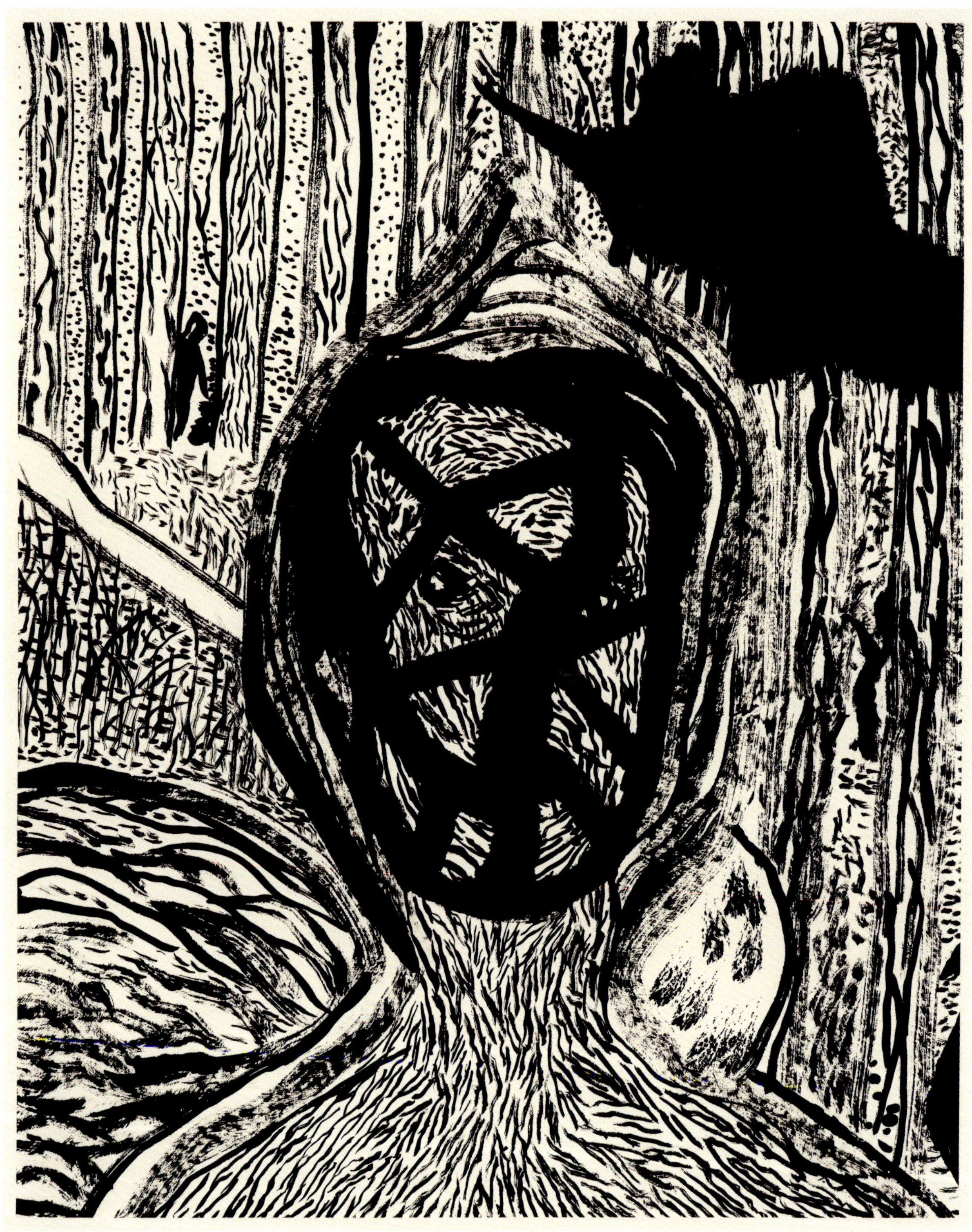

24 / Matthew Wong, *Untitled*, 2015
Ink on rice paper, 67.6 × 55.2 cm
Matthew Wong Foundation

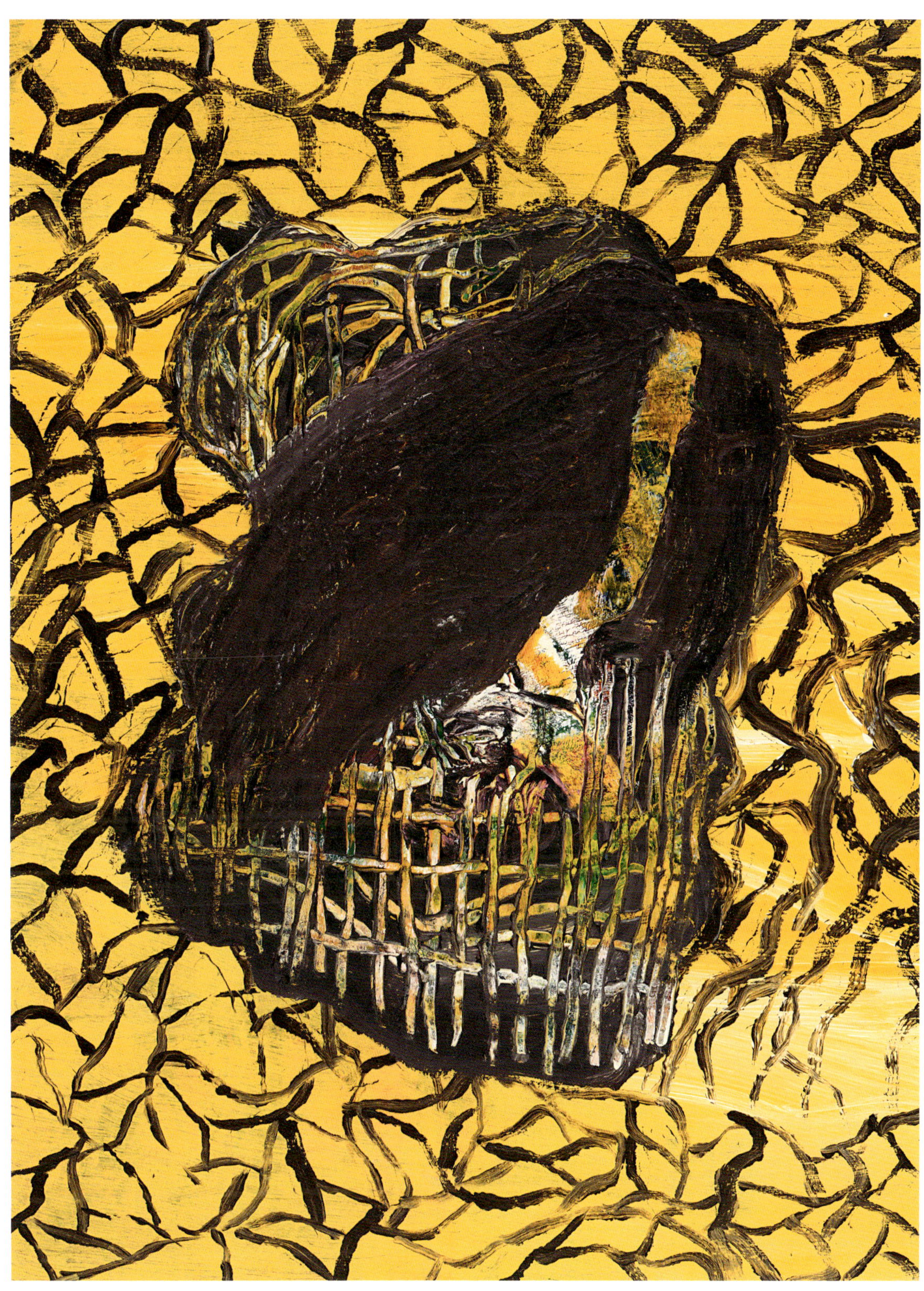

25 / Matthew Wong, *Memento*, 2015
Acrylic on paper, 76.2 × 55.9 cm
Collection of Phillip Meyer and Xing Yu Toh

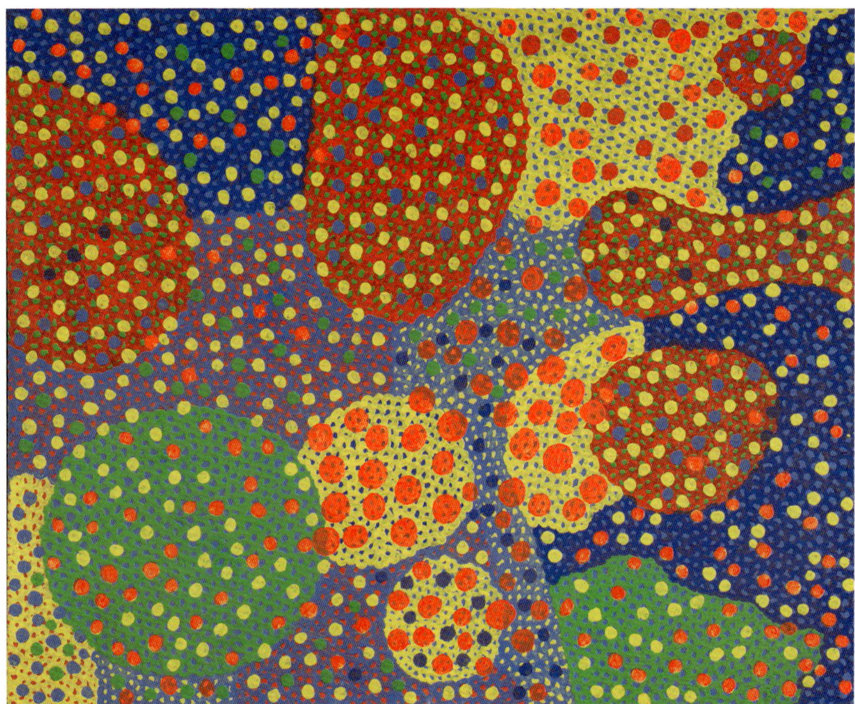

26 / Yayoi Kusama, *Untitled*, 1967
Oil on canvas, 101.6 × 127 cm
Minneapolis Institute of Art.
The John R. Van Derlip Fund

life he observed in Los Angeles. The result was an extensive series of modestly sized works in acrylic on paper, including *Bright Moment*, *Act of Faith* and *Sleeping on the Grass* (figs. 27, 29 and 30). It is apparent from the series that Wong's encounter with the Los Angeles lifestyle simultaneously cheered him while leaving him with a sense of emptiness: the positivity was infectious, yet also highlighted his own social shortcomings, which meant that the exuberant, Californian way of life was all but unattainable for him. To help express these contrary emotions, Wong looked to the nudes of artists like Matisse (fig. 28), prompting works in which freedom and sexual frustration go hand in hand.[68] He complemented this theme with less complicated paintings, such as the gouache *White Sea, White Sky* (fig. 1).

After their time in Los Angeles, Wong and his mother travelled to Edmonton, a large but quiet city surrounded by the endless prairies of the Canadian province of Alberta. The unpretentious and unremarkable life there came as a relief after the bustle of New York and Los Angeles. It had always been Wong's goal to associate himself with the art scenes of those metropolises, but it proved impossible for him to stay in them for any length of time. Like Van Gogh, who yearned for the countryside after his two years in Paris and in due course moved there, Wong was obliged to turn his back on the big city. Distance gave him the space he needed to focus on his art. Wong and his mother moved into a furnished apartment belonging to family friends in Edmonton. They felt good in the city and found pretty much everything they needed within walking distance. Canada was familiar because of the many years they had lived there previously, so they decided to stay and make Edmonton their home.[69]

The work Wong created shortly after arriving in Edmonton included *The Sun* (fig. 31). It was the first time he had painted the sun's intense rays in an expressive way, as Van Gogh had done before him. Not long thereafter, Wong had his first exhibition in the United States, entitled *Good Bad Brush*. The dual exhibition with work by Peter Shear opened on 16 July 2016 in a studio converted into an exhibition space belonging

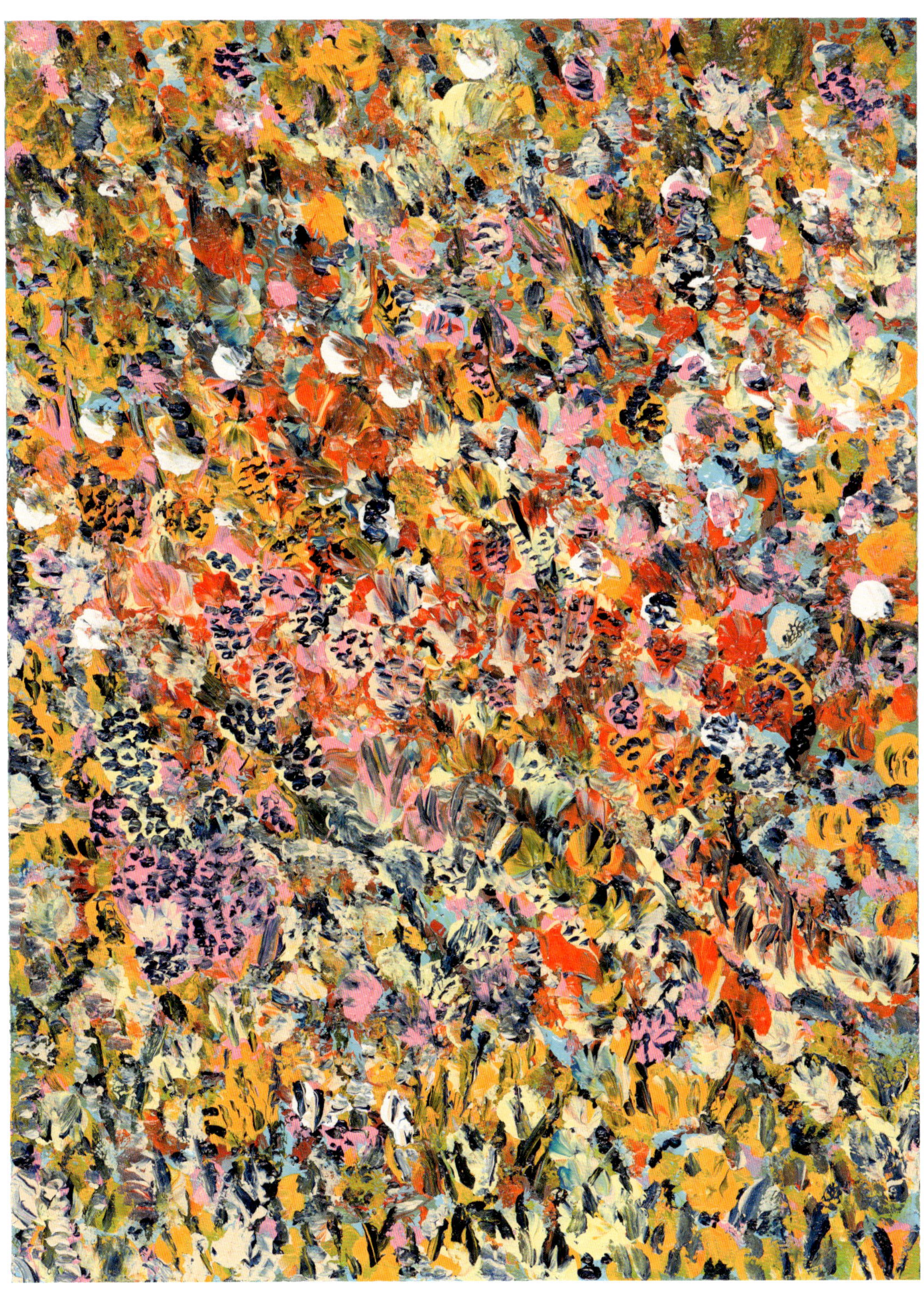

27 / Matthew Wong, *Bright Moment*, 2016
Acrylic on paper, 30.5 × 22.9 cm
Matthew Wong Foundation
and Cheim & Read, New York

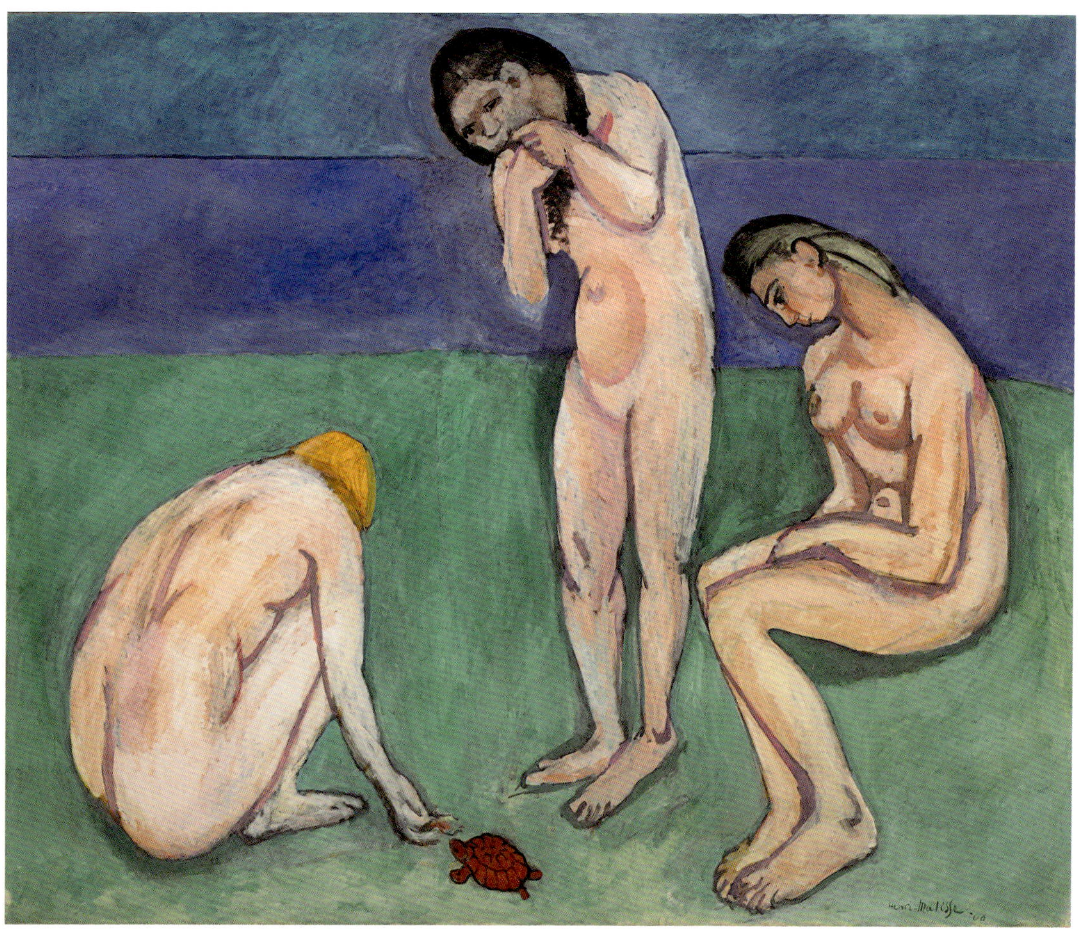

28 / Henri Matisse, *Bathers with a Turtle* (*Baigneuses à la tortue*), 1907–08
Oil on canvas, 181.6 × 221 cm
Saint Louis Art Museum.
Gift of Mr. and Mrs. Joseph Pulitzer Jr.

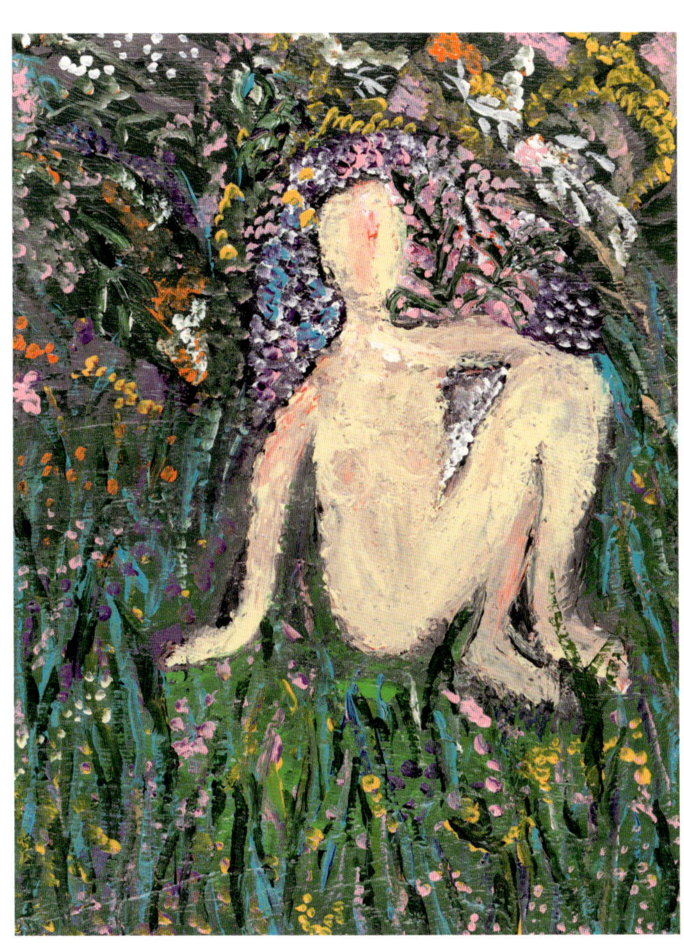

29 / Matthew Wong, *Act of Faith*, 2016
Acrylic on paper, 30.5 × 22.9 cm
Matthew Wong Foundation
and Cheim & Read, New York

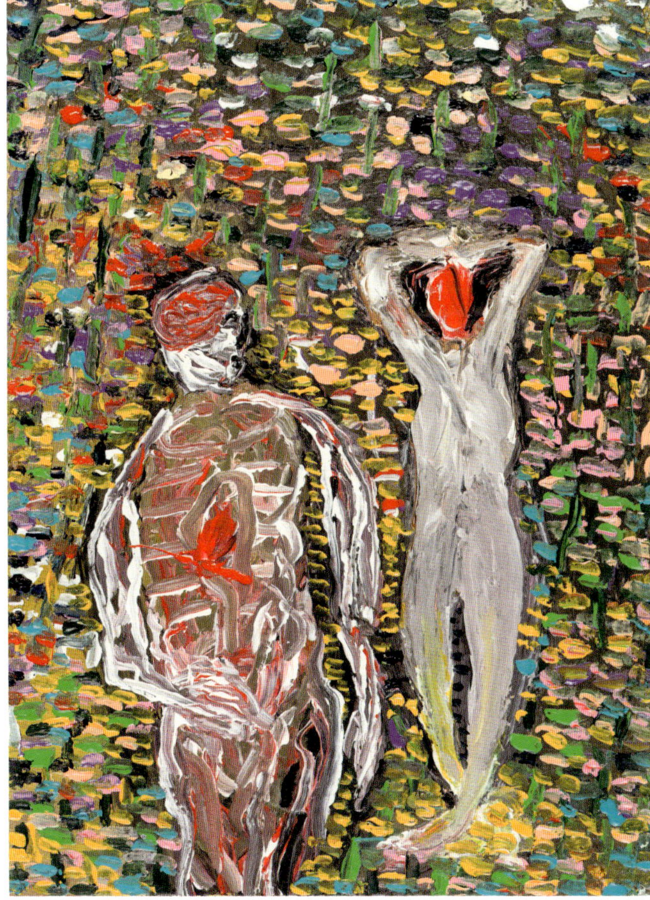

30 / Matthew Wong, *Sleeping on the Grass*, 2016
Acrylic on paper, 30.5 × 22.9 cm
Matthew Wong Foundation
and Cheim & Read, New York

to an artist friend in Burlington, Washington. Its title referred to the two artists' shared habit of working with cheap brushes.[70] Wong frequently threw them away after a single session.[71]

As preparations were underway for *Good Bad Brush*, Wong took the advice of John Cheim and introduced himself to Matthew Higgs in an e-mail accompanied by images of five of his paintings. The curator and director of White Columns, the New York art space, was so impressed that he selected two of the works for the group exhibition *Outside* at Karma's temporary gallery in Amagansett, Long Island.[72] The chosen paintings were similar in subject matter to the work Wong had produced in Los Angeles. Higgs was putting an exhibition together around landscapes that represented inner, experiential worlds rather than physical places and he felt that Wong's paintings fit his concept perfectly. The artists shown in *Outside* were mostly self-taught, lending the show a connotation of outsider art – a controversial label that Wong accepted with a mixture of reluctance and strategic calculation.[73] 'I'm technically an outsider artist', he wrote to Shear in 2015.[74]

Wong and his mother met Brendan Dugan, owner of Karma, at the exhibition opening. Wong had sold one of his paintings that day, which gave him the confidence he needed to approach the dealer.[75] While this did not immediately result in formal representation, Dugan agreed to show Wong's work to collectors. A number of sales swiftly followed and Dugan undertook to present some of Wong's paintings at the FIAC contemporary art fair in Paris towards the end of October 2016.[76]

The promise of success

This resounding success brought Wong a much-needed dose of happiness and satisfaction. Recognition lifted a little of the darkness and uncertainty that had plagued him since *Pulse of the Land*.[77] At the same time, though, success kindled a sense of responsibility now that he was no longer painting purely for the internet but also for a physical, art-loving public. It led him to review what he had done to date with an even more critical eye and to destroy anything that did not live up to his new requirements.[78] This was also the moment when he stopped sharing on Facebook every outburst of creativity that flowed from his brush. He limited his output to one painting a day – 'it still isn't really slow by any rational standards' – and embraced more reflection and contemplation in his working process.[79]

In the course of this realignment, Wong underwent a further leap in his development. He distilled a number of stylistic elements out of the many experiments he had performed up to that point and brought them together in a new way, making his work more open

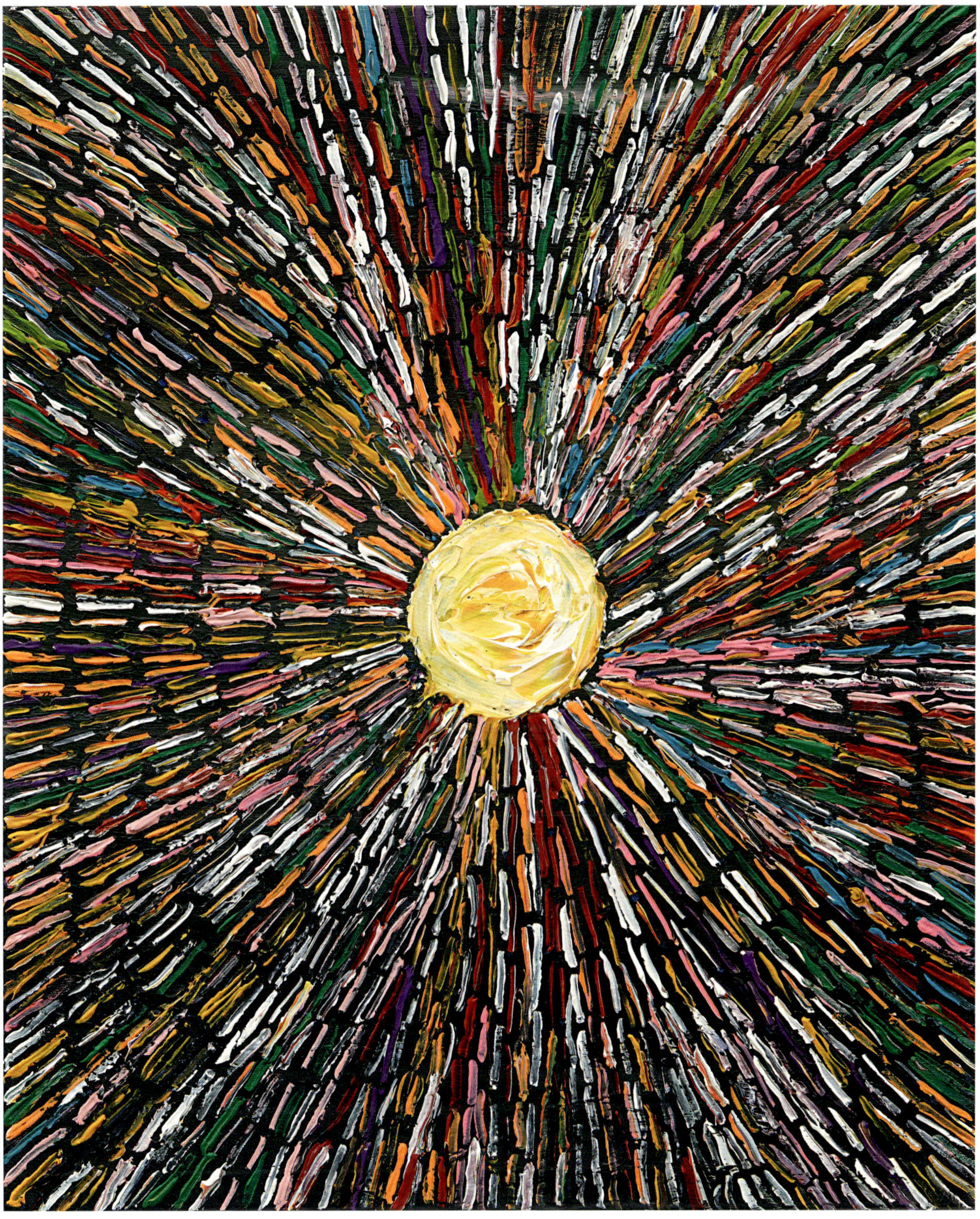

31 / Matthew Wong, *The Sun*, 2016
Acrylic on canvas, 61 × 50.8 cm
Courtesy of Level & Co

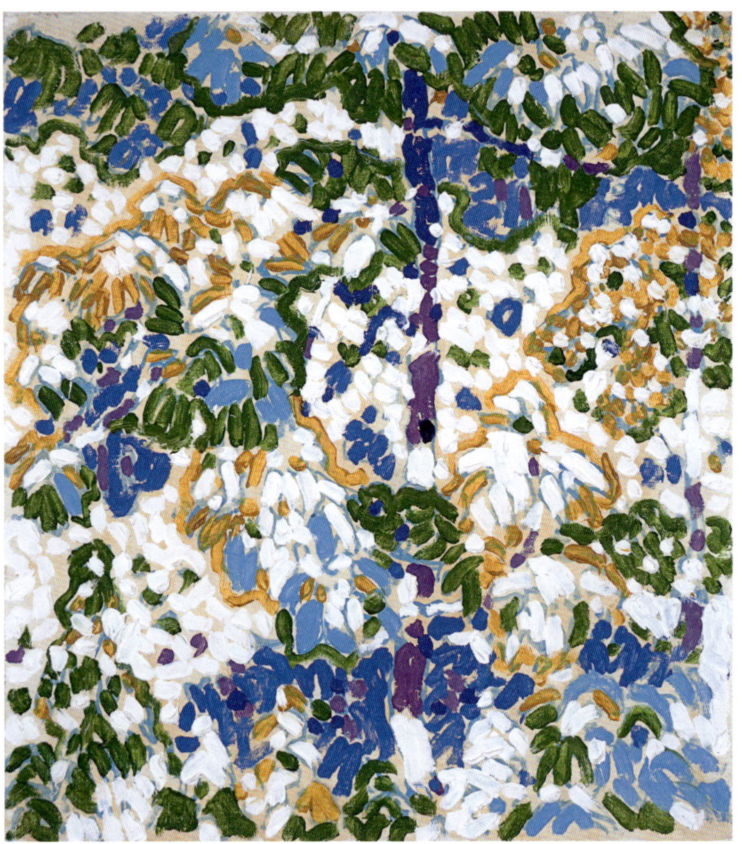

32 / David Milne, *Leaves in Sunlight*, 1914
Oil on canvas, 50.8 × 45.7 cm
John Shearer, Mayberry Fine Art

and accessible. The intense colour and emphasis on short brushstrokes and impasto from his 2016 work were retained, for instance, but he abandoned the palpable frustration of his nudes. He took the emotional charge of the imaginary landscape in the *Pulse of the Land* paintings, while omitting those works' heaviness. At the same time, Wong took stylistic elements from his ink paintings and introduced them in his painted work: an emphasis on line, for instance, the immense diversity of short, calligraphic touches and the high, distorted perspective he had borrowed from Shitao and Bada Shanren.[80]

In addition to this, Wong turned once more to a fresh series of names from Euro-American art history, among them Gustav Klimt, Egon Schiele, Forrest Bess and the Canadian David Milne (fig. 32). Contemporary artists like Jonas Wood (fig. 33) and Peter Doig were also valuable to Wong in this period.[81] Along with Chinese traditional painting, their examples helped him to lift his own work out of the raw, dark atmosphere in which it found itself and to shift it towards a visual language that was wider in scope and more accessible. To put a seal on his combination of Western and Chinese examples, Wong painted *The Realm of Appearances* (fig. 116) – a work featuring Schiele and Van Gogh-style sunflowers arranged in a Ming dynasty vase decorated with a Chinese mountain landscape.[82] The numerous references to the history of art lent his work a recognizable aesthetic, which was nevertheless original and innovative.

One of the most important early results of Wong's reorientation was *The Other Side of the Moon* (fig. 35): an imaginary landscape painted in early 2017 with a high horizon and an ominously yellow sky with a black moon. The piece might initially have been prompted by Bess's *Dedication to Van Gogh* (fig. 34).[83] *The Other Side of the Moon* was composed using a dark background applied in broad strokes, reminiscent of Wong's 2015 work, with luminous colours in all manner of different short touches applied on top of it. A tiny human figure can be made out in the upper left corner of the composition, all alone in this overwhelming fantasy world. It serves to intensify the eerie character of the work, which possesses an extraordinary beauty at the same time. The tension between these two aspects would become a central aspect of Wong's oeuvre.

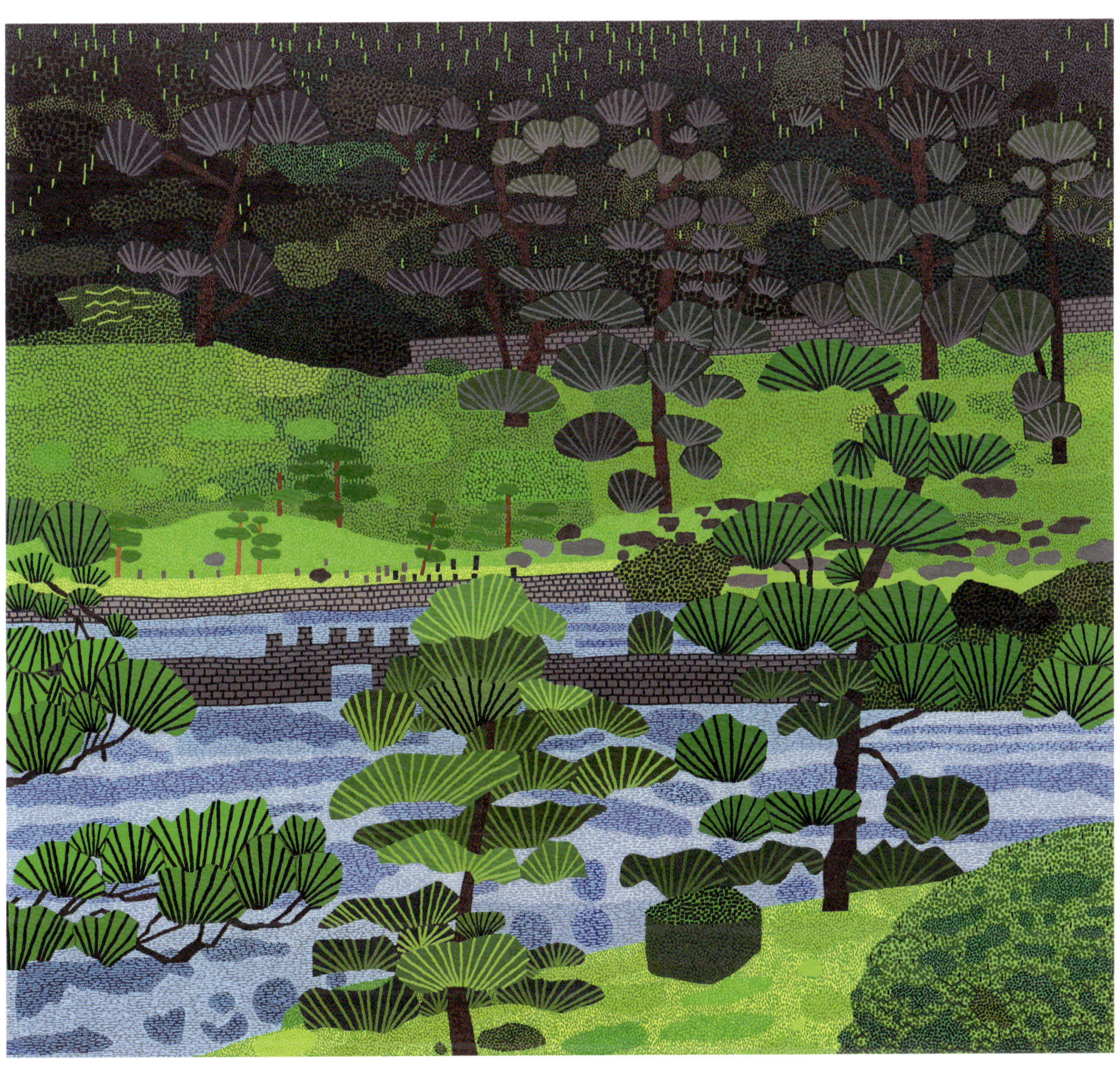

33 / Jonas Wood, *Japanese Garden 3*, 2019
Oil and acrylic on canvas, 223.5 × 248.9 cm
Courtesy of the artist

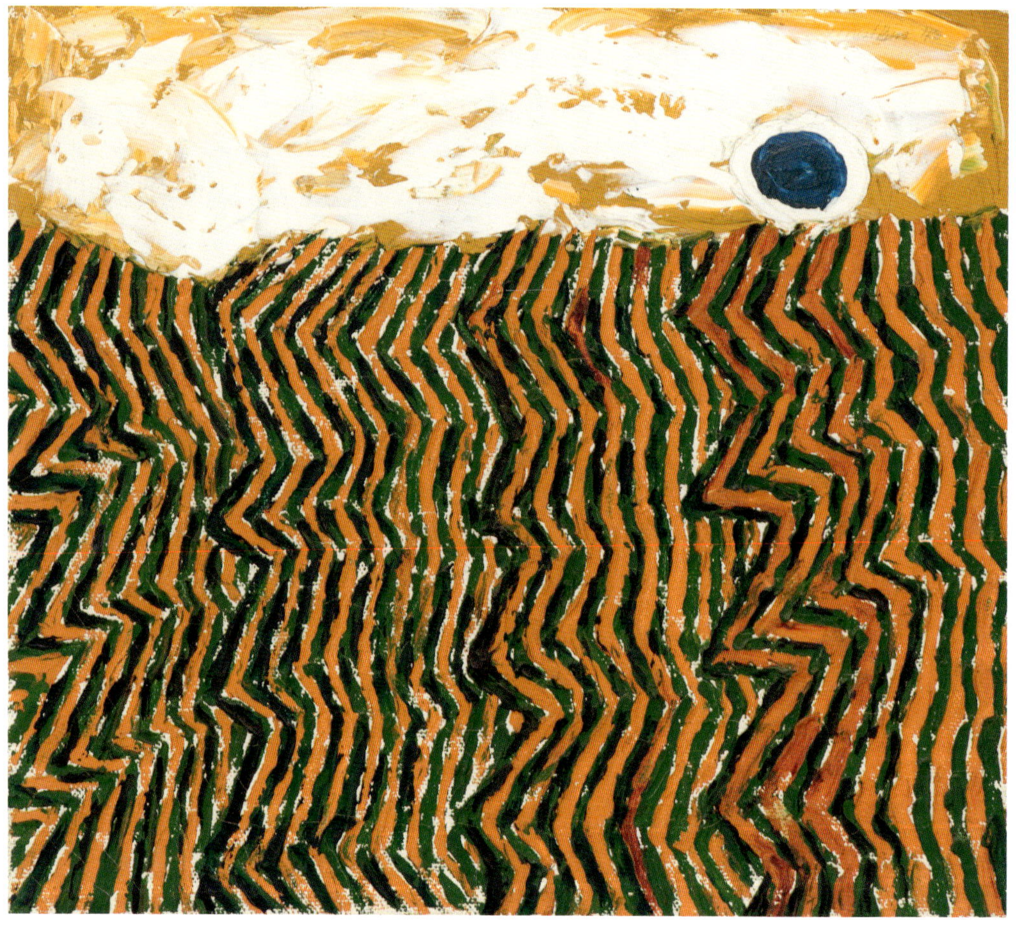

34 / Forrest Bess, *Dedication to Van Gogh*, 1946
Oil on canvas, 39.5 × 44.8 cm
Museum of Contemporary Art, Chicago.
Gift of Mary and Earle Ludgin Collection

35 / Matthew Wong, *The Other Side of the Moon*, 2017
Acrylic on canvas, 91.4 × 61 cm
Private collection

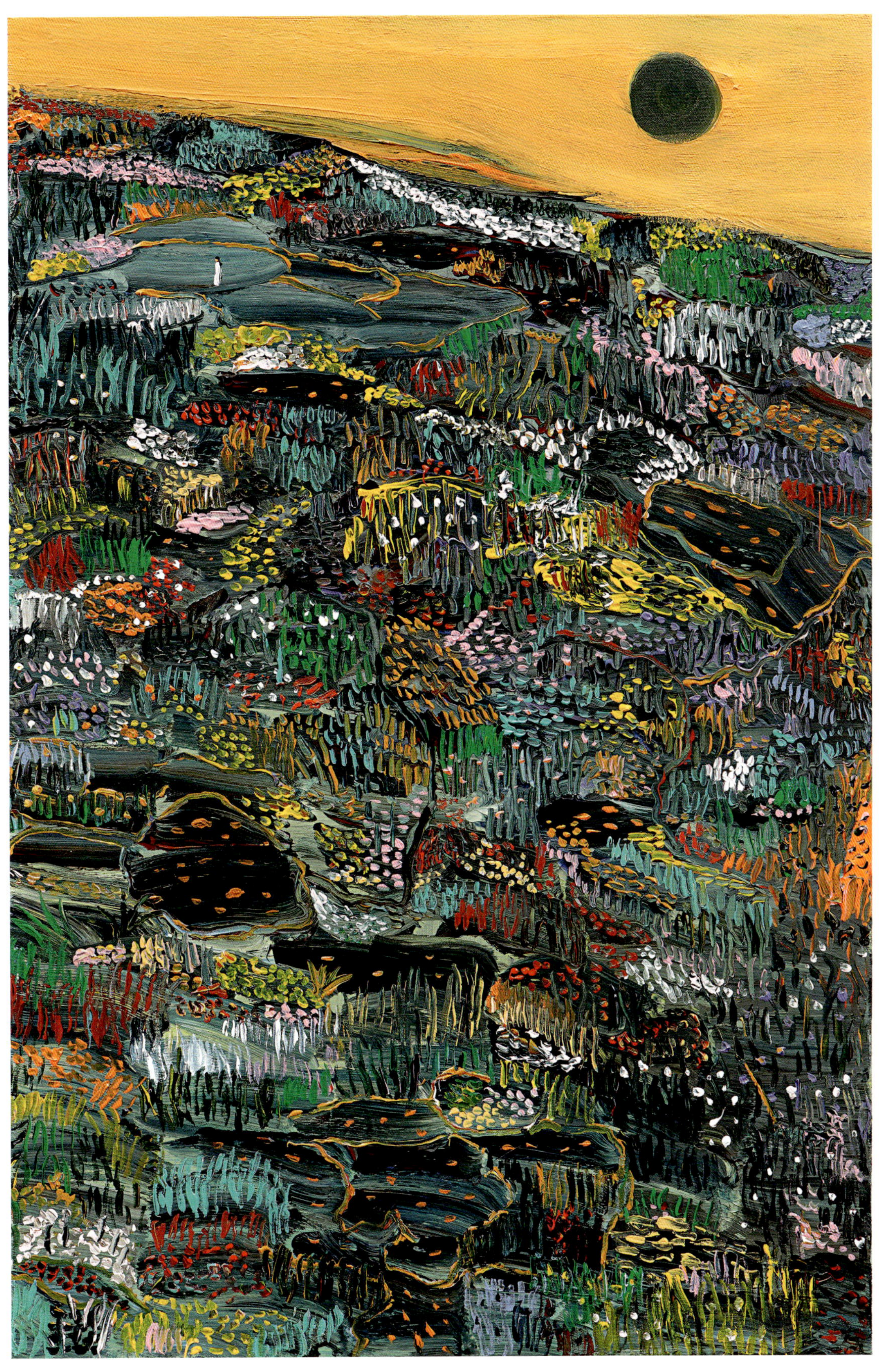

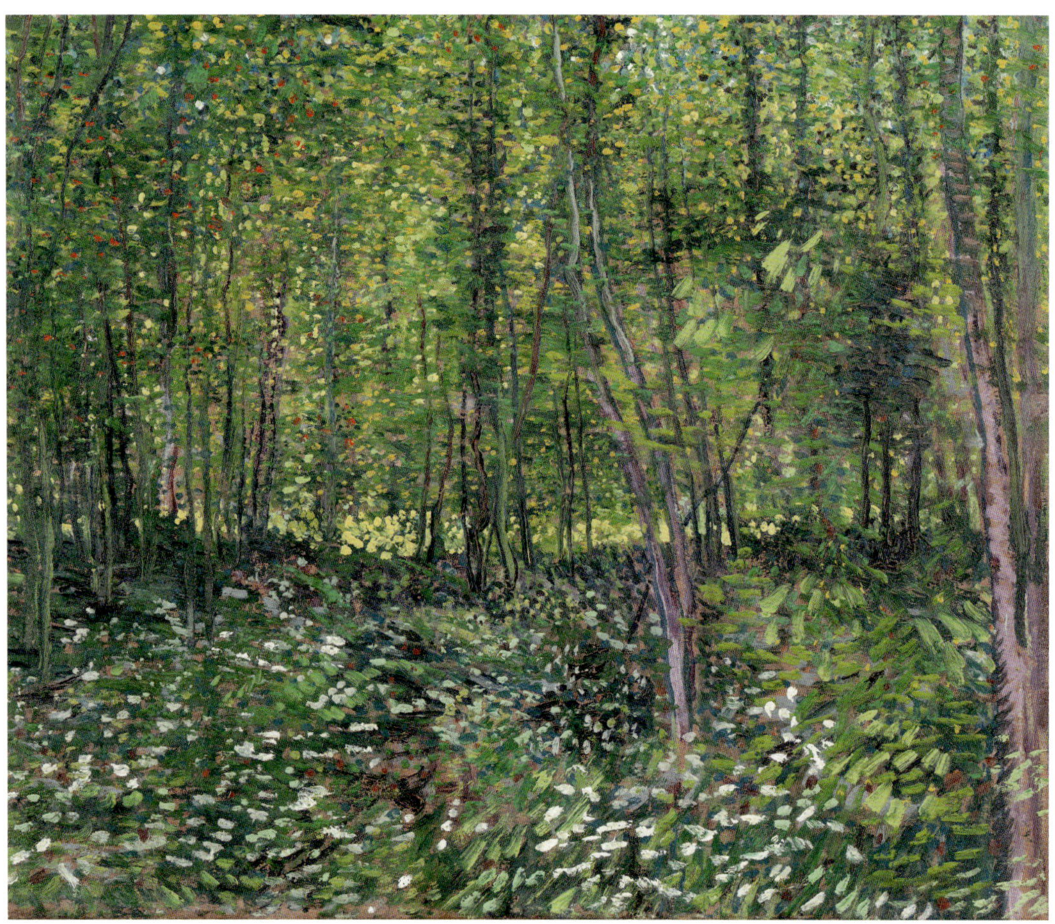

36 /Vincent van Gogh,
Trees and Undergrowth, 1887
Oil on canvas, 46.2 × 55.2 cm
Van Gogh Museum, Amsterdam
(Vincent van Gogh Foundation)

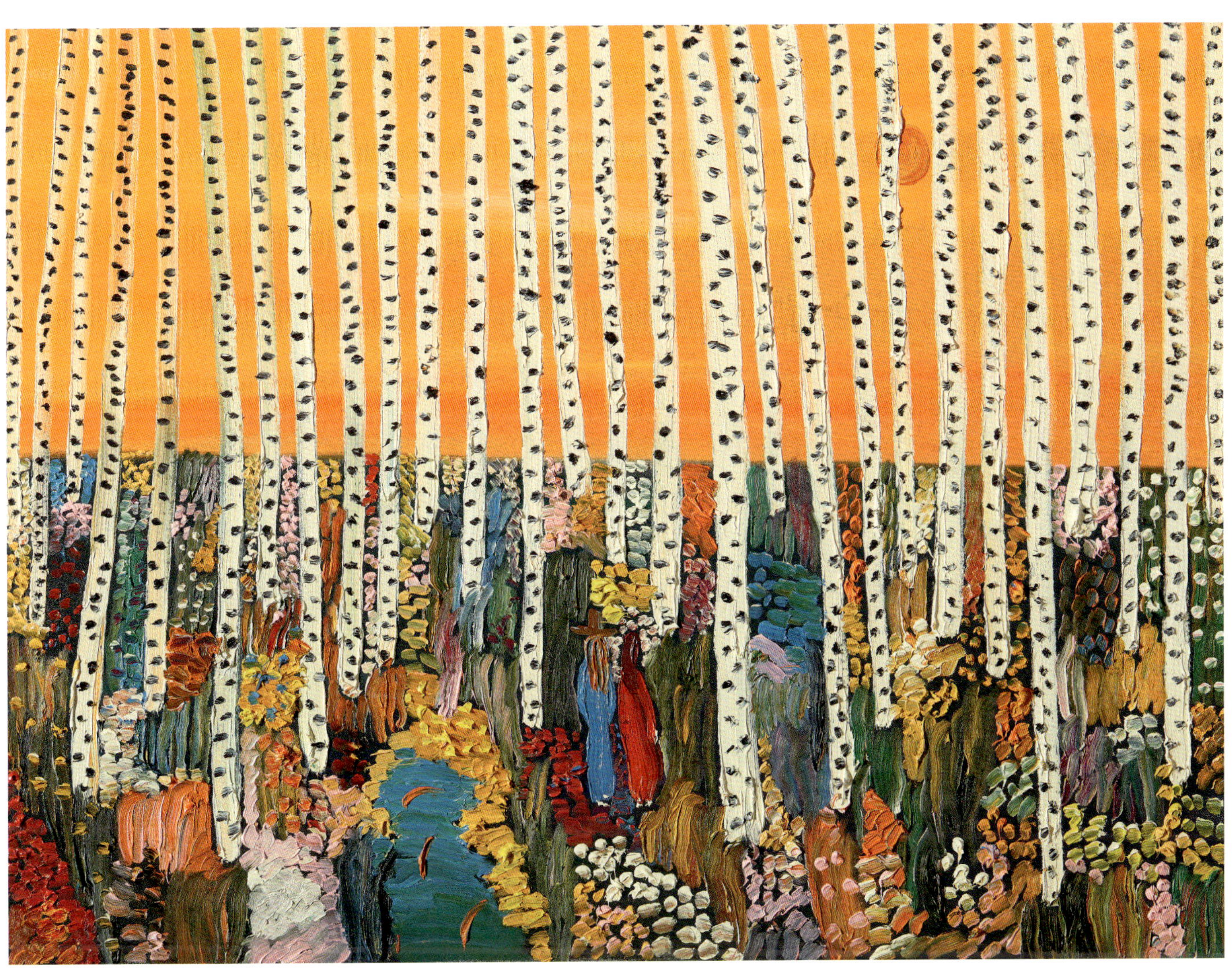

37 / Matthew Wong, *Dialogue*, 2018
Oil on canvas, 76.2 × 101.6 cm
Collection of Lisa and Michael Cotton

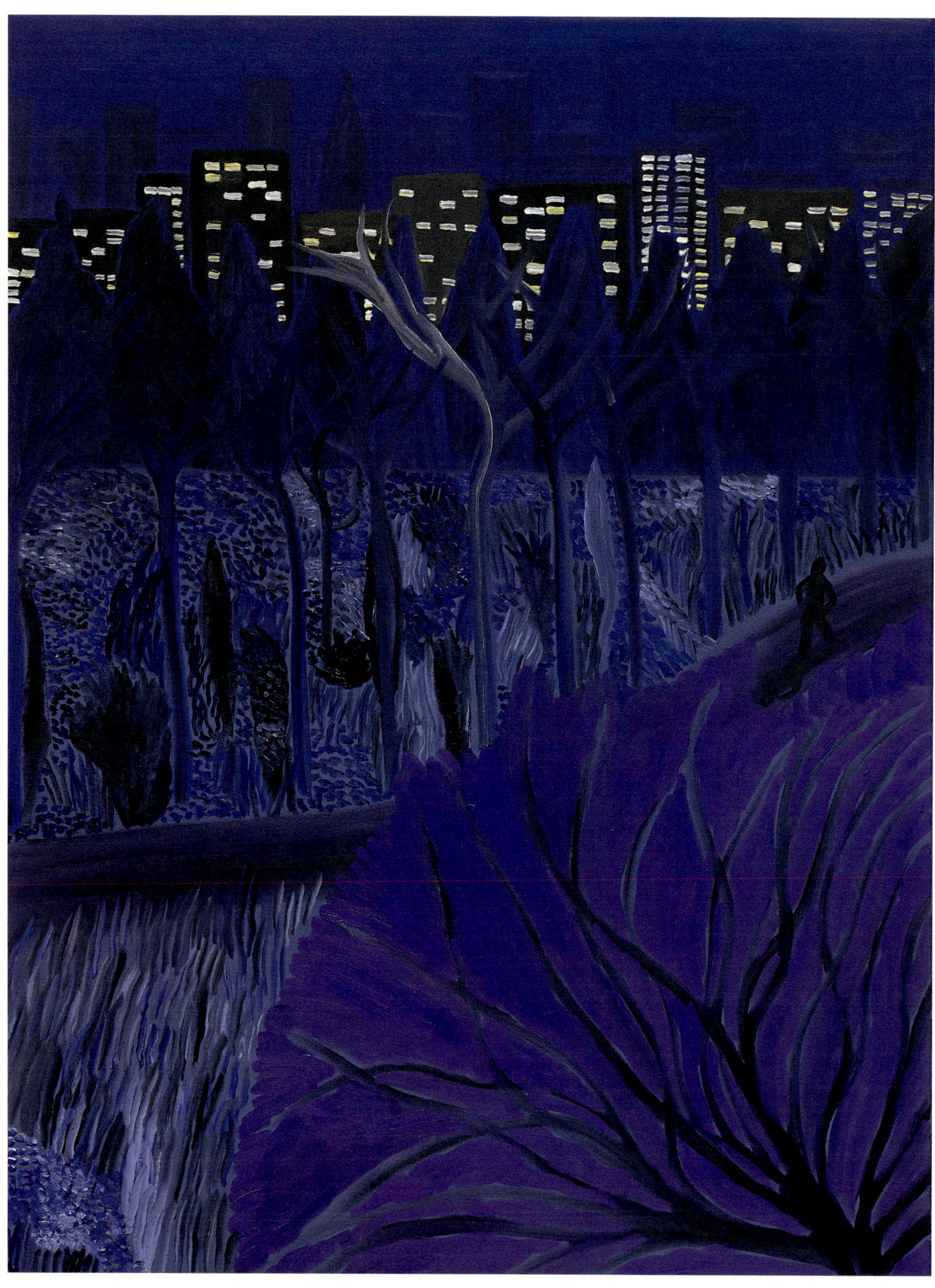

38 / Matthew Wong, *Solitude*, 2018
Oil on canvas, 121.9 × 91.4 cm
Matthew Wong Foundation

39 / Matthew Wong, *The West*, 2017
Oil on canvas, 99.1 × 78.7 cm
Dallas Museum of Art. Dallas Art Fair
Foundation Acquisition Fund

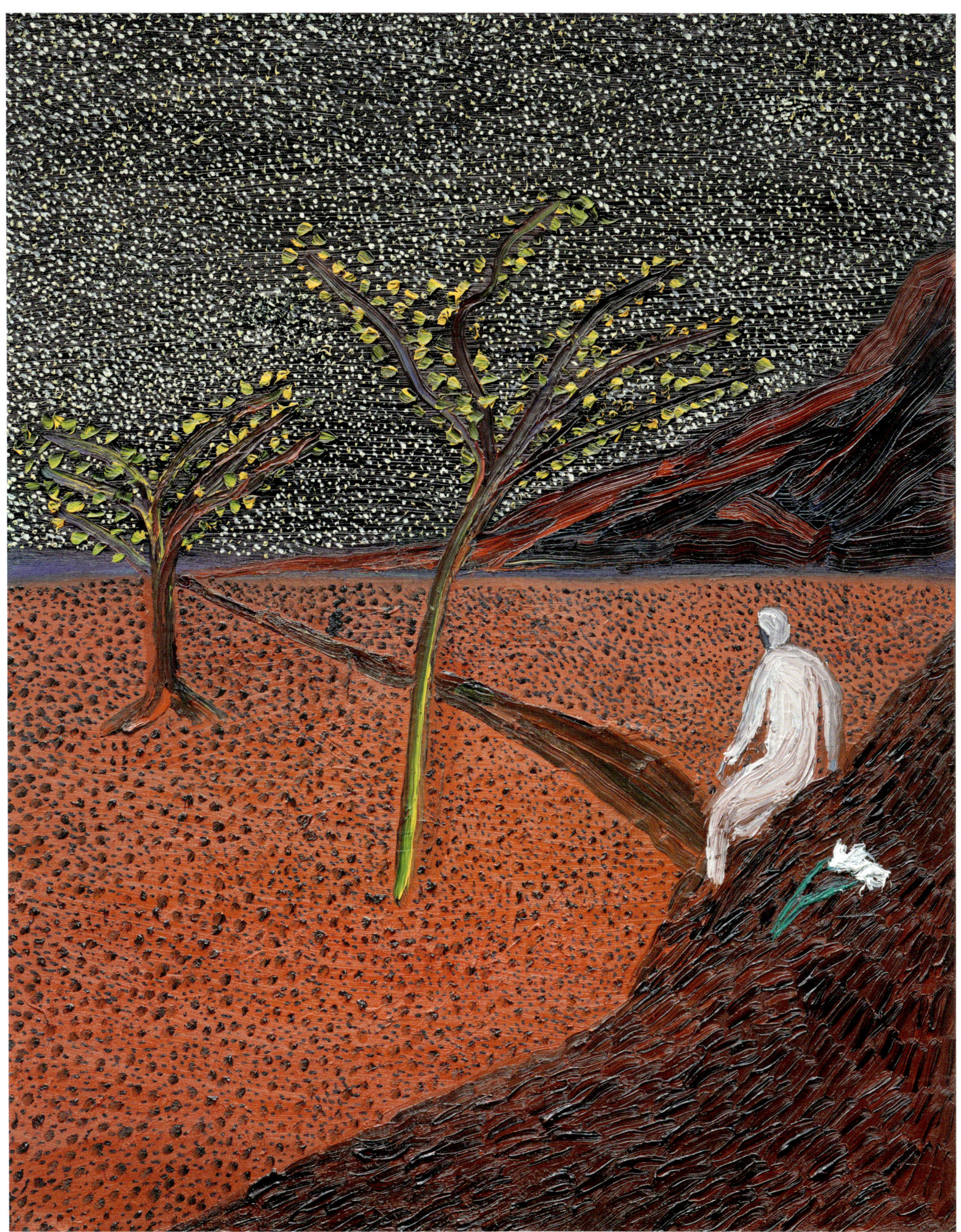

The Other Side of the Moon marked Wong's definitive breakthrough. It earned him the coveted formal representation by the Karma gallery and confirmation that his work was developing in the right direction. Together with the painting *The West* (fig. 39), among others, the work was taken to the Dallas Art Fair in early April 2017. As in *The Other Side of the Moon, The West* features a lonely figure in an otherwise empty landscape. The horizon is lower in this instance and the figure appears much larger in the foreground at the beginning of a path running into the distance. The quality of *The West* was recognized at the fair by the Dallas Museum of Art, which acquired it there and then, making it the only museum to purchase a work by Wong during his lifetime.[84]

Alone in the landscape

The solitary figures in *The Other Side of the Moon* and *The West* became a recurring theme for Wong. It was one drawn, like several motifs in his work, from traditional Chinese painting. While the figure was intended as a compositional reference point in the landscape, it also had symbolic meaning. In the first instance, it was autobiographical and alluded to Wong's own loneliness and isolation in the world.[85] *Solitude* (fig. 38), painted in 2018 and in which he depicted himself alone on a nocturnal riverbank in Edmonton, is one of the most explicit allusions to this. Another, later work in which the grandeur of the landscape contrasts beautifully with the solitude and insignificance of the figure is *End of the Day* (fig. 2). In some cases, Wong painted two figures, referring to the important role his mother played in his life. Examples include *Landscape with Mother and Child* (fig. 95) and *Dialogue* (fig. 37), works in which the two of them are shown together in an otherwise empty world.

All the same, most of Wong's canvases go beyond the depiction of solitude alone. He wanted the imaginary landscapes he painted in *The Other Side of the Moon, The West, Mother and Child* and *Dialogue* to evoke a certain sensation, which he liked to describe using the Portuguese word *saudade*: yearning, nostalgia and melancholy for a place, person or thing that no longer exists.[86] Wong himself expressed the intention behind his landscapes in the following terms: 'Visualizing the idea of that place or memory or thing that transcends its physical experience, but at the same time simply doesn't exist. Those perfect moments of heightened being.'[87]

Wong's landscapes visualize a nostalgic idea of a primordial world, in which human beings lived a simpler life, more in harmony with nature, as in *A Walk Through Primordial Garden* (fig. 40).[88] He yearned for a place far away from the complexities of twenty-first-century life, his relationship with which was difficult because of his tics and his mental

40 / Matthew Wong, *A Walk Through Primordial Garden*, 2018
Oil on canvas, 101.6 × 76.2 cm
Matthew Wong Foundation

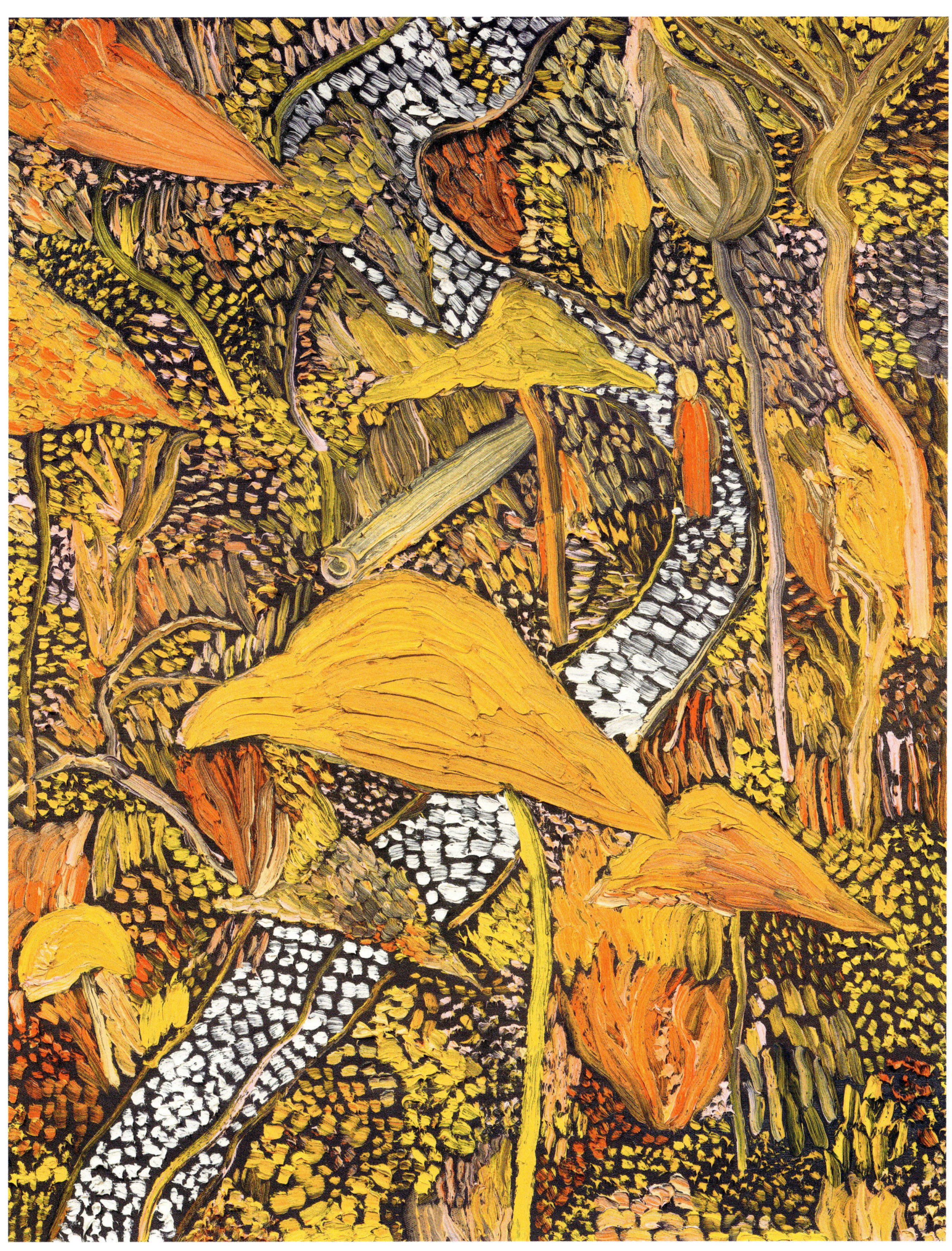

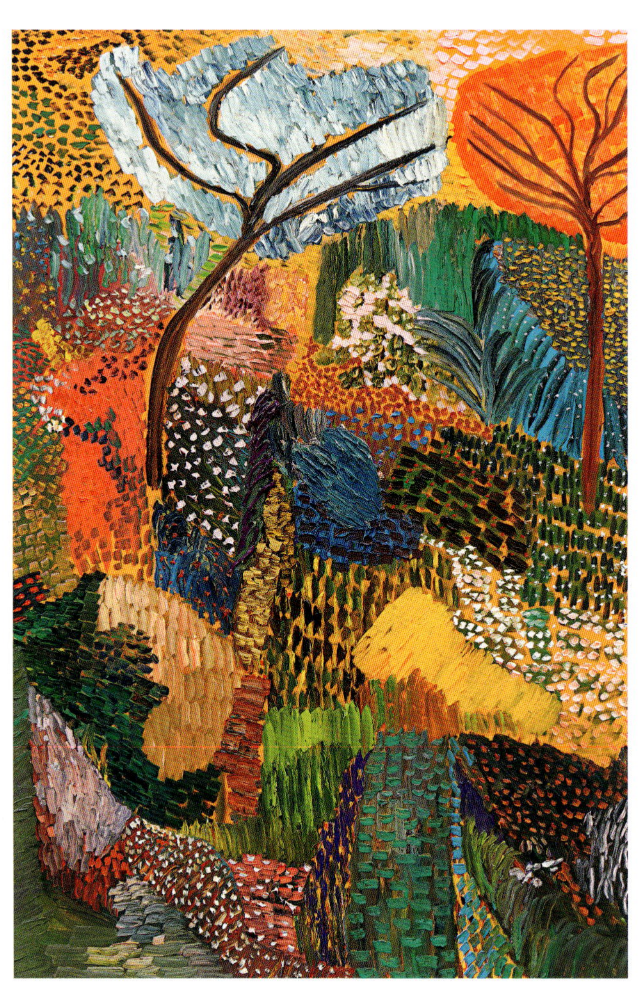

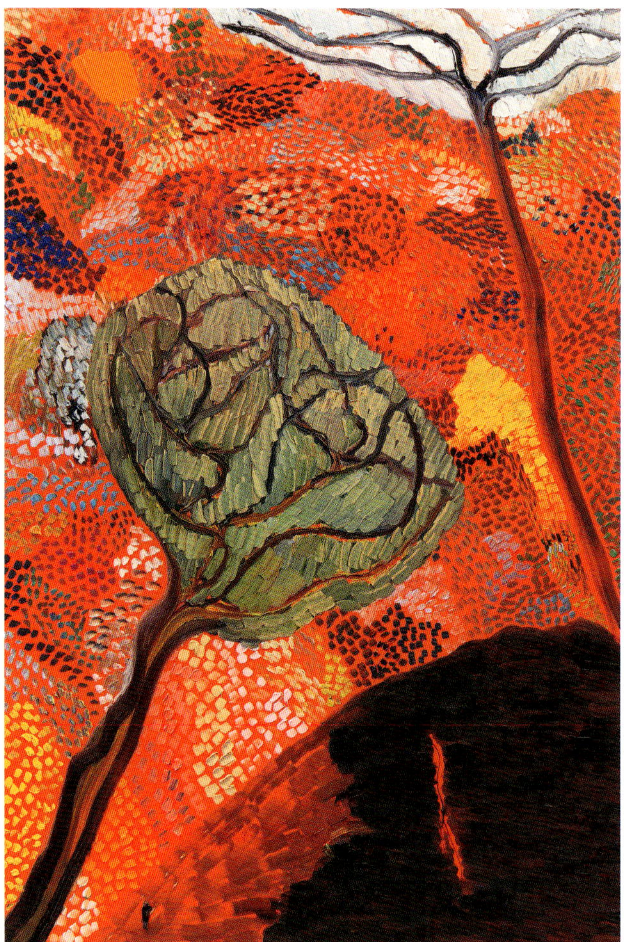

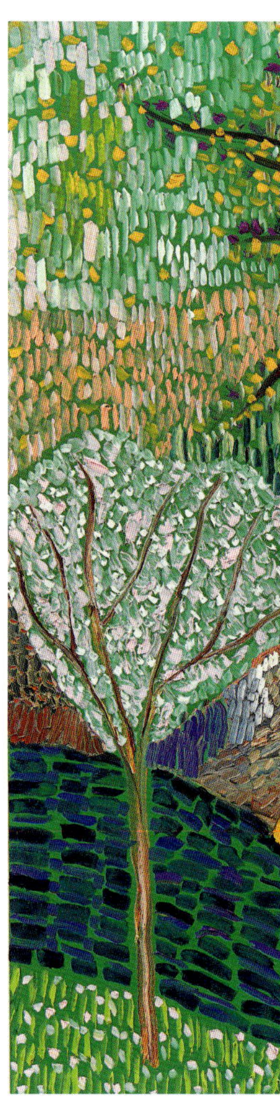

41 / Matthew Wong, *Untitled*, 2017
Oil on canvas, 182.9 × 121.9 cm
Private collection

42 / Matthew Wong, *Untitled*, 2017
Oil on canvas, 182.9 × 121.9 cm
Private collection

43 / Matthew Wong, *Untitled*, 2017
Oil on canvas, 182.9 × 121.9 cm
Private collection, courtesy of HomeArt

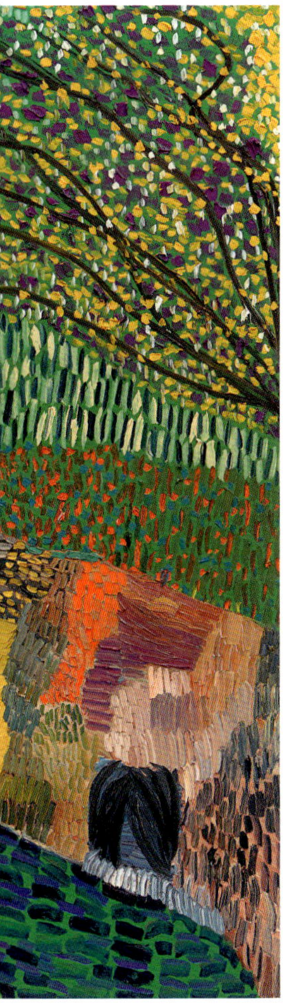

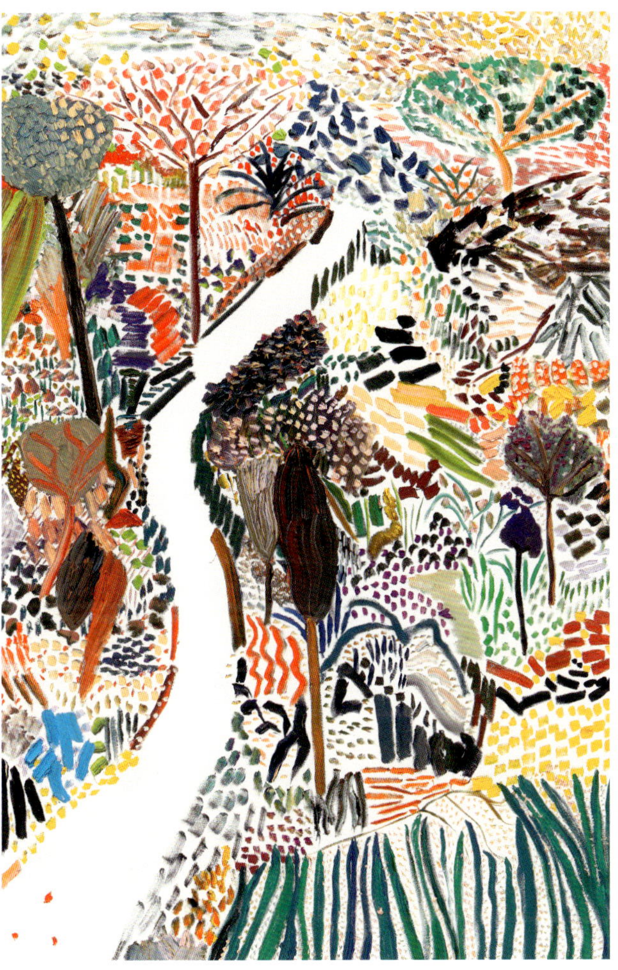

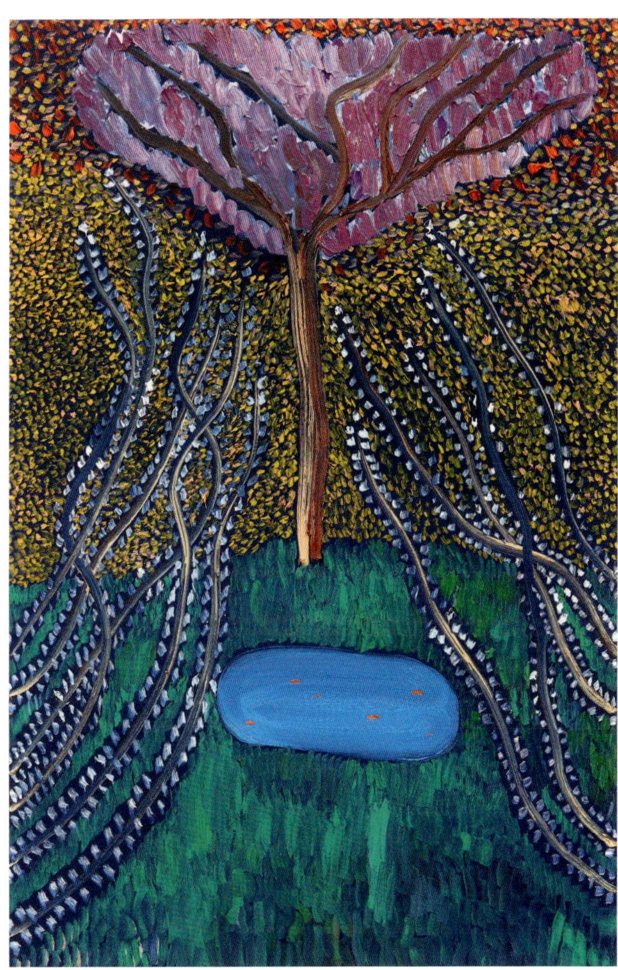

44 / Matthew Wong, *Untitled*, 2017
Oil on canvas, 182.9 × 121.9 cm
Private collection

45 / Matthew Wong, *Luminous Night*, 2017
Oil on canvas, 182.9 × 121.9 cm
Private collection

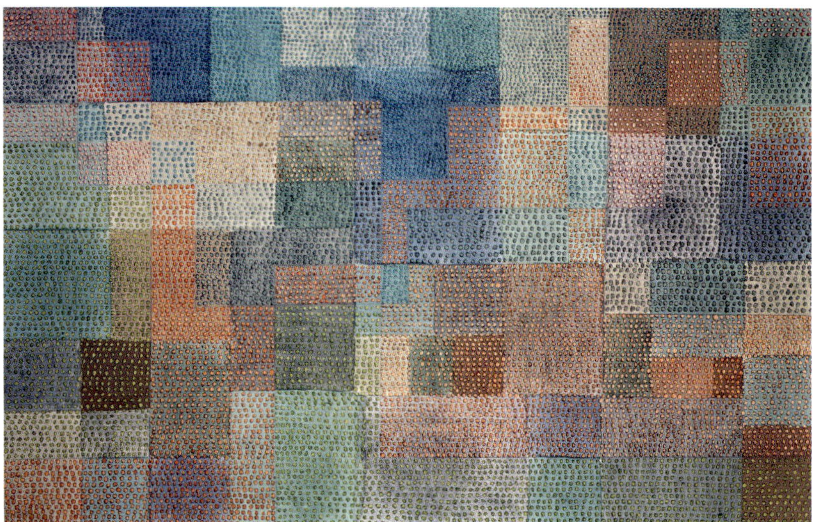

46 / Paul Klee, *Polyphony*, 1932
Tempera on linen, 66.5 × 106 cm
Kunstmuseum Basel.
Emanuel Hoffmann Foundation, Basel

health. His imaginary landscapes were a perfect world he created for himself, into which he could escape. By placing himself within them, he was essentially depicting the release from everyday reality that he experienced as he painted. Wong created his own dream world in a later painting titled *A Dream* (fig. 106). The fact that these landscapes do not exist while still fostering a desire to enter them evokes feelings of melancholy.

Like the figure in a landscape, another recurring theme in Wong's work was the path or road, as seen in *The West*, *A Walk Through Primordial Garden* and *A Dream*. The motif symbolized the path he followed as an artist.[89] The destination is invariably undefined in Wong's work. Sometimes the road is empty, sometimes a solitary figure can be seen walking in the distance. In *Path to the Sea* (fig. 122), which he painted in 2019, Wong placed himself firmly on the path, and we look over his shoulder as he makes his journey.

An explosion of colour

While symbolism played a central role in Wong's work, not all of the paintings he created had a narrative charge. Shortly after completing *The West*, he painted a series of five monumental landscapes – four of them *Untitled* (figs. 41–44), and *Luminous Night* (fig. 45) – that consisted entirely of the pure, expressive power of colour and paint. 'I think my main strengths are colour and brushwork.'[90] It became clear at this point that he truly was made of the same stuff as Van Gogh, for whom colour and touch were at least as important. He painted the five canvases in four days at a Brooklyn studio arranged for him by his art dealer.[91] For Wong, who had not worked in a studio since leaving Hong Kong, it must have come as a genuine liberation. He seems to have cast off his shackles in this brief period, resulting in five bravura works – explosions of colour that demonstrate the full potential of the direction in which he was taking his art.

As he worked in Brooklyn, Wong and others took a large number of photographs, which offer an insight into his studio practice (fig. 92). He began each work, for instance, with a ground layer consisting of a single, brightly coloured and inexpensive type of paint, and then allowed this to guide him in his characteristic, intuitive way. There is no trace of an underdrawing or a preliminary study – things that Wong never did: he began work without hesitation and continued until he was finished. These extremely direct paintings look to David Hockney in terms of palette, and Paul Klee in terms of combining short touches and patches of colour (fig. 46). Wong initially viewed the five works as a series to be shown together at Karma, but this did not come to much as the paintings sold almost straight away.[92]

Following this brief episode of unbridled creativity, Wong would have to wait a further two months before finally securing a studio of his own in Edmonton. His mother had arranged a space for him in a business park to the south of the city, but administrative delays meant that Wong had to wait a while longer before he could get down to work. Being unable to paint the way he wanted made him 'restless as hell', so he produced another oil painting at home – a panorama of a Chinese landscape that he named after the Rolling Stones song *Far Away Eyes* (fig. 124).[93] When he finally got access to his studio, a creative explosion occurred similar to the one previously witnessed in New York. Wong painted with such verve that the walls ended up spattered and the space was swiftly transformed into a chaos of paint tubes, trays of brushes and piles of paper towels, which he used as makeshift palettes. Despite the apparent disorder, he was soon painting one large colourful canvas after another, including *Morning Landscape* and *The Kingdom* (figs. 123 and 47).

The Kingdom presents the visual spectacle of tree trunks in a birch forest, a familiar motif through which Wong alluded to the many artists who had depicted it before him, including Klimt (fig. 48), Hockney and Van Gogh (fig. 49).[94] At the same time, the trees refer to his own surroundings in Edmonton, where birch forests of this type are found all around the city. By calling the work *The Kingdom*, Wong was declaring that he felt like a king in his new home and his new studio. He often used the word 'king' in his titles, possibly in reference to rap artists like Notorious B.I.G., who declared himself to be 'The King of New York'.[95] In 2018, meanwhile, Wong painted a smaller canvas titled *The King Returns to his Boyhood Home* (private collection).

It was during this period that Wong created the huge work *Old Town* (fig. 52), with a folded perspective that recalls the work of Wayne Thiebaud (fig. 53).[96] The canvas is one of a series of seven, each measuring almost 245 by 185 centimetres, the largest format he ever painted, and seemingly an indication of the boundless ambition he felt at this point in his career. Painting large canvases rather than small ones came to him more naturally anyway, although he continued to produce smaller works in his studio too, such as *Figure in a Landscape* (fig. 54), *So Much Depends...* (fig. 15) and the triptych *The Journey Home* (fig. 5).[97]

>> 47 / Matthew Wong,
The Kingdom, 2017
Oil on canvas, 121.9 × 182.9 cm
Liz Lange and David Shapiro

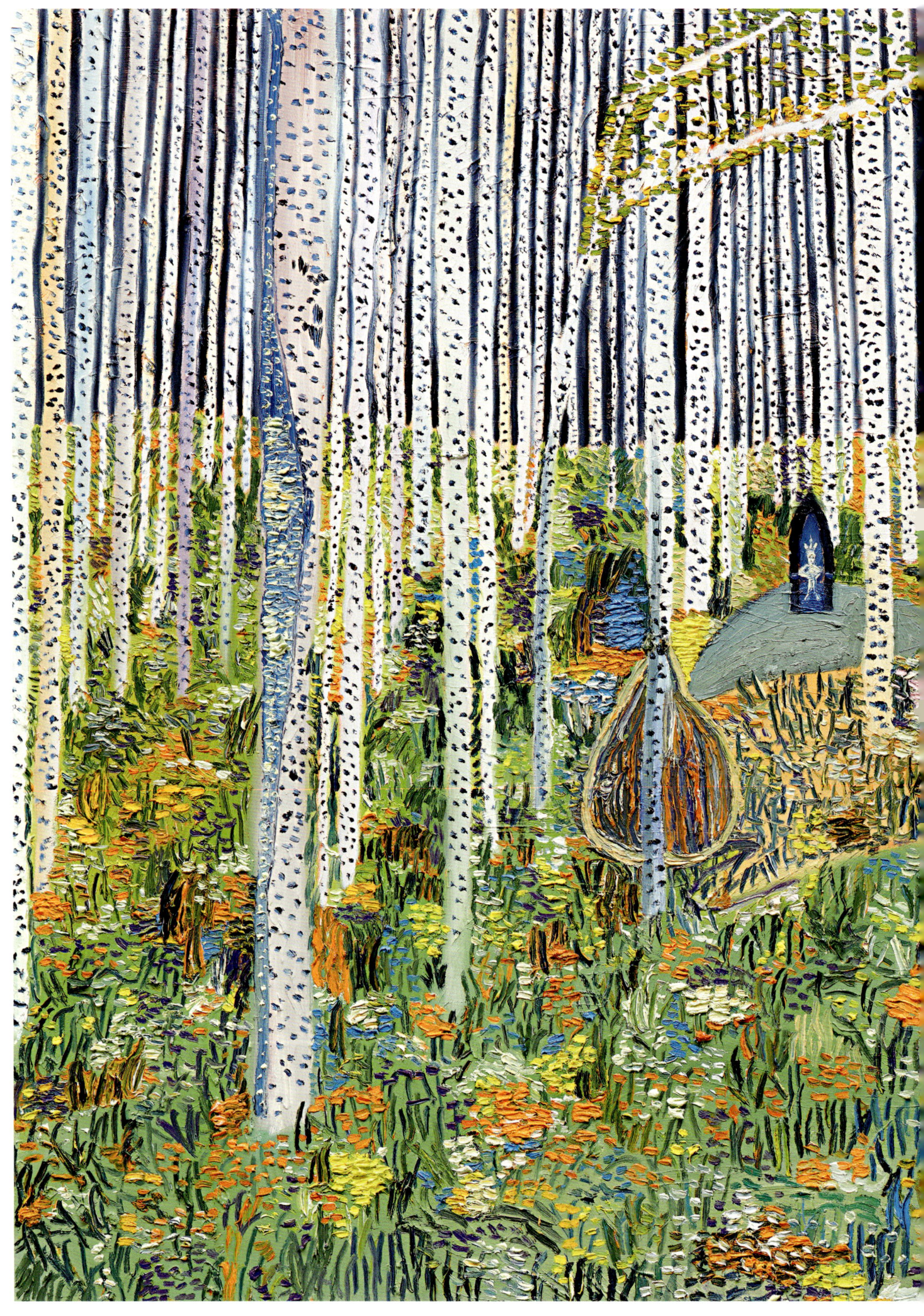

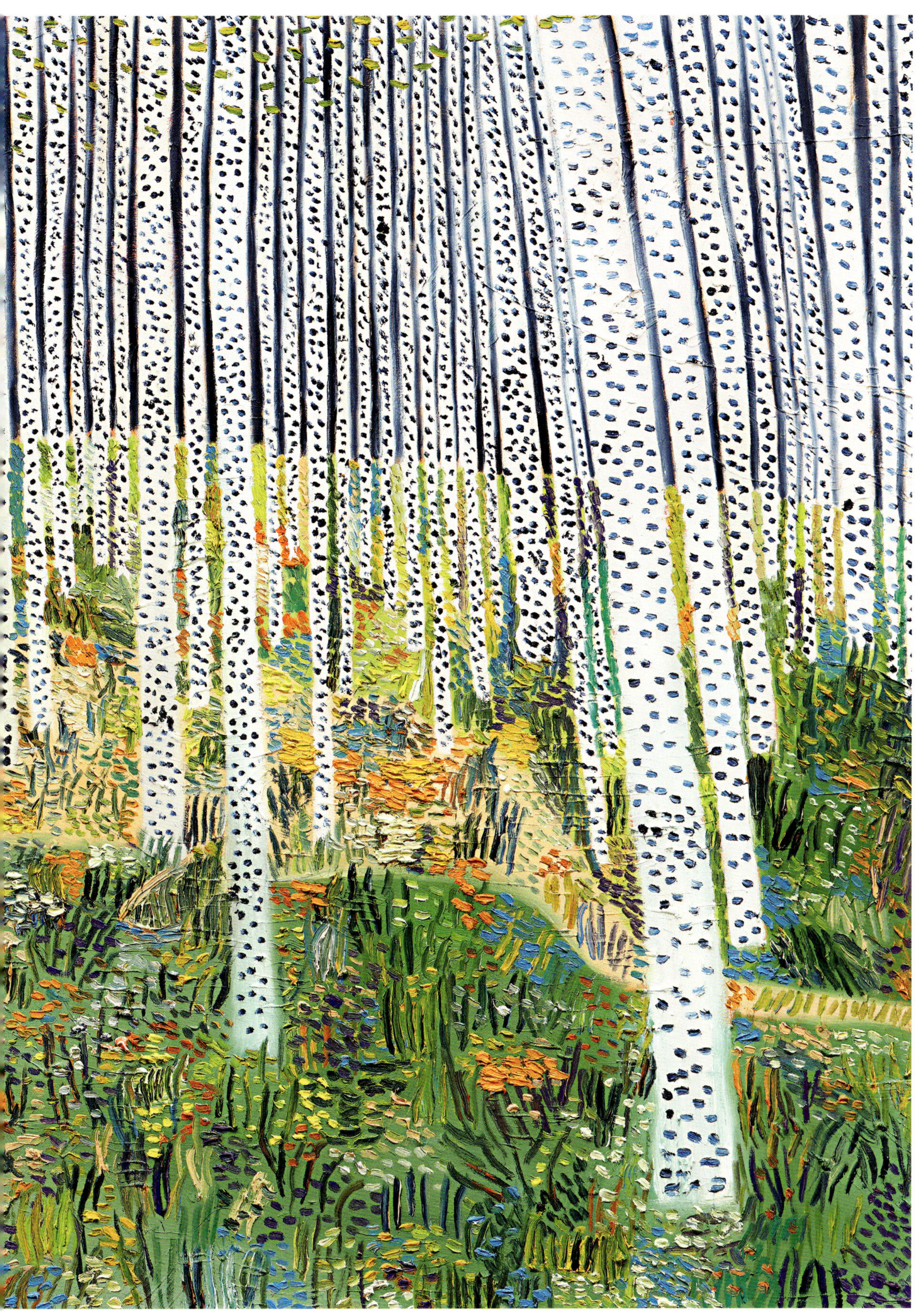

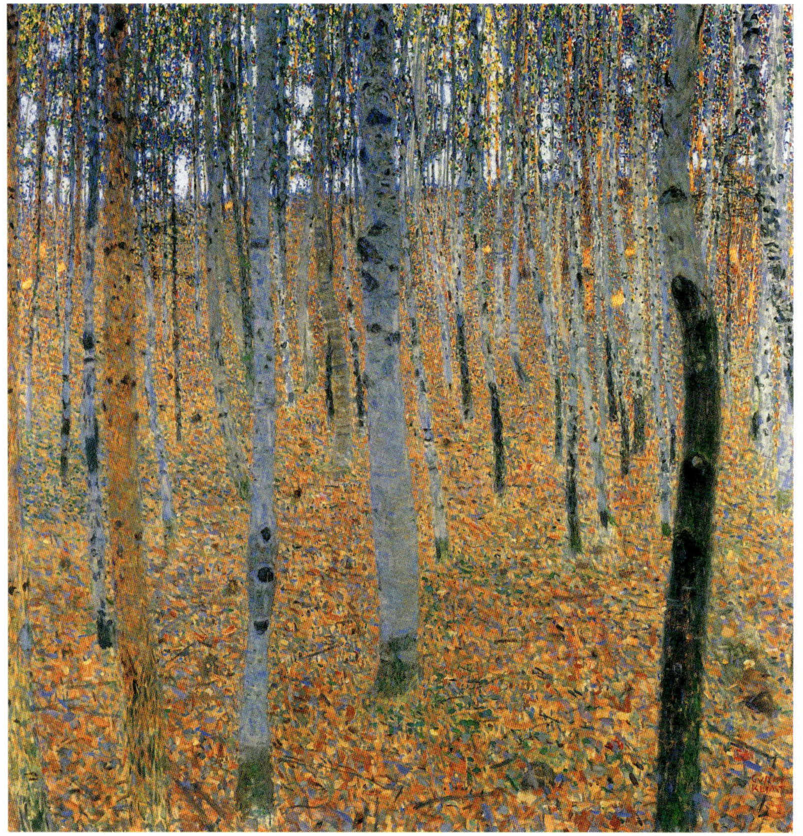

48 / Gustav Klimt, *Beechwood Forest I* (*Buchenwald I*), 1903
Oil on canvas, 100 × 100 cm
Gemäldegalerie Neue Meister, Staatliche Kunstsammlungen, Dresden

Imaginary landscapes

After the summer of 2017, Wong started to think about his solo exhibition at Karma, which was scheduled for the spring of 2018. The high bar he set himself led him to probe the extremes of the style in which he was working, yielding several of his most celebrated paintings, *The Realm of Appearances* (fig. 50) and *Somewhere* (fig. 126) among them. In the first of these works, Wong painted a stylized and aesthetically harmonious fantasy forest in all sorts of different colours and touches over a warm orange-red ground layer. The jumble of brushstrokes and planes of colour in the landscape contrasts beautifully with the cool evening sky over the horizon. While the painting leans heavily towards the work of his friend Scott Kahn (fig. 55), it is also one of Wong's most successful evocations of the *saudade* concept. The landscape is a place we can yearn for and into which we would like to disappear, but the realization that this is not possible fills us with melancholy and loss. This is what Wong is alluding to with the title *The Realm of Appearances*. The landscape appears as an ideal, dreamed-of form, yet ultimately exists only in the imagination. 'Something of profound feeling yet at once at an impossible irreconcilable remove – the paradox that I feel is at the heart of my vision.'[98] The same goes for *Somewhere*, in which it remains unclear whether this 'somewhere' really exists or is merely a figment of the imagination. Wong proved to himself with this work, reminiscent of a woodcut, that he was able to create a fantasy world full of beauty just as well with two colours as he could with a full palette.

The titles *The Realm of Appearances* and *Somewhere* place the emphasis on the imaginary character of Wong's landscapes. The fact that he worked from his imagination in the studio is a key difference between his practice and that of Van Gogh, who based himself overwhelmingly on the observation of reality. Van Gogh wrote in this regard to his friend Bernard: 'I sometimes regret that I can't decide to work more at home and from the imagination.'[99] But working in that way simply was not in his nature. He much preferred to set up his easel outdoors and to paint what he saw – his *Wheatfield* (fig. 51), for instance.

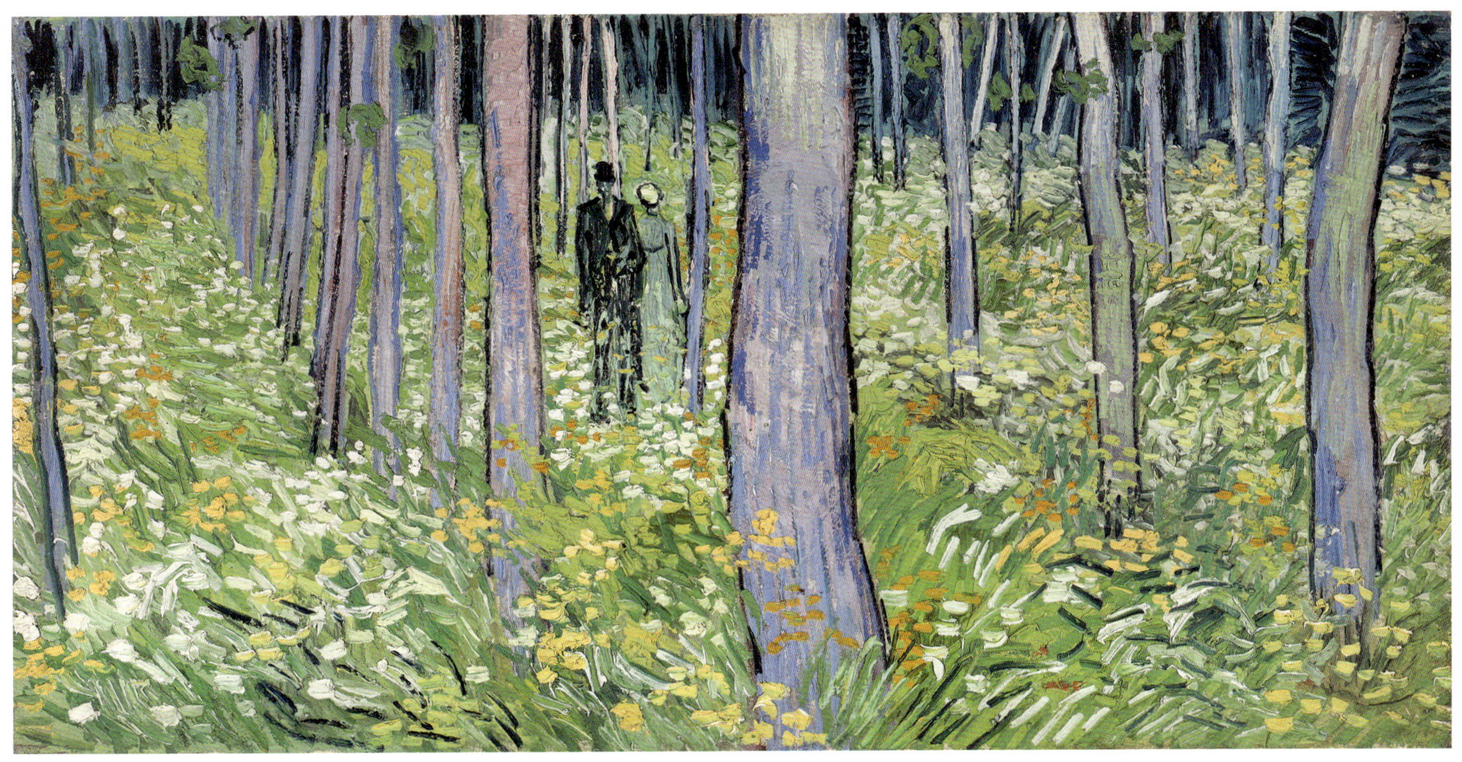

49 / Vincent van Gogh,
Undergrowth with Two Figures, 1890
Oil on canvas, 49.5 x 99.7 cm
Cincinnati Art Museum.
Bequest of Mary E. Johnston

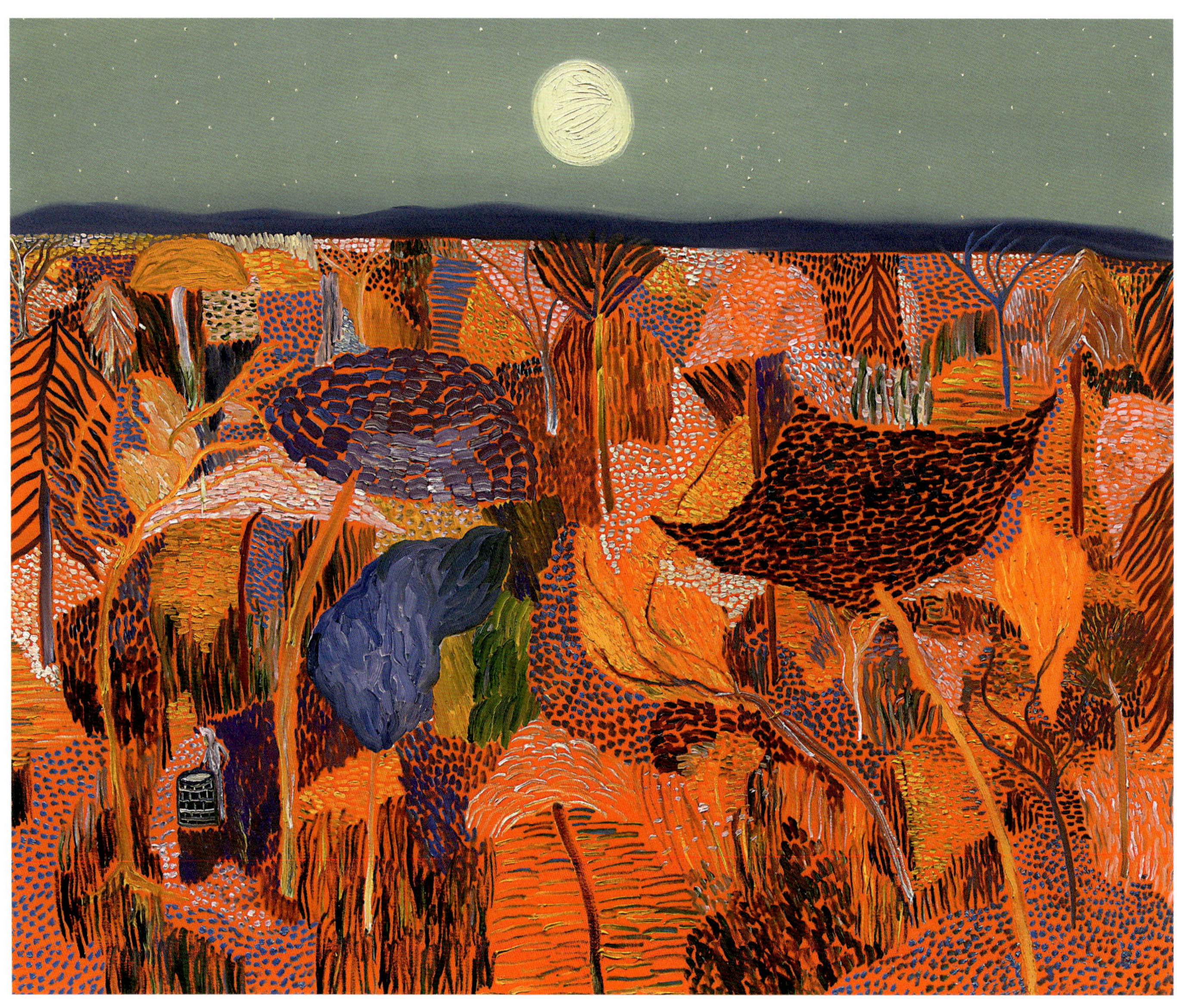

50 / Matthew Wong, *The Realm of Appearances*, 2018
Oil on canvas, 165.1 × 203.2 cm
Private collection

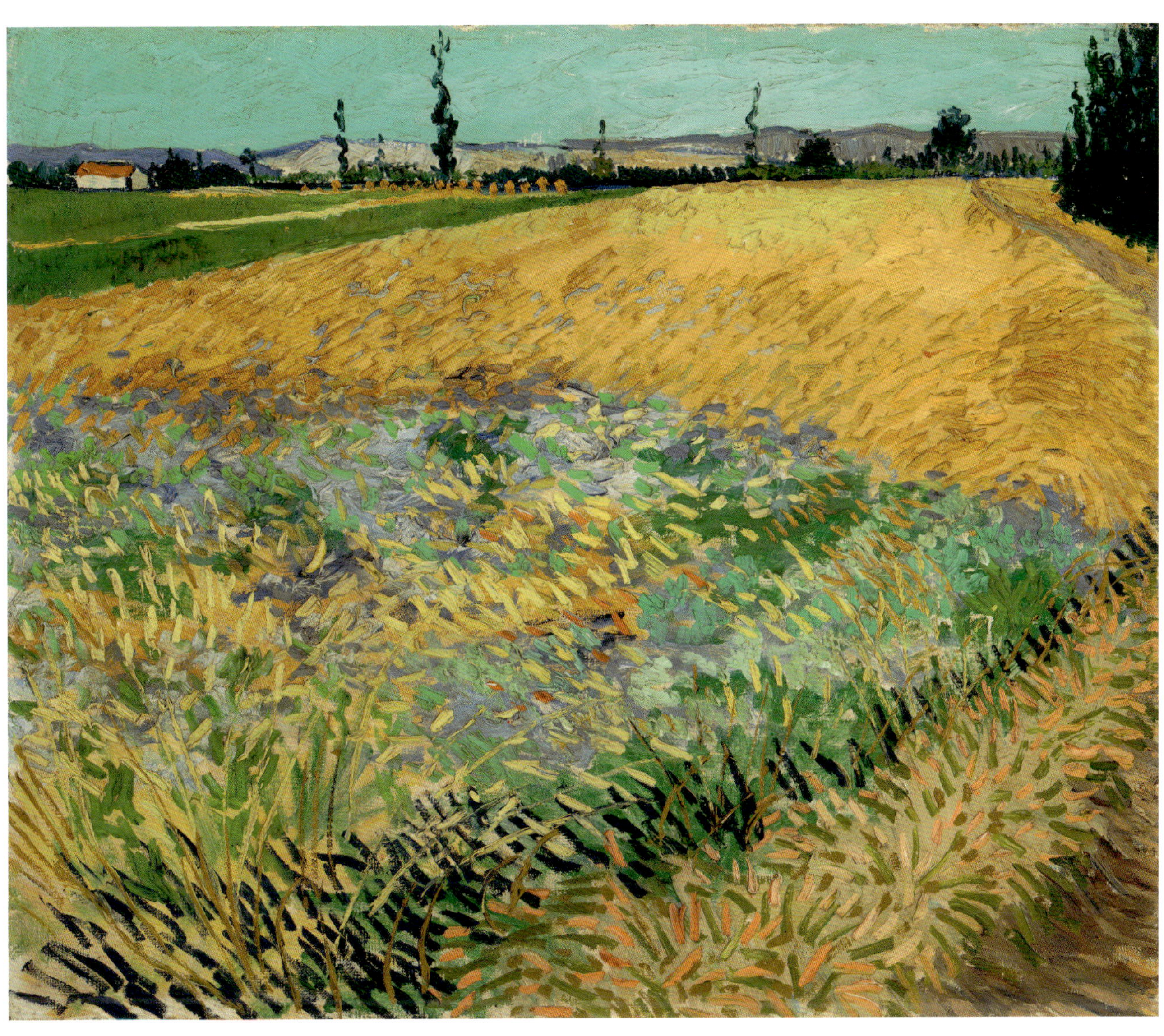

51 / Vincent van Gogh, *Wheatfield*, 1888
Oil on canvas, 54 × 65 cm
Van Gogh Museum, Amsterdam
(Vincent van Gogh Foundation)

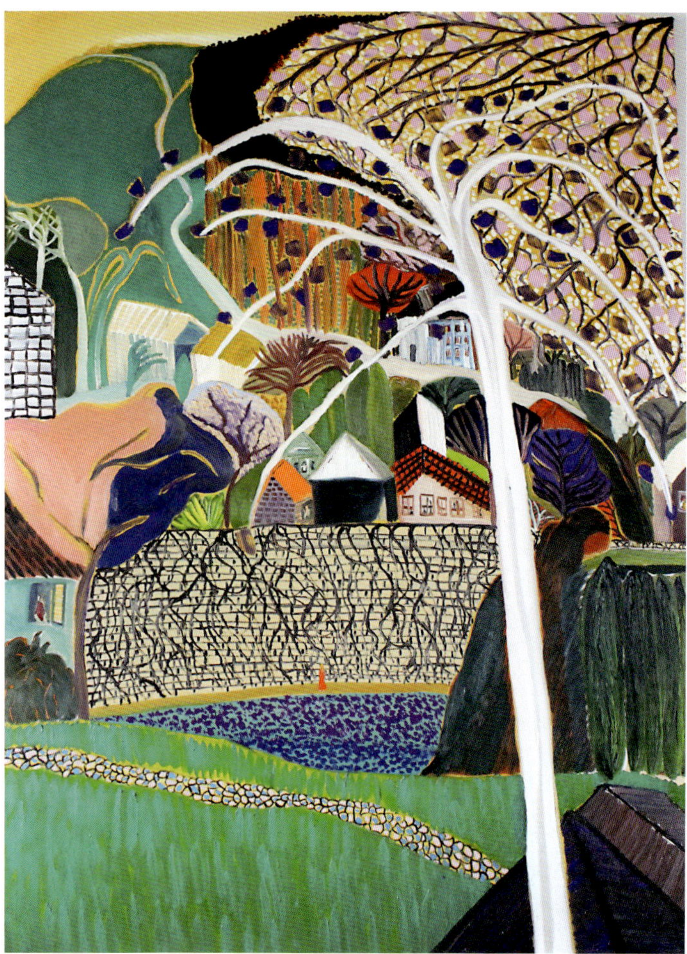

While Van Gogh did imbue his work with a symbolic charge, he found his symbols in the physical world around him. In the *Garden of the Asylum* (fig. 56), he painted a tree from which a large branch had been sawn off, which he interpreted as 'a proud man brought low' – the way he had felt when he was admitted to the institution in Saint-Rémy.[100] The colours he used in the painting likewise carried an emotional charge. The ochre of the soil and the garden walls and the 'green saddened with grey' expressed the feelings of anxiety that he and his fellow patients experienced.[101] Wong used colour in a similarly expressive way. *Dark Reverie* (fig. 57), for instance, is painted with an intensely dark palette and conveys with great immediacy the depression with which Wong constantly had to contend.[102]

The turning point

Wong showed *The Realm of Appearances*, *Somewhere* and *The Kingdom* together with six other paintings and twenty-two gouaches at his solo debut at Karma (22 March–29 April 2018) (see p. 164, fig. G). The exhibition was, as mentioned, a great success and garnered glowing reviews. His popularity now reached even greater heights and things began to move so quickly that he could barely keep up. At one point during the opening, he found himself outside, smoking and thinking about his next painting. He would have preferred to have nothing to do with the praise coming his way and sought to distance himself from his work as much as possible. The catalogue that was produced was extremely discreet, without his name on the cover or any accompanying text. Nor did Wong give any interviews in the run-up to the opening.[103]

All this resulted from a jarring realization on Wong's part in the summer of 2017 after the high of his first success had begun to fade. He had hoped that prosperity and recognition would prove a lasting remedy for his severely (in fact chronically) depressed mental state and that success would bring him a greater sense of connection with the art world. Neither of these came to pass and even the resounding success of his exhibition at Karma left him cold: 'Things like sales or even recognition turn out in the end not to assuage any of the bumpiness. You think they do or would but they don't.'[104] On the contrary, he realized that he was ill-equipped to deal with all the attention, admiration and change. He

52 / Matthew Wong, *Old Town*, 2017
Oil on canvas, 243.8 × 183.9 cm
Green Family Art Foundation;
courtesy Adam Green Art Advisory

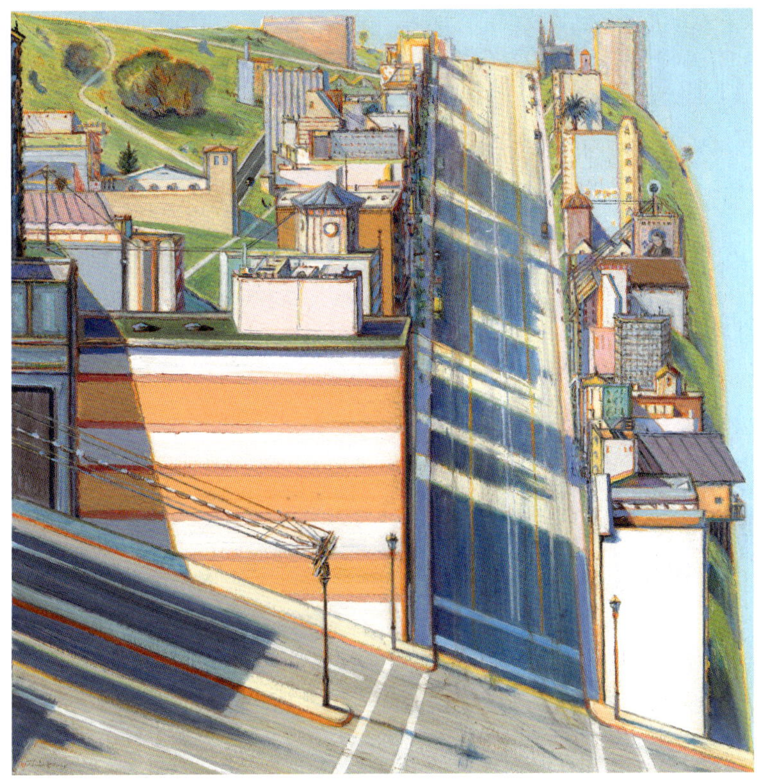

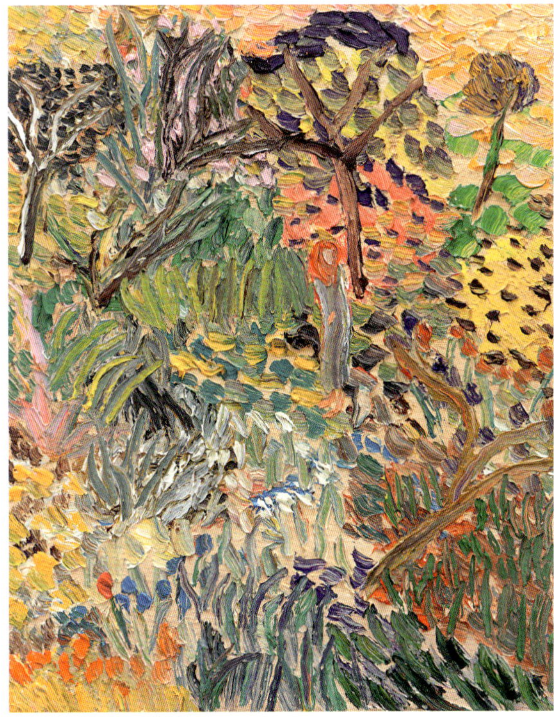

53 / Wayne Thiebaud,
San Francisco West Side Ridge, 2001
Oil on canvas, 91.4 × 91.4 cm
Smithsonian American Art Museum, Washington. Gift of Sam Rose and Julie Walters

54 / Matthew Wong,
Figure in a Landscape, 2017
Oil on canvas, 50.8 × 40.6 cm
Collection of John Cheim

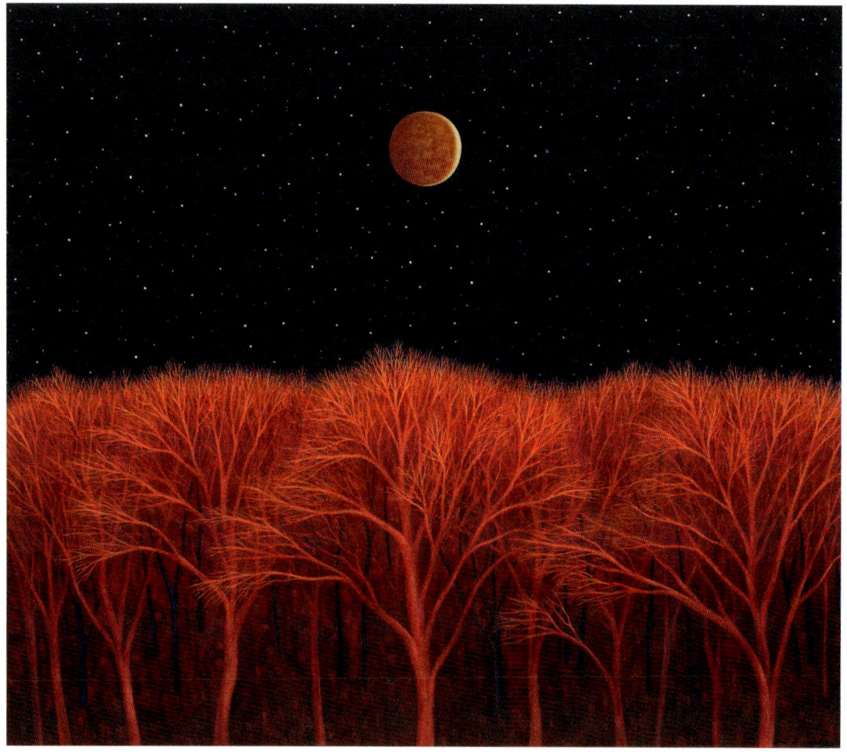

55 / Scott Kahn, *Lunar Eclipse*, 2008
Oil on canvas, 61 × 71.1 cm
Private collection
Courtesy of the artist

now faced jealousy within his Facebook community and was suspicious of people who only began to pay him attention after his breakthrough.[105] Wong wrote to Shear at this point: 'I'm not comfortable with the attention really. It was different in the past mostly just other painters on FB or whatever looking at and responding to the work. Now I don't want to be so exposed. I just kinda wanna be invisible – do the shows make some sales so I can afford to live and keep working.'[106]

Wong had looked up to the New York art world in his early years in Hong Kong and wanted nothing more than to become part of it. Having succeeded, however, he found that all he wanted to do now was to withdraw into his studio in Edmonton and paint. He only travelled to New York when absolutely necessary, such as the opening of his exhibition at Karma. 'This city [New York] is too cool for my blood', he wrote. 'The longer I stay the lonelier I feel which is strange considering in Edmonton I'm completely and utterly alone lol.'[107] Viewed in this light, the painting *Solitude* (fig. 38) can be read more as a celebration than an indictment of his solitude. Edmonton was his 'kingdom', the place where he wielded his craft with complete confidence, where the act of painting was the genuine remedy, and where he could escape into his self-created worlds.

It was at this turning point in Wong's career that he found comfort in the story of Van Gogh's life. In his correspondence with his Facebook friend Sofia Silva, he described what he had been through as the 'Van Gogh effect': '[I am] not saying I'm Van Gogh or as good as Van Gogh but [I'm on] a weird path where most people don't like you.'[108] Realizing that he would never become part of the art world or be truly understood, Wong increasingly identified with and drew strength from the story of his predecessor a hundred and thirty years earlier. 'Man that must've sucked to be Van Gogh', he wrote to Shear: the knowledge that there had been another artist who went through something similar offered him support.[109]

Wong's perception of Van Gogh seems to have been based largely on the popular image of the tormented and plagued artist who received

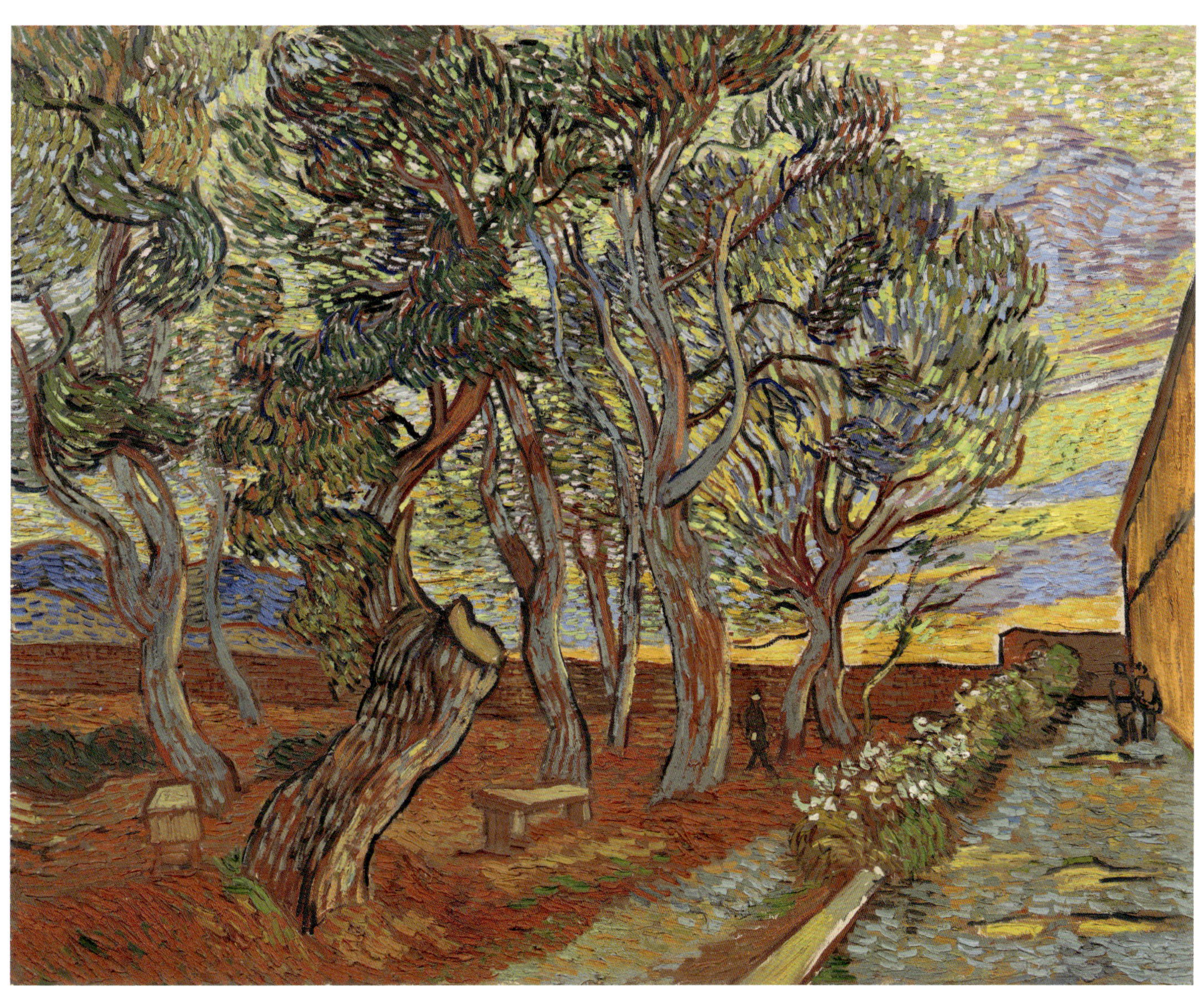

56 / Vincent van Gogh,
Garden of the Asylum, 1889
Oil on canvas, 72 × 91 cm
Van Gogh Museum, Amsterdam
(Vincent van Gogh Foundation,
gift of Paul Gachet jr.)

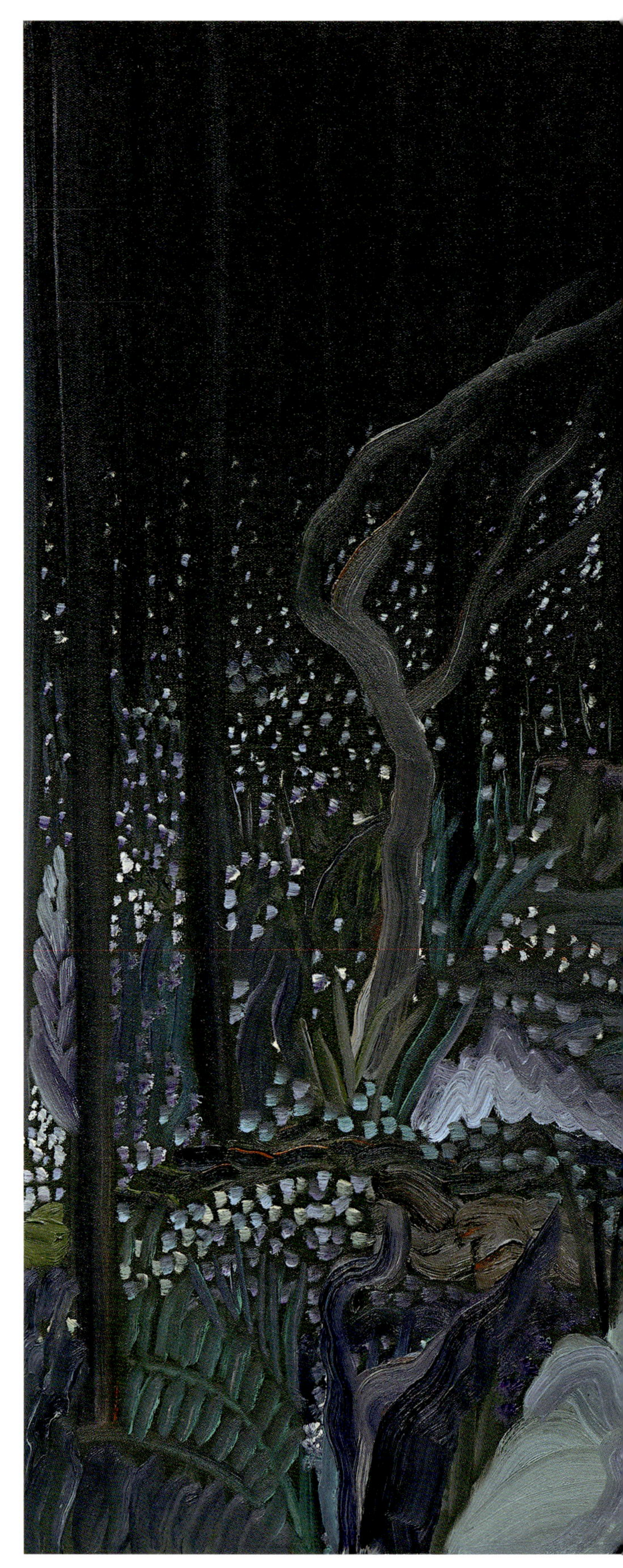

57 / Matthew Wong, *Dark Reverie*, 2018
Oil on canvas, 76.2 × 101.6 cm
THE EKARD COLLECTION

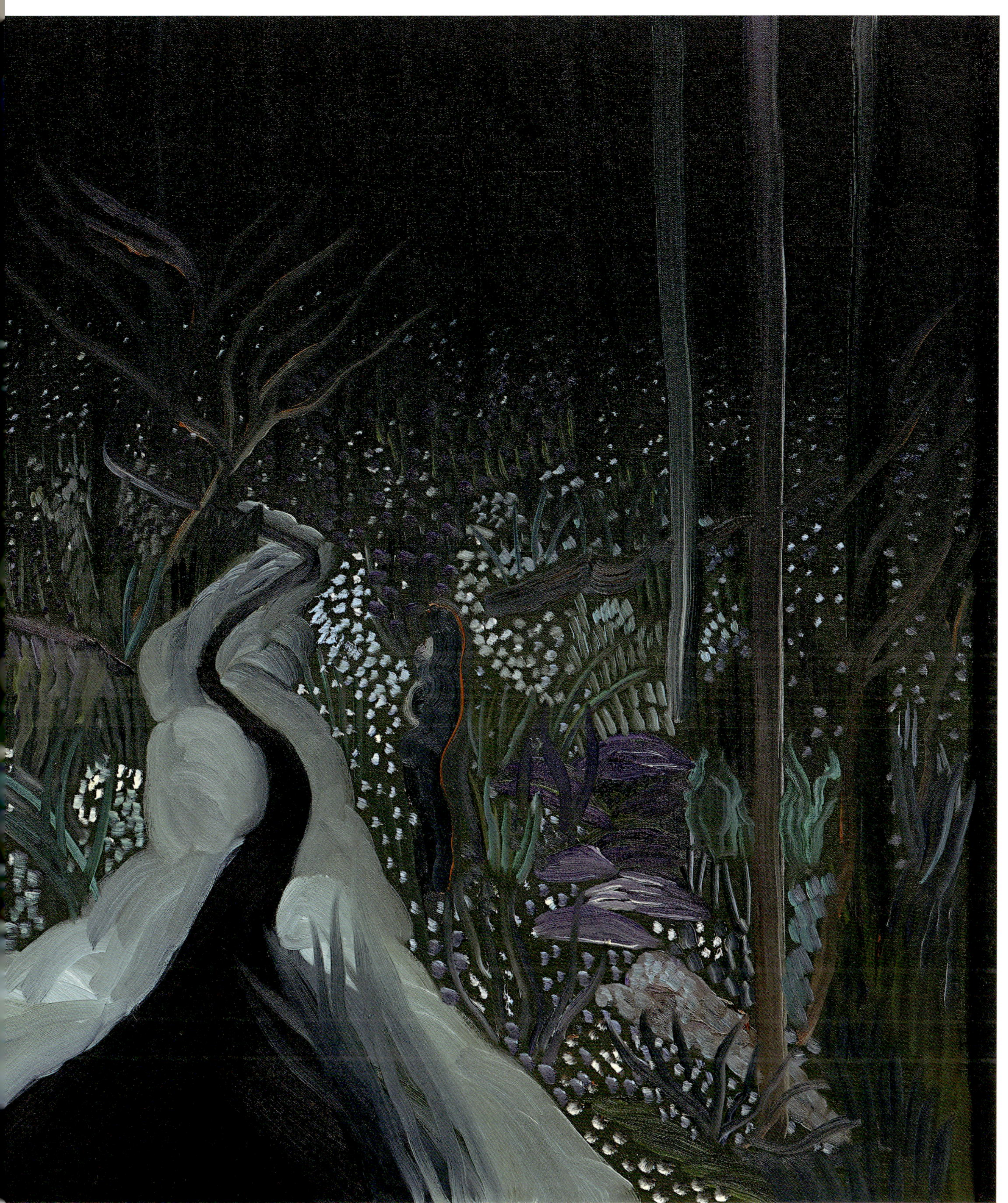

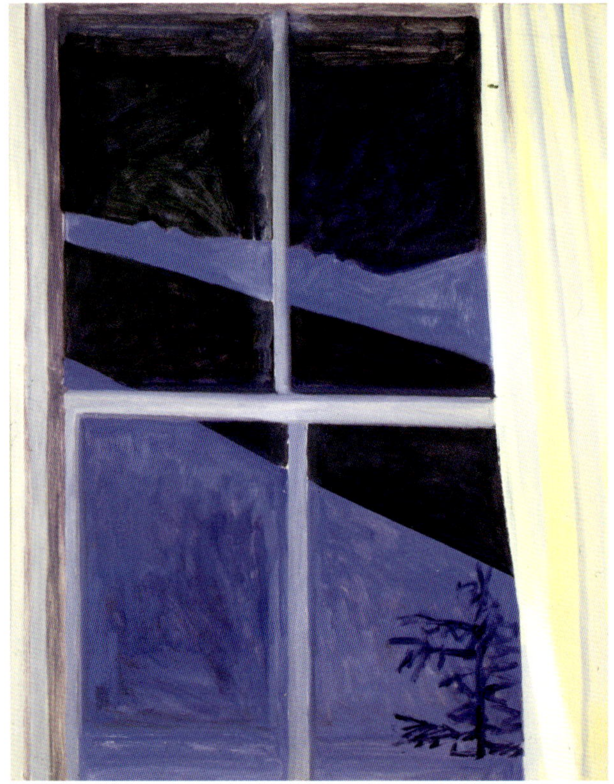

little appreciation for his work during his lifetime. He was aware that 'the legend is too familiar to the point of cliché', but that did not stop him from stating that: 'I see myself in him. The impossibility of belonging in this world.'[110] Wong was in touch with and inspired by all manner of figures in the artistic field, but during the final two years of his life it was Van Gogh's story that helped him to cope with his isolation and his troubled relationship with the art world.

It is not clear whether Wong was aware that Van Gogh too struggled to accept the first serious recognition to come his way.[111] In 1890, Albert Aurier wrote a long article about the Dutch painter, whom he praised as a 'terrible and demented genius. Often sublime, sometimes grotesque'.[112] Van Gogh responded with a letter, in which he told the French critic: 'I feel ill at ease when I reflect that what you say should be applied to others rather than to me'.[113] The challenges posed by the painter's mental health prevented him from embracing the offered recognition.

Simplification and tranquillity

Wong continued to work hard, despite his realization that success had done nothing – other than on the financial front – to alleviate his sombre situation. Besides the comfort offered by Van Gogh, working in his studio remained the most important remedy for his depression. Following his exhibition at Karma, he took the time to instil a greater tranquillity in his paintings. He had spent over a year investigating how far he could go with mark-making, but now sensed that this almost compulsive technique was no longer sufficient. To him, his heavily stippled paintings were 'crowd pleasers'.[114] As he searched for greater restraint, Wong found examples in the work of artists such as Lois Dodd (fig. 58) and Eleanor Ray, and the landscapes of Alex Katz and Milton Avery (fig. 60) – all of whom paint landscapes or interiors with limited means but with a powerful sense of colour and a great sense of calm.[115] He produced two interiors at this point that exude a similar atmosphere: *Time after Time* (fig. 62) and *Round About Midnight* (fig. 63). The spectacles in the latter work are Wong's own, while the prominent windows in both interiors seem to refer to the work of Dodd, who is known for her paintings of this motif.

58 / Lois Dodd, *Blue Night Window*, 1983
Oil on Masonite, 50.8 × 40.5 cm
Private collection, courtesy Alexandre Gallery, New York

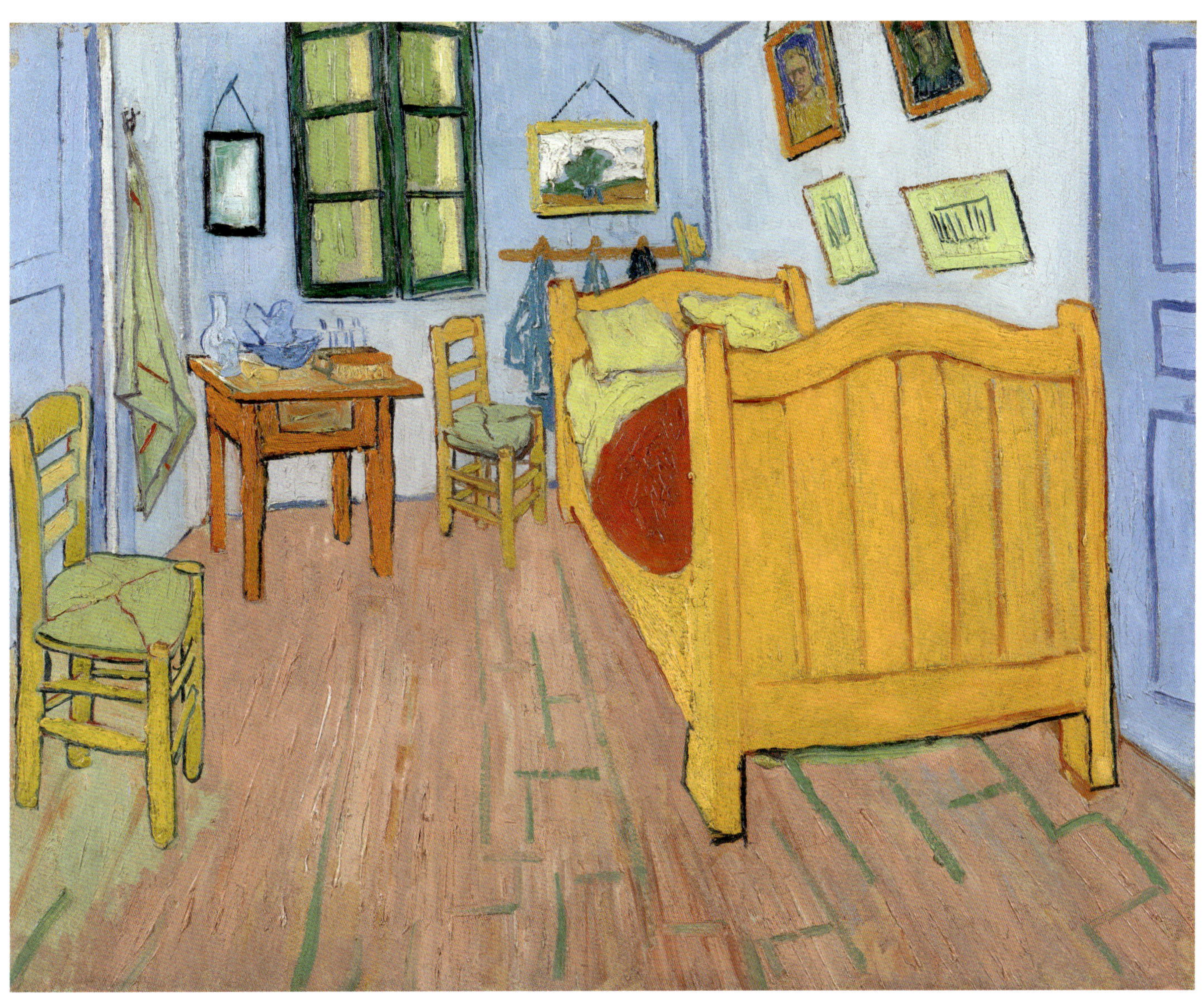

59 / Vincent van Gogh, *The Bedroom*, 1888
Oil on canvas, 72.4 × 91.3 cm
Van Gogh Museum, Amsterdam
(Vincent van Gogh Foundation)

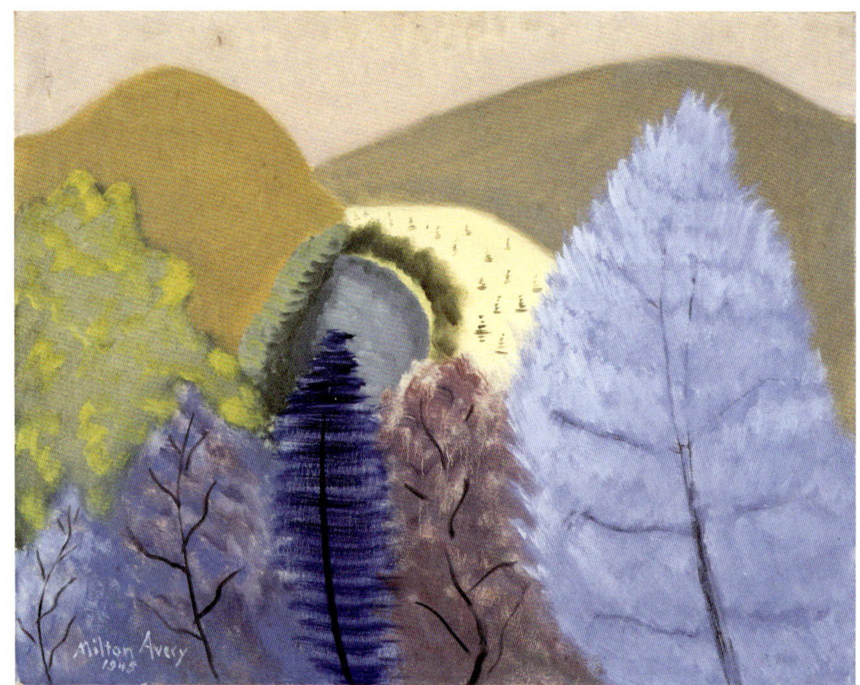

Wong might have painted these interiors to calm himself down, just as Van Gogh had done with *The Bedroom* (fig. 59). The latter painted this soothing motif to recharge his batteries after a period of intensive outdoor painting.[116] As he had done with *Garden of the Asylum*, Van Gogh chose a subject from reality, onto which he then projected a symbolic meaning. Wong's interiors, by contrast, were the product of his imagination, as was the rest of his work.

Wong's evaluation of his painting style did not mean that he had abandoned his stippling technique altogether, but he now applied it more fluidly and combined it with other techniques, such as zones painted with a wide brush and robustly executed lines. Good examples can be found in *Night Crossing* (fig. 61) and *Unknown Pleasures* (fig. 125). At times he nevertheless felt the need to paint a canvas like *The Night Watcher* (fig. 83), almost the entire surface of which was worked with dots of yellow paint applied directly from the tube, or *Night Moods* (fig. 65), a challenging combination of decorative patterns. The latter might have been inspired by Matisse's *Interior with Aubergines* (fig. 64).[117]

Wong must have felt that he had achieved a level of 'maturity' in his work when he found himself freely able from 2018 onwards to handle and combine the techniques he had now mastered. He marked this pivotal moment with his appropriately titled *Coming of Age Landscape* (fig. 66), in which he juxtaposed a broadly painted sky with an iridescent sun and a free and decoratively rendered landscape, which nevertheless retains a certain tranquillity. What is more, the colours of the work convey a shimmering heat in a comparable manner to a number of works that Van Gogh painted in the summers of 1888 and 1889 in southern France, including *Wheatfield with a Reaper* (fig. 67).

In addition to the serenity of his brushwork, Wong instilled calm in the canvas by means of a more restricted palette. The earliest results of these experiments included *Somewhere* (fig. 126) done in early 2018, which consists entirely of orange and dark-blue paint. That same year, he created the luminous *Good Morning* (fig. 96) in pink and orange paint

60 / Milton Avery, *Blue Trees*, 1945
Oil on canvas, 71.1 × 91.4 cm
Collection Neuberger Museum of Art, Purchase College, State University of New York. Gift of Roy R. Neuberger

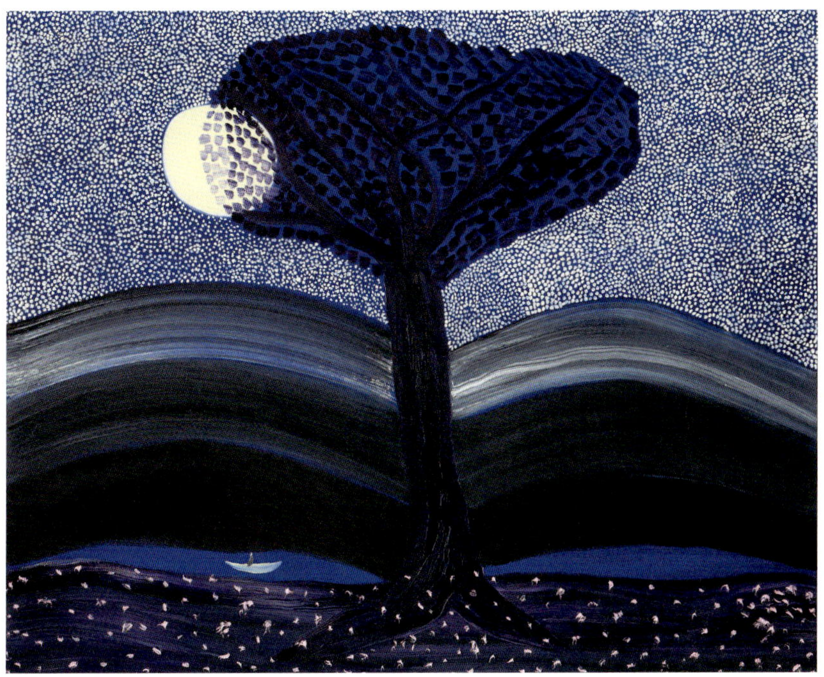

61 / Matthew Wong, *Night Crossing*, 2018
Oil on canvas, 121.9 × 152.4 cm
Collection of Nancy and Sean Cotton

on a white ground. By the end of 2018, Wong was pushing at the limits of the restricted palette with *Day 4* (fig. 68) – a monochrome work constructed from different shades of the same yellow – and in the work's blue counterpart *Night 4* (fig. 69). It is fairly likely that these paintings were done after the example of the landscapes of Alex Katz, who frequently uses a few variations of the same colour, as in *Golden Image* (fig. 71). *Day 4* and *Night 4* featured in a second solo exhibition held in early 2019 at Massimo De Carlo's Hong Kong gallery, for which Wong made a series of four day and night views (see p. 164, fig. F).[118]

In 2019, Wong focused primarily on a single colour: blue. With its connotations of melancholy and gloom, it became the subject of his second major exhibition at Karma, which ultimately took place posthumously in November 2019.[119] Through his series of blue paintings, Wong placed himself once more within 'the greater dialogue between artists throughout time', this time with artists who had a particular affinity with the colour, such as Pablo Picasso, Yves Klein and Ad Reinhardt.[120] He also looked to Van Gogh for his blue paintings in this period. Wong painted a blue gouache, for instance, in which he referred to *Van Gogh's Chair* (fig. 8) and produced his own variation on the Dutch artist's bluest and best-known painting, *Starry Night* (fig. 12). In his version of the latter work (fig. 13), Wong reduced the houses and mountain ridge to archaic forms, added a dark lake and painted the starry sky with a pattern borrowed from Kusama's *Infinity Nets*, for example *Nets Blue* (fig. 70). At the same time, however, he maintained the relationship between night and the colour blue, which had been so important to Van Gogh. That Wong chose to emulate a work like *Starry Night* shows he was still as ambitious as he had been at the outset and that he was not afraid of clichés or of harming his reputation. He might have been insecure in the world around him, but not so in his art.[121]

The bench

In Edmonton, Wong developed fixed routines to lend structure to his life. He began each day as ever, by creating a work on paper. After getting up in the morning, he installed himself at a table set up for

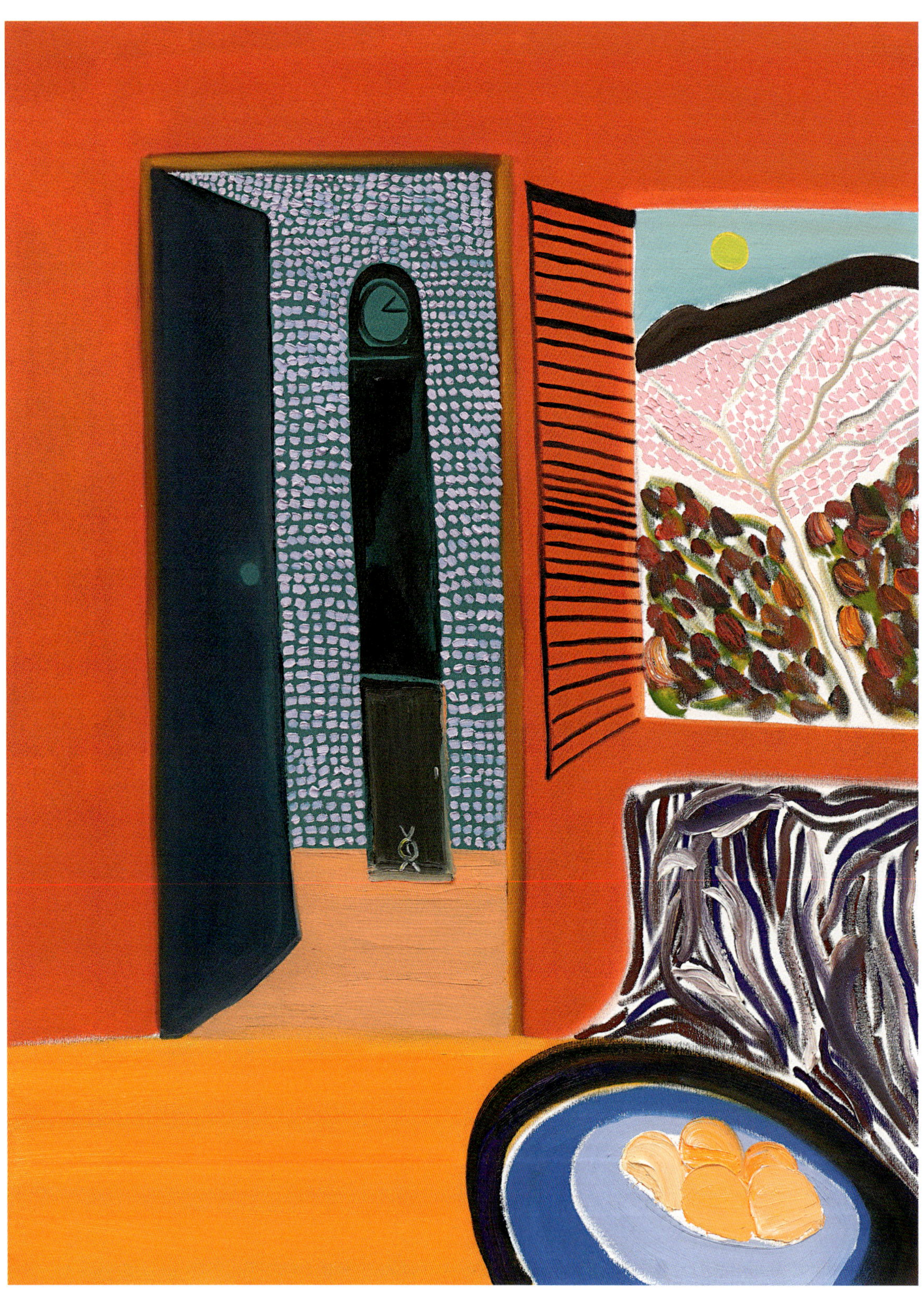

62 / Matthew Wong, *Time after Time*, 2018
Oil on canvas, 121.9 × 91.4 cm
Collection of Nancy and Sean Cotton

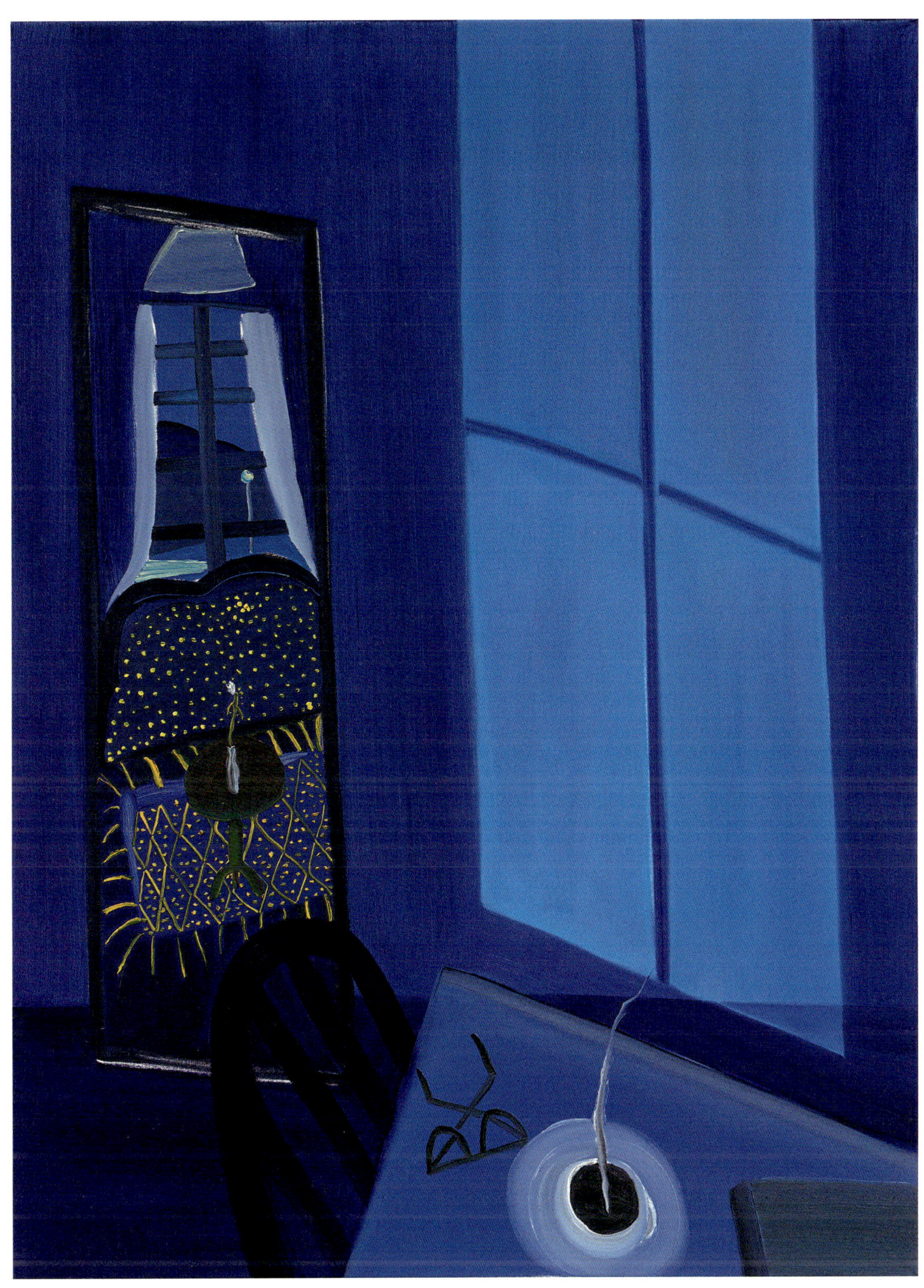

63 / Matthew Wong, *Round About Midnight*, 2019
Oil on canvas, 121.9 × 91.4 cm
Matthew Wong Foundation

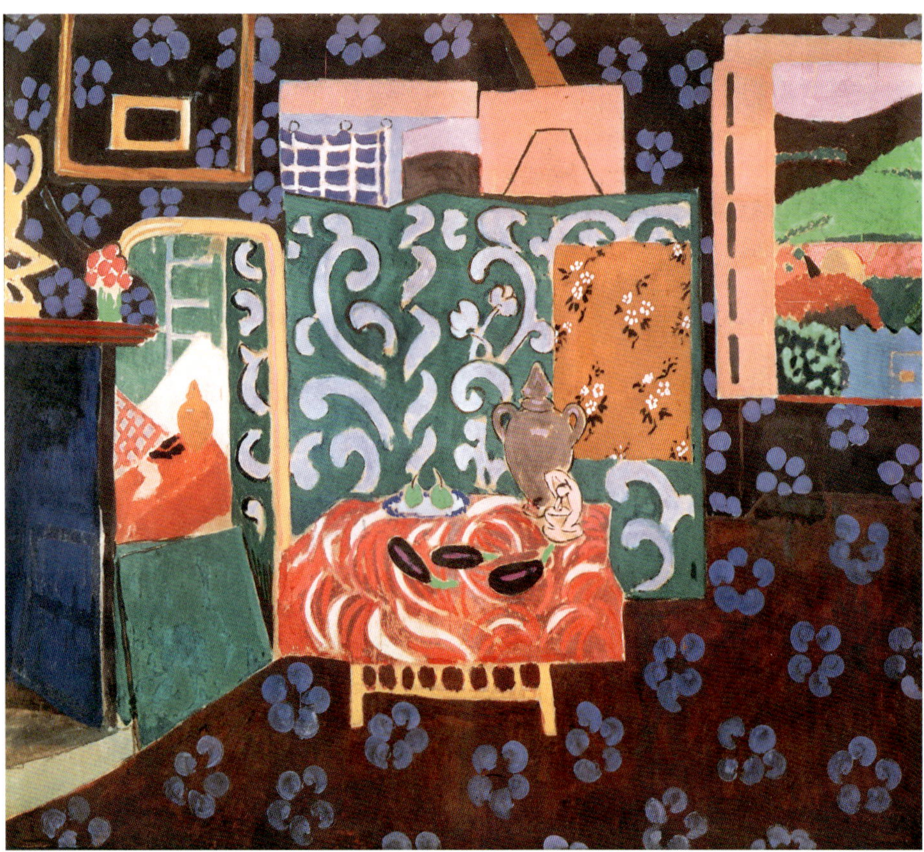

64 / Henri Matisse, *Interior with Aubergines* (*Intérieur aux aubergines*), 1911
Distemper on canvas, 212 × 246 cm
Musée de Grenoble-J.L. Lacroix,
Ville de Grenoble

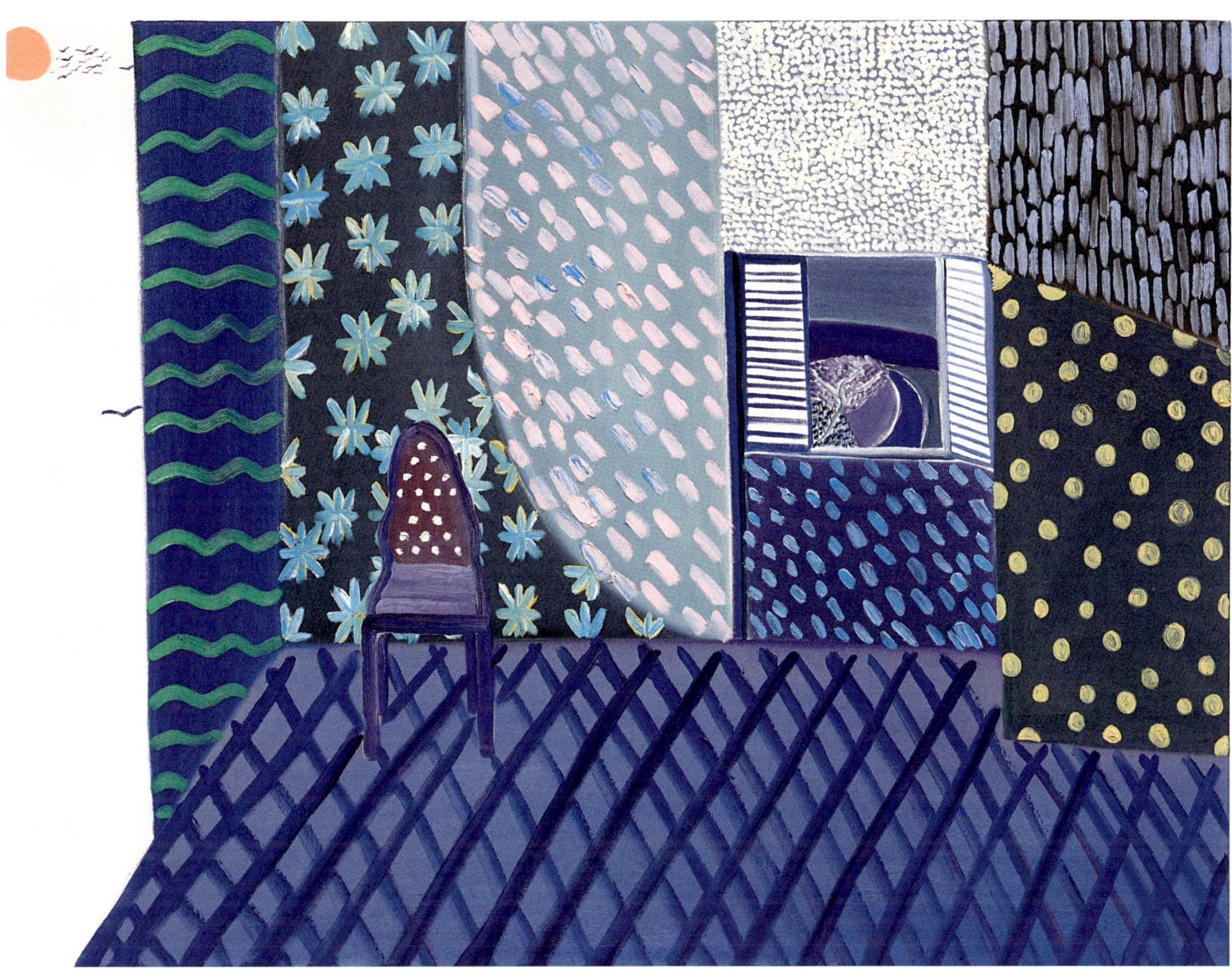

65 / Matthew Wong, *Night Moods*, 2018
Oil on canvas, 91.4 × 121.9 cm
Matthew Wong Foundation

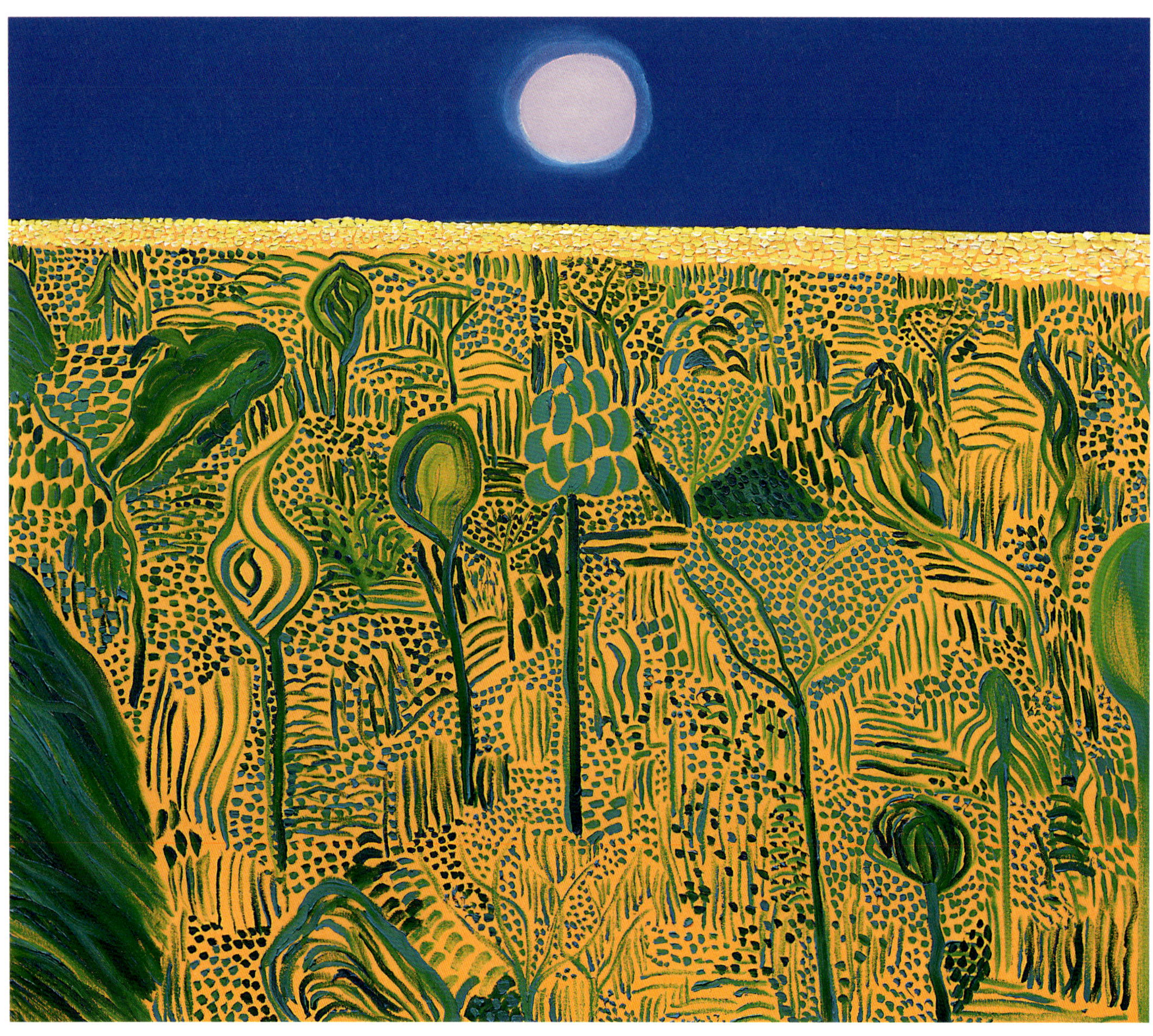

66 / Matthew Wong, *Coming of Age Landscape*, 2018
Oil on canvas, 152.4 × 177.8 cm
Private collection, courtesy of HomeArt

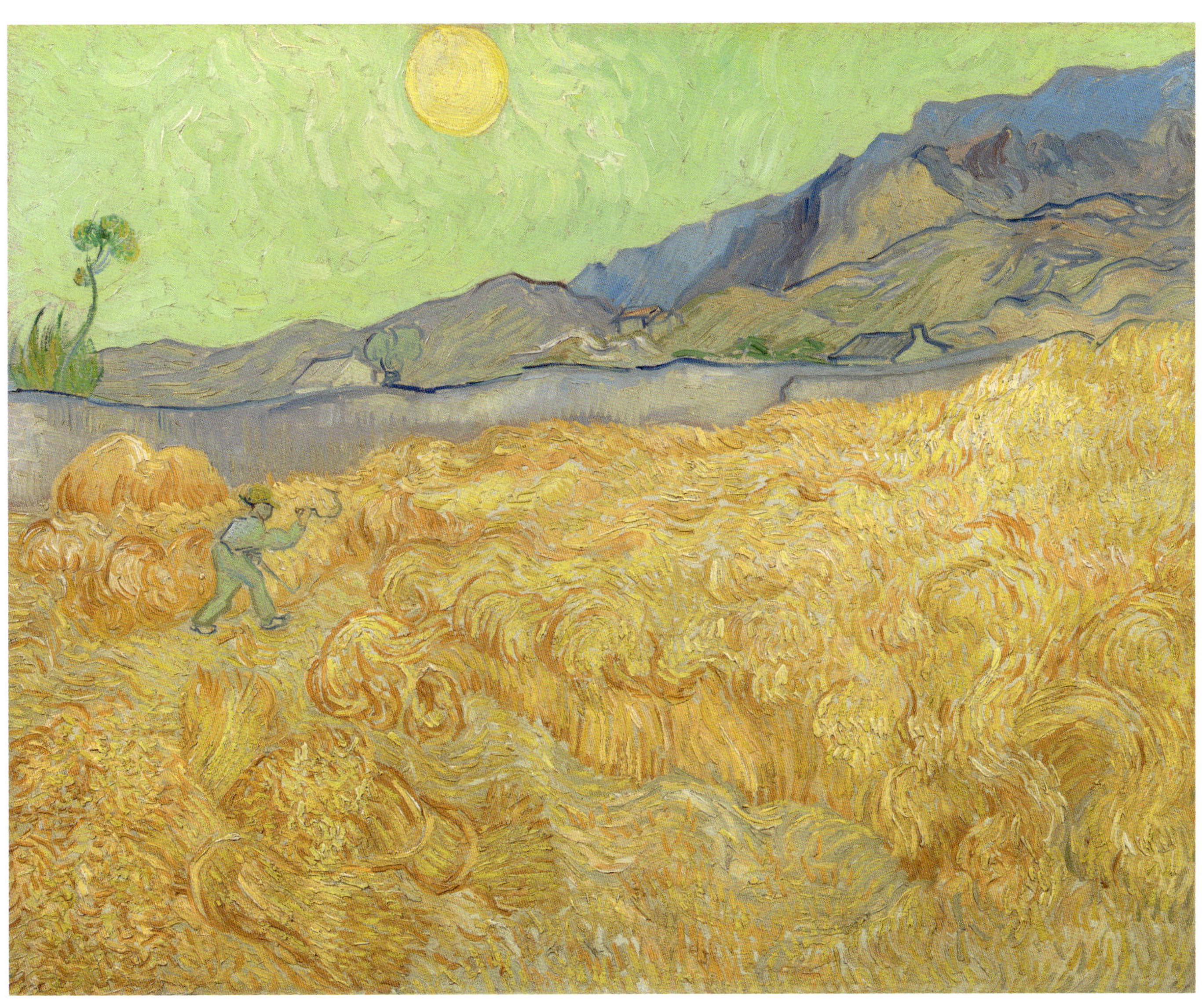

67 / Vincent van Gogh, *Wheatfield with a Reaper*, 1889
Oil on canvas, 73.2 × 92.7 cm
Van Gogh Museum, Amsterdam
(Vincent van Gogh Foundation)

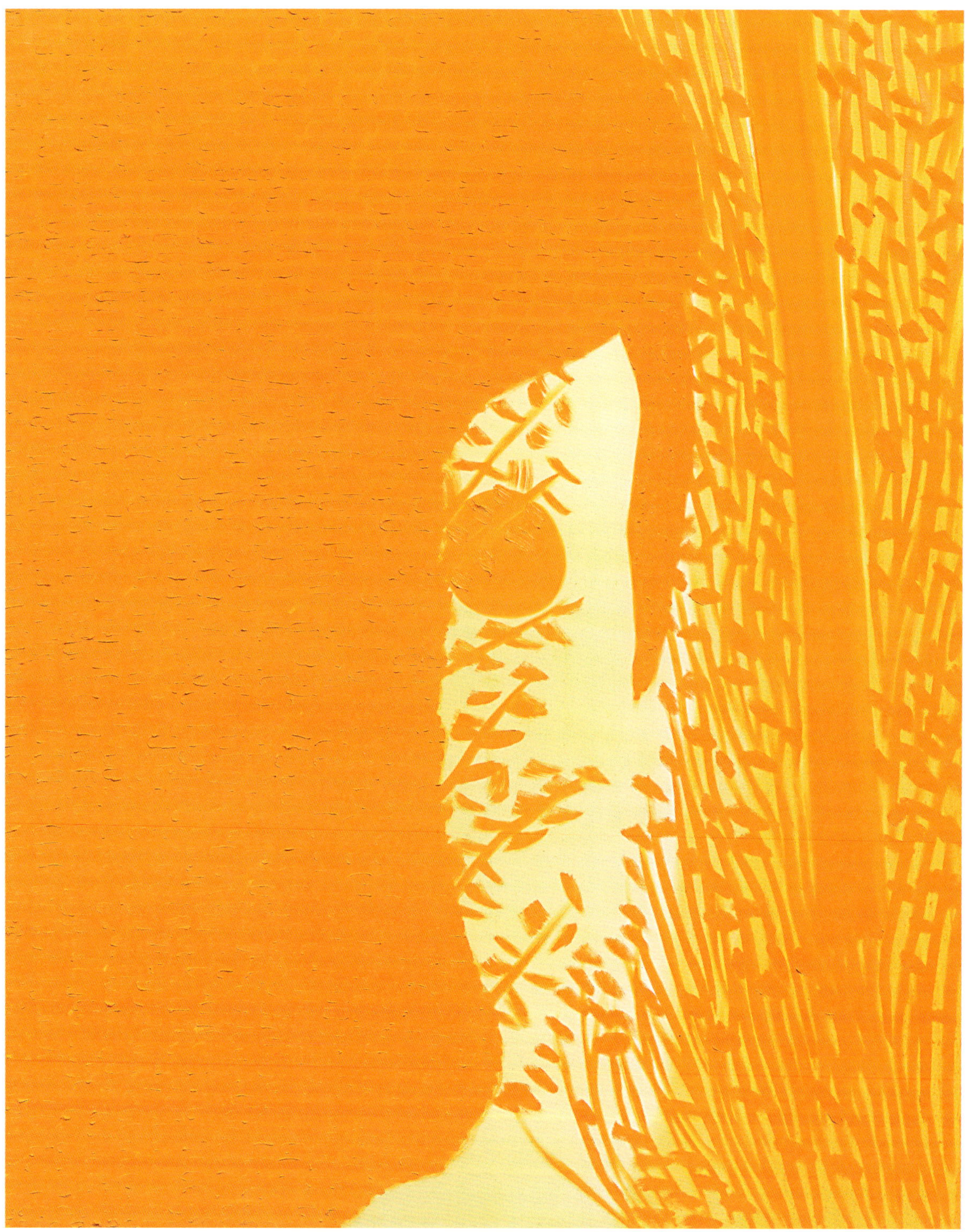

68 / Matthew Wong, *Day 4*, 2018
Oil on canvas, 203.2 × 165.1 cm
Josh Abraham

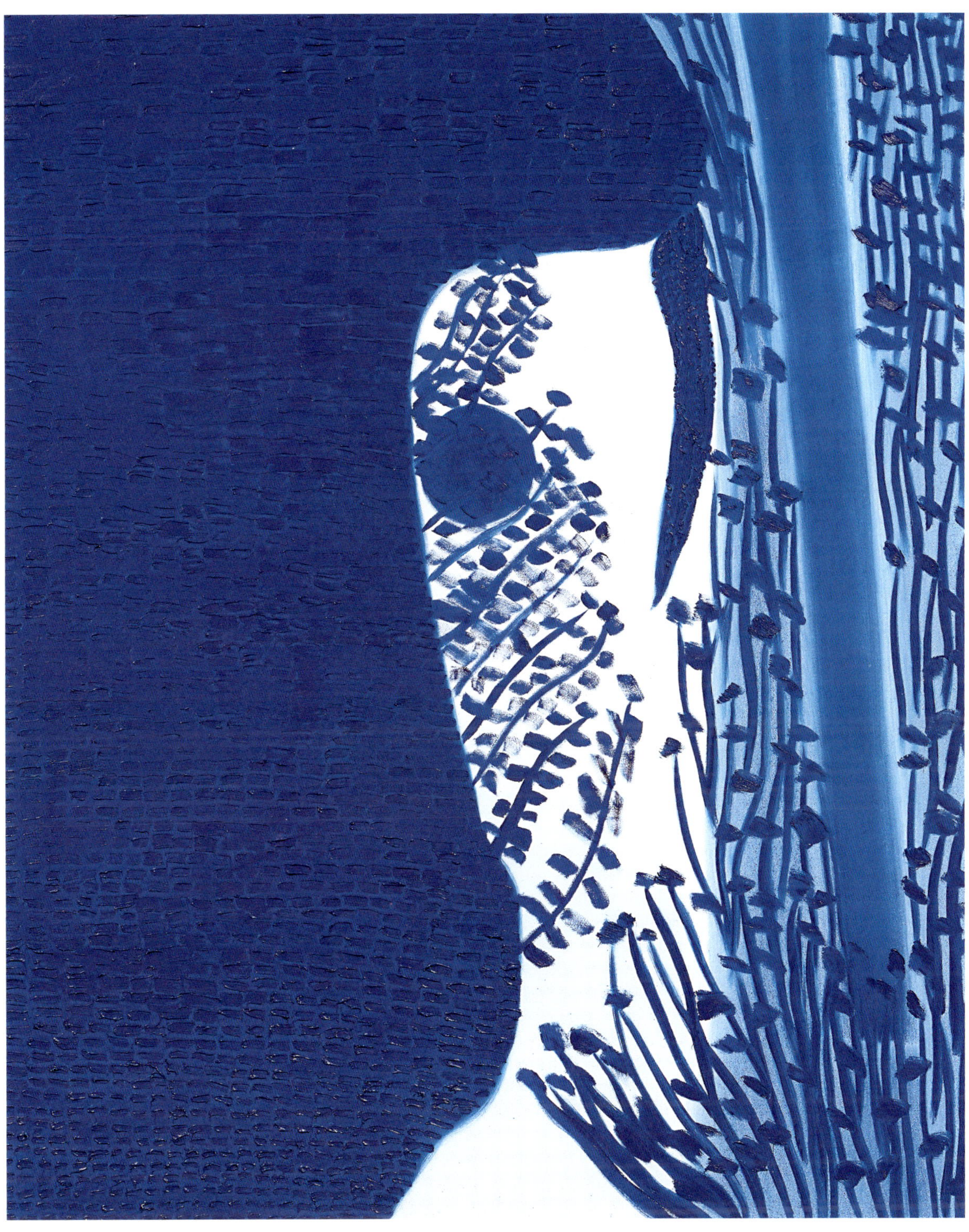

69 / Matthew Wong, *Night 4*, 2018
Oil on canvas, 203.2 × 165.1 cm
Private collection

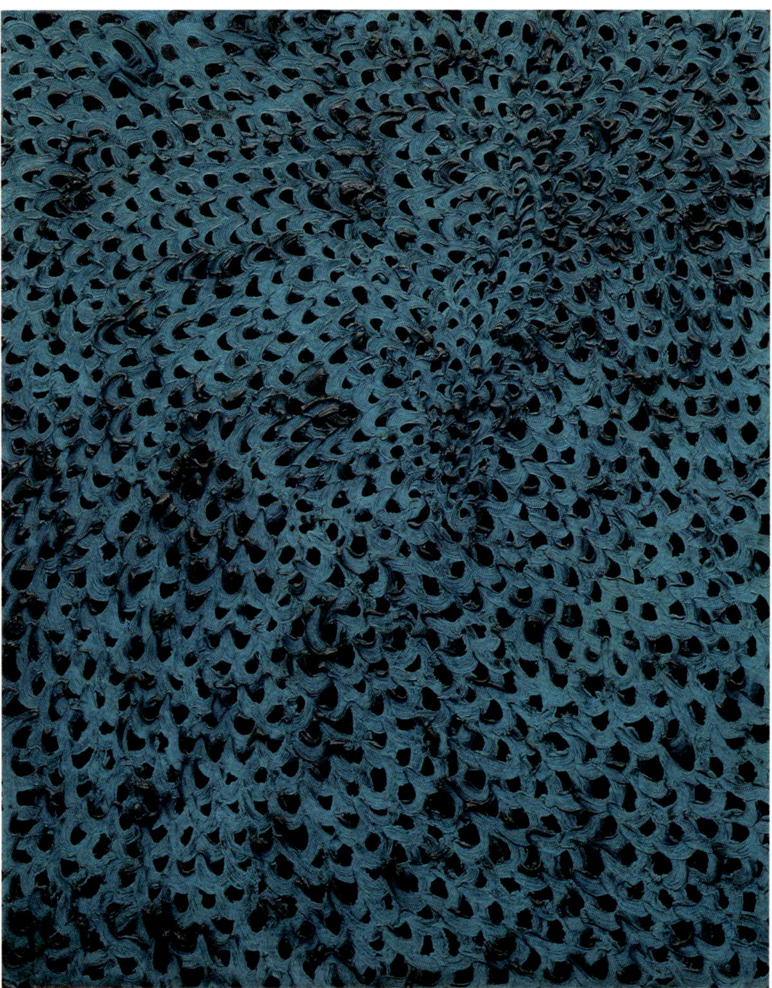

70 / Yayoi Kusama, *Nets Blue*, 1960
Oil on board, 51.4 × 42.2 cm
Private collection

that purpose and painted the first thing that came to mind in what were more frequently colourful gouaches now than ink paintings (figs. 72–77). He had no need of external stimuli: his imagination and memories were more than enough. These works are the most telling and direct examples of his inwardly derived creative process. In keeping with his quest for tranquillity in his work, he was no longer going to the studio every day, working there instead about three days a week in 2018 and 2019.[122] On other days he spent a great deal of time on a bench in a nearby park, which offers a beautiful view of the North Saskatchewan River as it flows through Edmonton. As he sat, Wong smoked and pondered. Reflections on paintings completed or yet to be made will have passed through his mind, as well as musings on his unconventional position in the art world as a big-selling but misunderstood outsider living far away in self-imposed isolation. Depressive – and quite possibly suicidal – thoughts will also have occupied much of this contemplation. When evening came, he took a walk, ate dessert at his favourite restaurant, The Cactus Club, or spent more time on the bench. Experiences from everyday life and the associations they evoked in him increasingly found their way into his work.[123]

Alongside his studio, the bench became a cornerstone of Wong's life in Edmonton. It appears frequently in paintings such as *Untitled* (fig. 79) and *Stage* (fig. 78) and began to assume the symbolic charge of a self-portrait, as *Van Gogh's Chair* had done (fig. 8).[124] In the summer of 2019, Wong painted *The Space Between Trees* (fig. 11), an explicit reference to Van Gogh's *Painter on the Road to Tarascon* (fig. 10), which was destroyed during the Second World War. Wong replaced the walking painter in Van Gogh's work – likewise intended as a self-portrait – with the bench as a self-portrait of his own. In doing so, he inserted himself in Van Gogh's work, creating a painting that is not only a tribute to his predecessor, but also a visual expression of his deep-rooted identification with the Dutchman's life. Wong will

71 / Alex Katz, *Golden Image*, 2017
Oil on linen, 365.8 × 274.3 cm
Courtesy of the artist and Gavin Brown's
Enterprise, New York/Rome

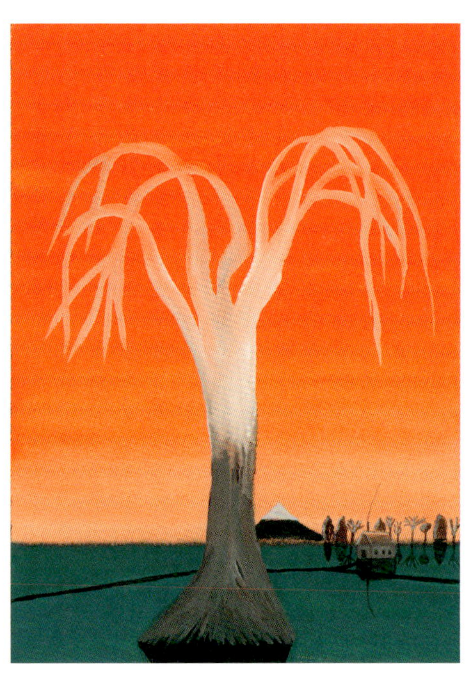

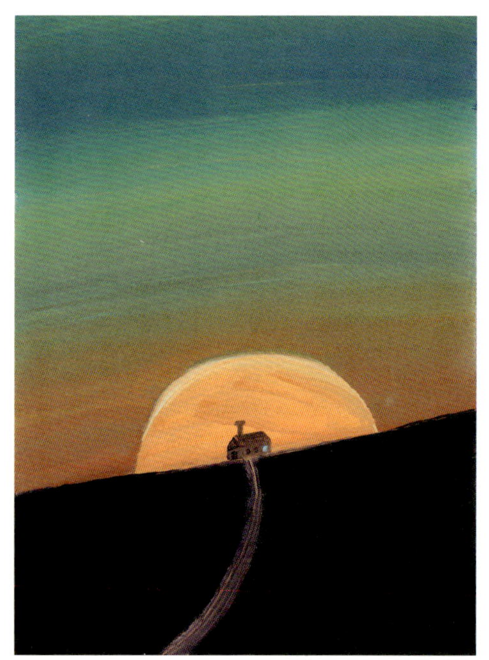

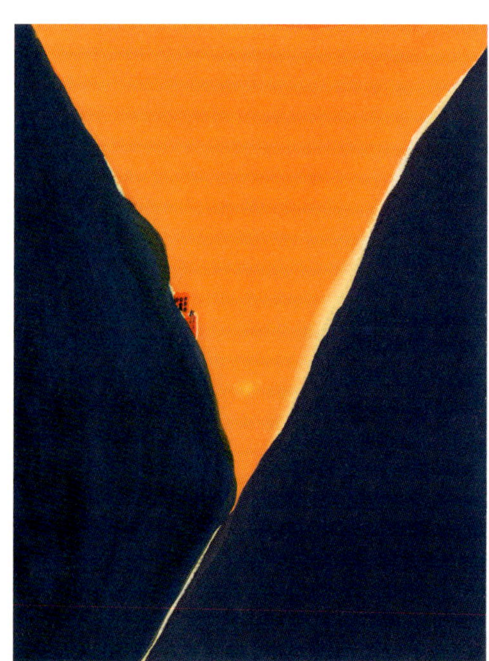

72 / Matthew Wong, *Untitled*, 2018
Gouache on paper, 35.6 × 25.4 cm
Matthew Wong Foundation

73 / Matthew Wong, *Last Light*, 2019
Gouache on paper, 41 × 31.1 cm
Matthew Wong Foundation

74 / Matthew Wong, *Red House*, 2018
Gouache on paper, 40.6 × 30.5 cm
Matthew Wong Foundation

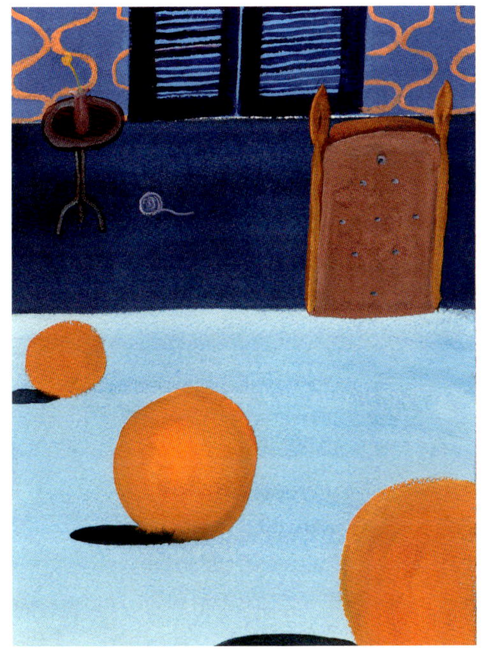

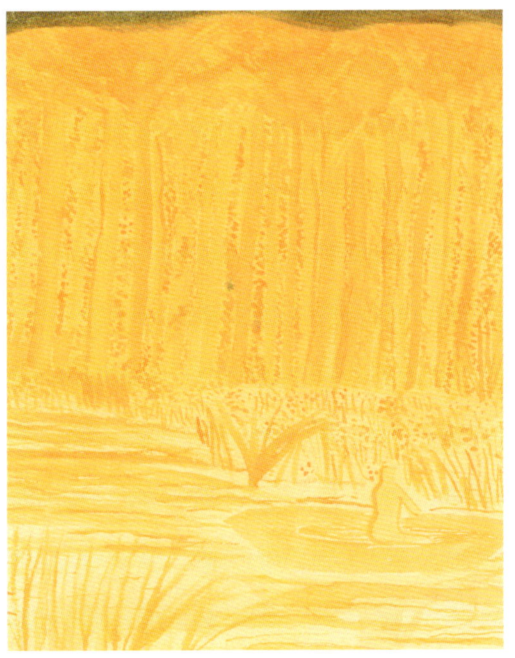

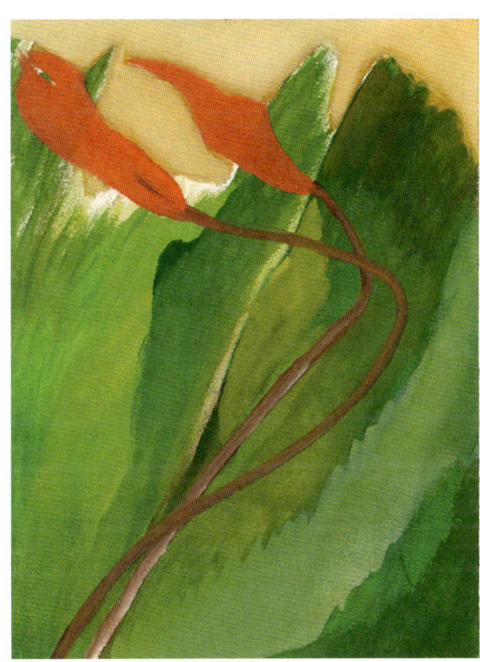

75 / Matthew Wong, *Untitled*, 2019
Gouache on paper, 30.5 × 22.9 cm
Matthew Wong Foundation

76 / Matthew Wong, *Illumination*, 2018
Gouache on paper, 30.1 × 27.3 cm
Matthew Wong Foundation

77 / Matthew Wong, *The Twins*, 2019
Gouache on paper, 30.8 × 22.9 cm
Matthew Wong Foundation

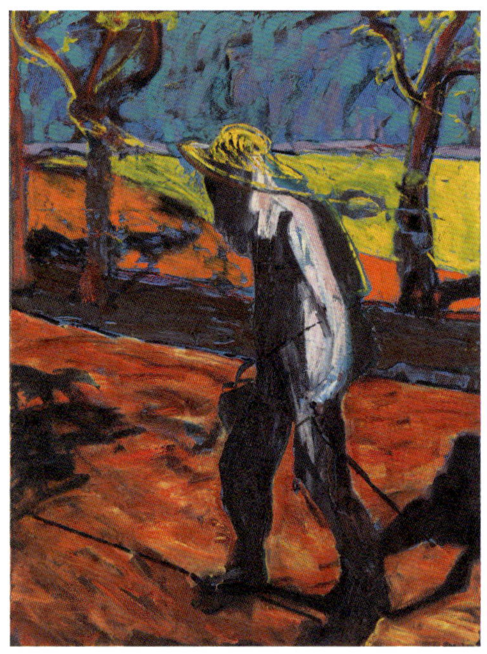

place for himself in 'the greater dialogue between artists throughout time' and in that he succeeded. Despite his depression and anxiety, Wong painted constantly, wherever he was, resulting in an oeuvre that is large (some 1,300 works) in terms of the timeframe in which it was produced, especially when we remember that a great deal was destroyed or painted over. Like Van Gogh, he put every atom of himself into his work, with no trace of reserve or irony. The sincerity of the art is total. Even though he is no longer here, his presence can be sensed in every work, direct and unfiltered. Jonas Wood, an important example for Wong and who became a close friend of his, once called him 'the modern day Van Gogh'.[127] Perhaps he was right. —

Much of the research for this essay consisted of conversations with Matthew Wong's family and friends. I am sincerely grateful to everyone who was willing to talk to me: the generosity and openness of the community that Wong left behind is exceptional. Special thanks are due to Monita Wong, who was an inexhaustible source of assistance and support and taught me an immense amount about her son in the course of our long conversations; to John Cheim, without whom this project would not have been possible; to Peter Shear, Sofia Silva, Brendan Dugan and Benjamin Styer, for sharing specific passages or all of their correspondence with Matthew Wong and their contribution to my research; and to Vivian Li, curator of the first retrospective of Wong's work, for her advice and generous help.

80 / Francis Bacon,
Study for 'Portrait of Van Gogh IV', 1957
Oil on canvas, 152.4 × 116.8 cm
Tate, London

81 / Matthew Wong,
See You On the Other Side, 2019
Oil on canvas, 152.4 × 121.9 cm
Matthew Wong Foundation

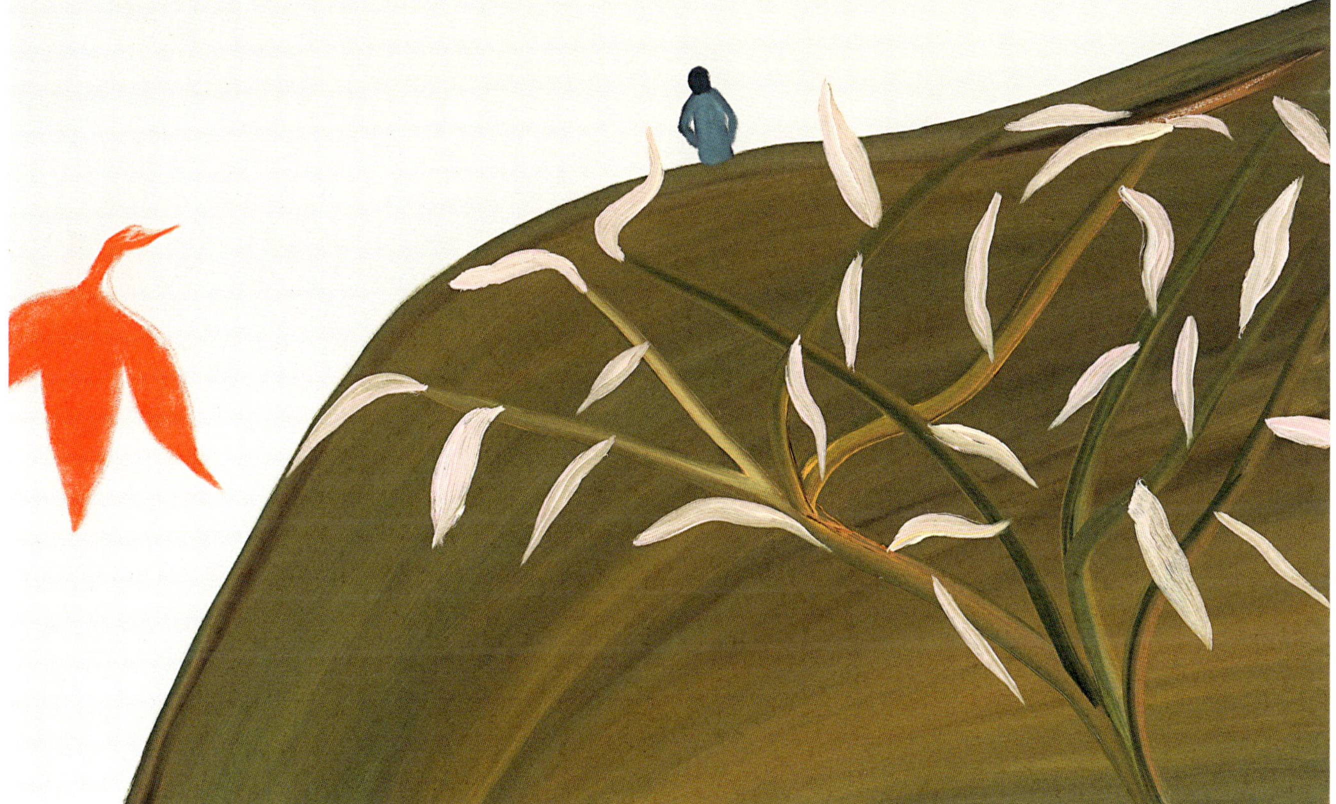

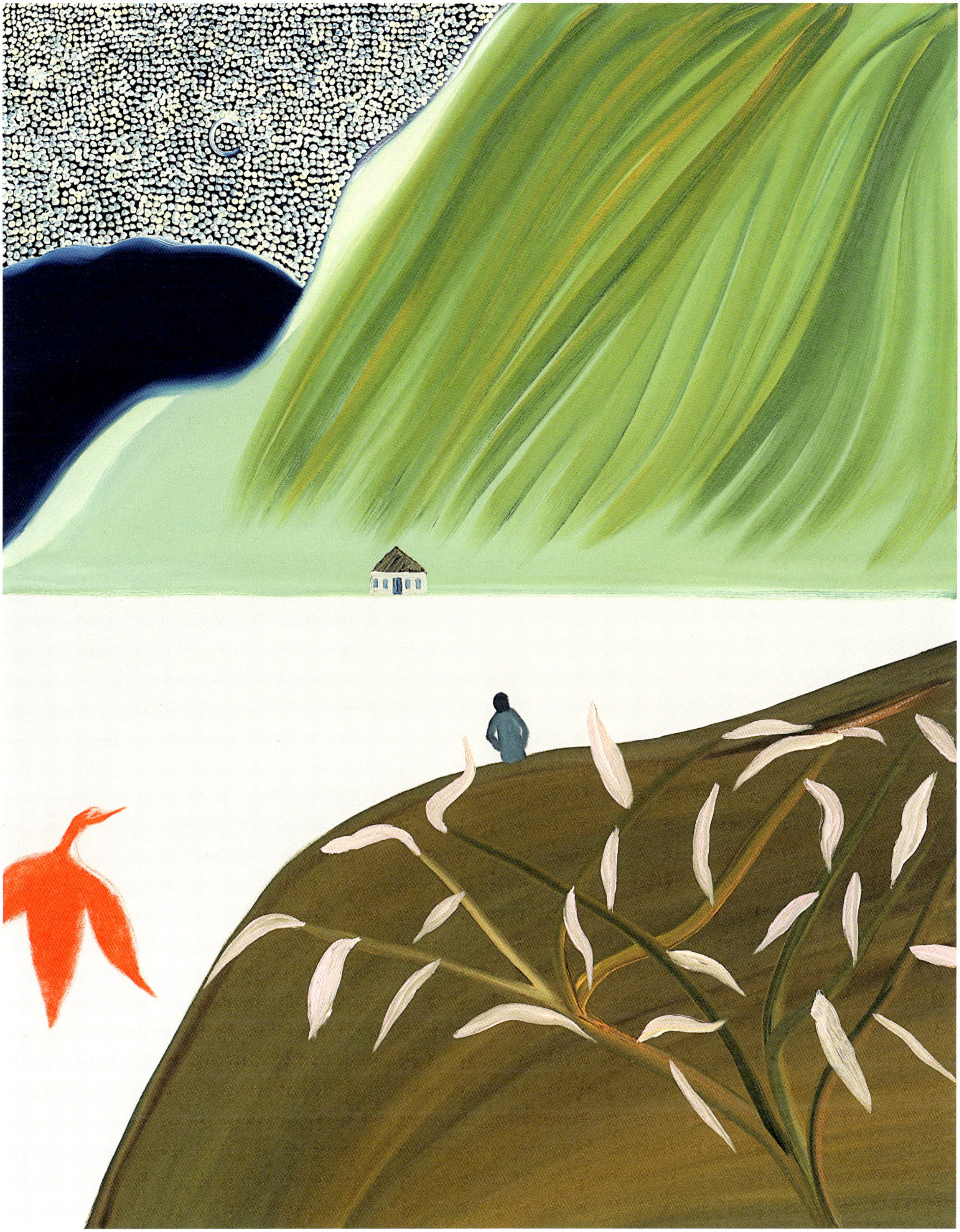

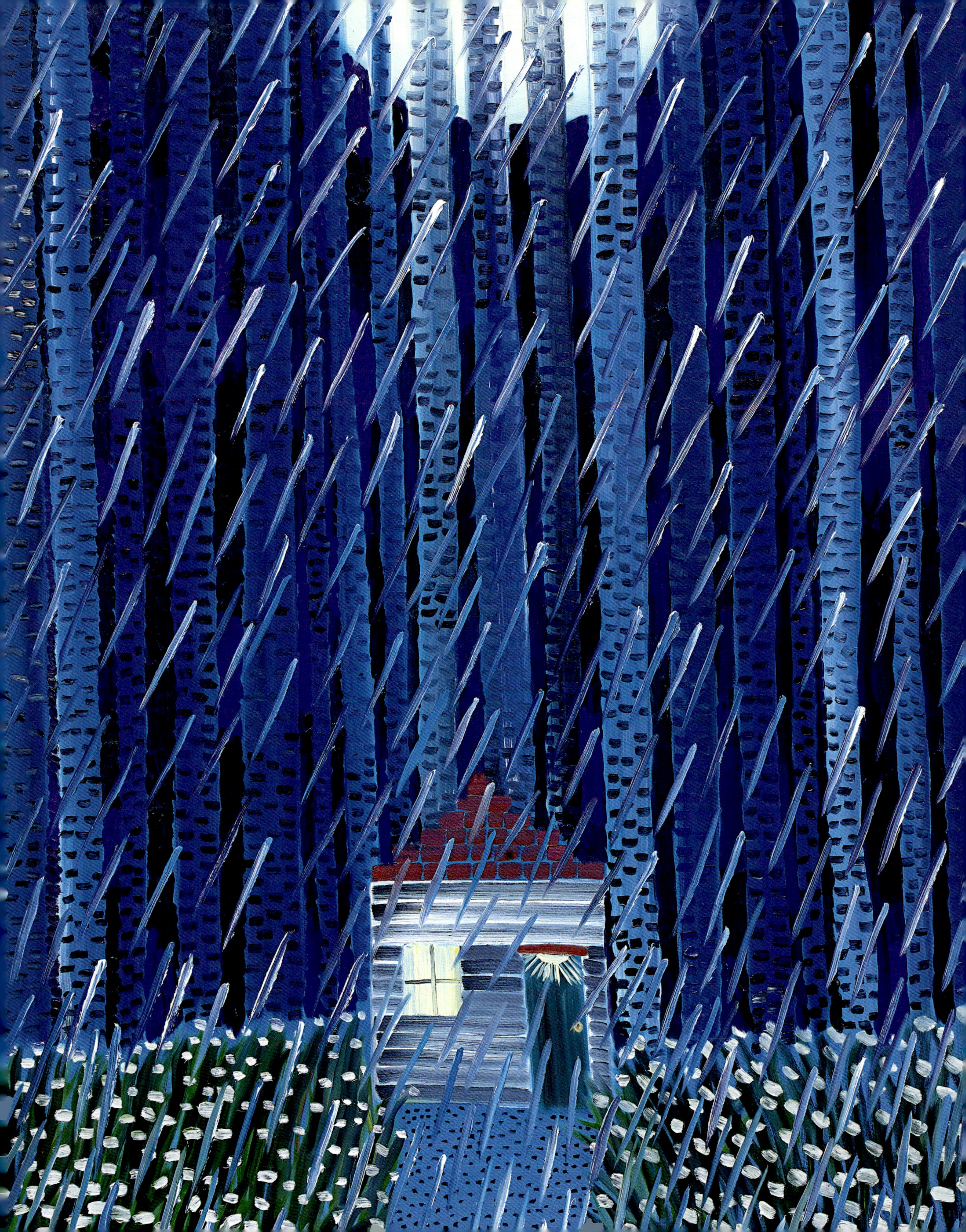

Richard Shiff

Rain Rising

Matthew Wong, *Blue Rain*, 2018 (detail of fig. 102)

Matthew Wong produced his art quickly, intuitively, 'listening to your gut and going from there'.[1] Resorting to an organic metaphor, he said that his imagery developed within 'the flow from hand to surface'.[2] A flow has already changed before thought is able to conceptualize and compartmentalize its contents. By this understanding, Wong's art could find its purpose only in the midst of his action, as if at least some of the creative impetus derived from his contact with materials. The physicality of paint, brush and scraper would contribute to the trajectory, 'hand to surface'. As an alternative, Wong might have conceptualized his organic action at such an extraordinary pace that he kept abreast of his instincts. If he accomplished this superhuman feat, he was too modest to say so.

Some of Wong's rapidly made works are of ink, watercolour or gouache on paper; these were not preparatory studies for larger oils or acrylics on canvas but independent expressions in a variety of media. Working without a plan may have been the only option for someone whose imaginative mind spewed thoughts and images at an accelerating rate, even altering nominally finished compositions. The same mentality absorbed the abundant store of discursive and sensory information that the cultural environment offered. Much of what Wong internalized through libraries, cinema, social media and an array of print and electronic sources belonged to the established history of modern art, Asian and Euro-American. The contemporary artists with whose works he became acquainted electronically – many as yet uncelebrated, perhaps never to be celebrated – were products of a hyper-productive

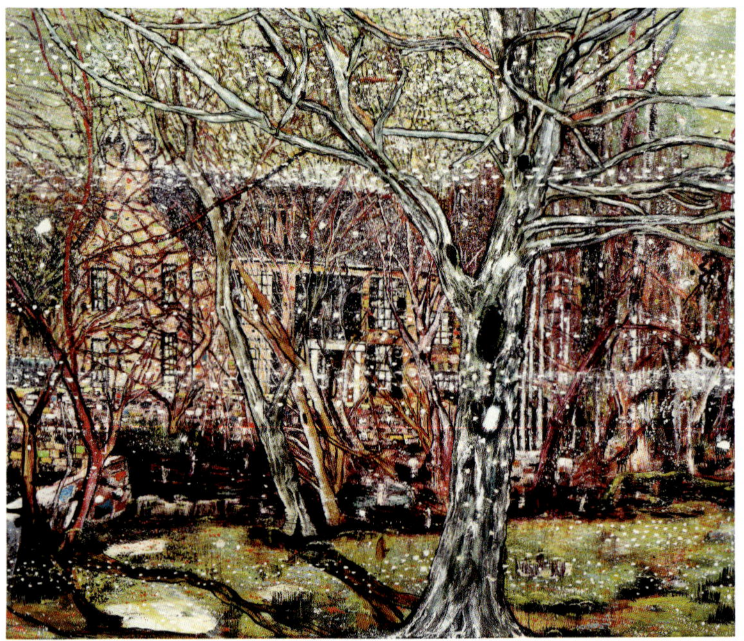

cultural system, the macrocosm of which Wong became the microcosm, a nexus of aesthetic distillation. Few artists have so efficiently absorbed past and present sensitivities as Wong did. He generated imagery that was novel, yet uncannily familiar – accessible, yet seeming to lack a specific time or place of origin.

Art in and out of history

Wong seems to have concealed nothing, and critics have noted the range and eclecticism of his stated interests.[3] The art of Vincent van Gogh was a recurrent reference, often implicit, always relevant ('I just posted one of my own paintings next to a Van Gogh').[4] Among others, Wong engaged with Edvard Munch, Henri Matisse, Gustav Klimt, Andrei Tarkovsky, Miyoko Ito, Raoul De Keyser, Lois Dodd and Peter Doig. As an example, the bands of spotting and the web of trees in Wong's *The Night Watcher* (fig. 83), recall the motifs of Doig's *Rosedale* (fig. 82).[5] Observations of this kind, however, contribute little to our understanding, for Wong's capacity to transform pictorial information cannot account for his aesthetic distinction. It may be more profitable to speculate that Wong derived his art from sources more natural than cultural.

To this end, a warning, or at least an advisory. In our era of increasingly refined articulations of social grouping, with individuals located at the intersection of multiple lines of ethnic, gender, economic and political identity, some will reduce Wong to a creature of cultural inheritance, filtered through both Western and Eastern systems of education – canonical lineages that mask social and political tensions. Much current scholarship focuses on revealing the causes of tension, raising issues of gender bias, racism, income inequality, cultural appropriation and colonialism. Within the course of my own academic education, I sensed an undertone of distrust of the cultural value accorded to some of the most revered artists, those whose careers had eventually generated a secondary commercial industry of reproductive prints and posters, and even clothing and household items. A colourful life contributed to the commercial appeal, as in the case of Van Gogh and Munch, or later (but to a lesser extent), Jackson Pollock. To hyper-critical minds, broad popular acceptance renders an art suspect, as if it reflected an ideological syndrome so ingrained as to escape questioning.

82 / Peter Doig, *Rosedale*, 1991
Oil on canvas, 199.4 × 239.4 cm
Private collection

83 / Matthew Wong, *The Night Watcher*, 2018
Oil on canvas, 152.4 × 122 cm
Private collection

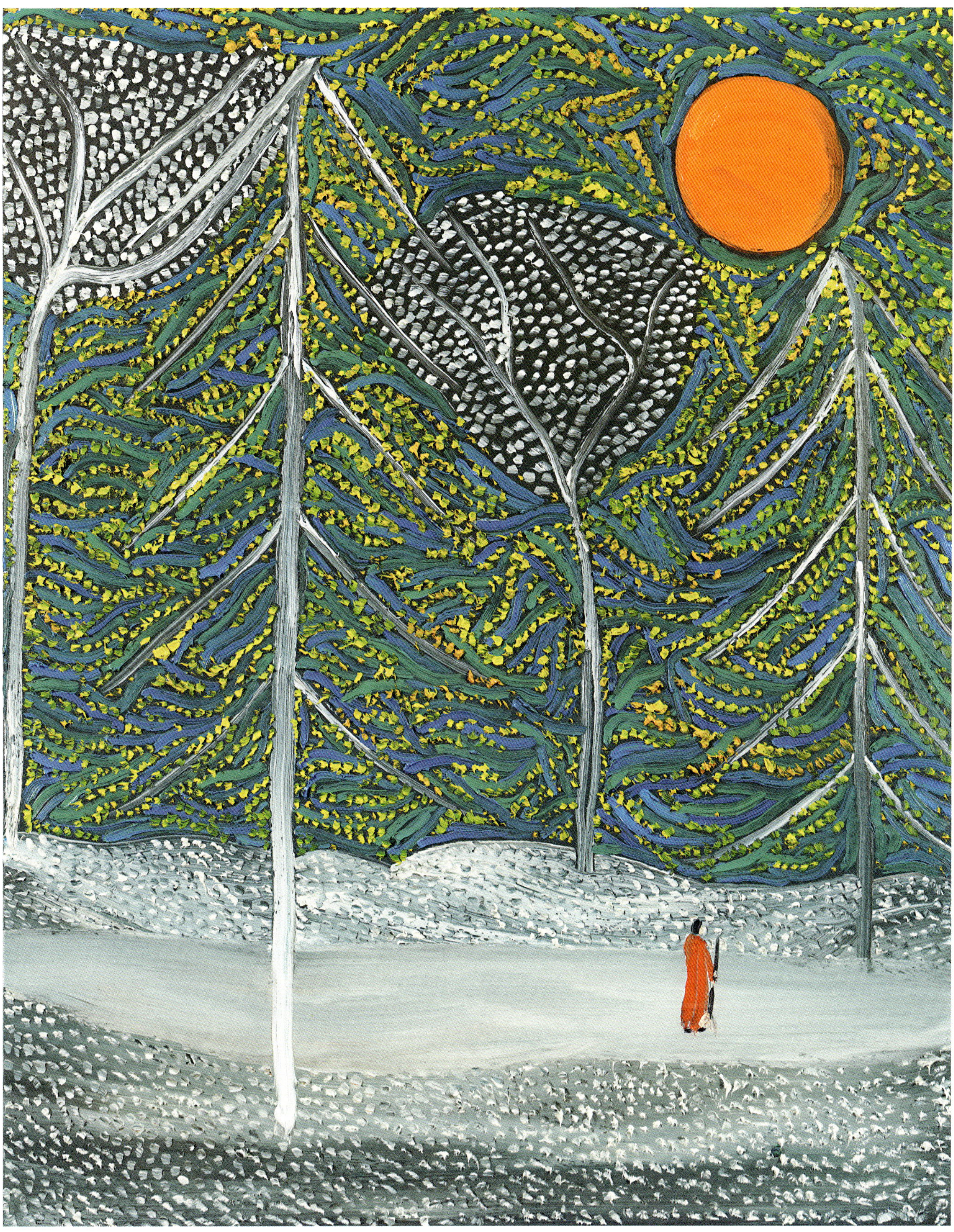

No art, the argument goes, transcends social difference. In Wong's case, because of his migrations, his formation was hybrid and inclusive at its core.[6] By embodying some of the cultural contradictions that otherwise divide East from West, he demonstrated that the aesthetics of the two worlds were not irredeemably at odds. Accordingly, in both Hong Kong and North America, Wong received institutional support within a global network of art fairs, public exhibitions and commercial representation. As his achievement gained increasing acknowledgement, he came to inhabit the rhizomatic web of a contemporary art machine set to accommodate not only Matthew Wong but every aesthetic possibility. Some will claim that Wong's individualized professional ambition was a product of the twenty-first-century gallery system, itself a derivative of the history of bourgeois society and its market economy – a system geared to absorb and neutralize the many instances of deviance from de facto norms. So much is current critical orthodoxy, applied especially to those who choose painting as the primary medium.[7] When experiencing art, I try not to be distracted by such disabling scepticism, whatever its political merits; it prejudices the specific situation.

Like Van Gogh, Wong profited from the available archives of imagery in several media yet even more from being self-taught as a painter. In Hong Kong, he received an MFA degree in photography but never studied painting in an institutional context. An isolated studio practice can open the artist to spontaneous impulses, which bypass theoretical guides to work. In 1888, writing to his brother Theo, Van Gogh acknowledged a twofold conflict (vision versus emotion, theory versus practice): 'instead of trying to render exactly what I have before my eyes, I use colour more arbitrarily in order to express myself forcefully. Well, let's let that lie as far as theory goes.'[8] Van Gogh proceeded to describe a portrait that he began as 'faithfully' as possible, only to exaggerate its chromatic intensity and contrasts, substituting his subjective feelings for objective observations. His abortive theorizing could hardly stabilize the distinction. His critical supporter Albert Aurier finessed the matter by arguing that Van Gogh manifested 'realism', though of a personal kind, affected by emotional excesses.[9]

We may need to set aside issues of historical context and theories of aesthetic expression to grasp the character of Wong who, ironically, was so deeply conscious of the history of modern and contemporary art. For comparison, think of how knowledgeable Van Gogh – avid reader and correspondent – was with respect to his past and present, yet how singular was his accomplishment, as if he had been as 'isolated' in his brand of 'realism' as his admirer Aurier implied.[10] Van Gogh's version of 'reality' was idiosyncratic but proved to connect with masses

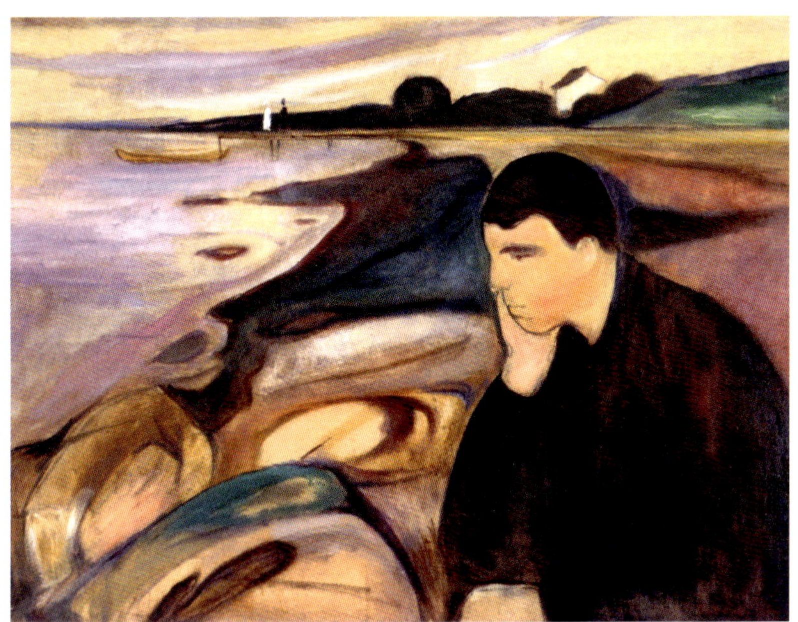

84 / Edvard Munch, *Melancholy* (*Melankoli*), 1894–96
Oil on canvas, 81 × 100.5 cm
KODE, Art Museums of Bergen

of viewers. His letter-writing corresponds to Wong's engagement with social media as links to established culture. Yet, like a force of nature, Wong's art (Van Gogh's too) attracts the senses and emotions of viewers, whatever their consciousness of history. This imagery is for everyone – in all places, at all times – its parentage hardly a concern.[11]

Modern melancholia

For the moment, consider a less sweeping judgement of Wong's significance, acknowledging his personal belief that he embodied the social dynamic of his contemporaneity. In 2018, during an interview, he merged two thoughts into a declaration resembling a manifesto, though an inadvertent one. 'I would like my paintings to have something in them people across the spectrum can find things they identify with.' Then he added: 'I do believe that there is an inherent loneliness or melancholy to much of contemporary life, and on a broader level I feel my work speaks to this quality in addition to being a reflection of my thoughts, fascinations and impulses.'[12] The second proposition, which conjoins the emotional needs of the individual to those of the society, renders realizable the first proposition, which invokes the collective longing for a common aesthetic language. For if the great majority of Wong's contemporaries were experiencing melancholia (loneliness, social detachment, lingering sadness) as their dominant emotional state, an art speaking to this condition would reach 'people across the spectrum'. The theme seems to have fallen to Wong naturally, without his having set out to represent it.[13]

Such had been the case with two of the late nineteenth-century painters whom Wong especially admired, Van Gogh and Munch – modernist predecessors in producing images for a melancholic era. Significantly, Van Gogh and Munch have long been favourites of the general population, now even globally. Long after their deaths the two artists continue to touch a universal nerve. Works such as Van Gogh's *Doctor Paul Gachet* (fig. 85), and Munch's *Melancholy* (fig. 84), address the pathology of melancholia and may even have sensitized Wong to the ubiquity of the syndrome. Van Gogh described his *Gachet* as bearing 'the deeply sad expression of our time'.[14] Munch narrated his scene of *Melancholy*, as a story of separation and jealousy, emotional states he knew from personal experience, perhaps having become all the more

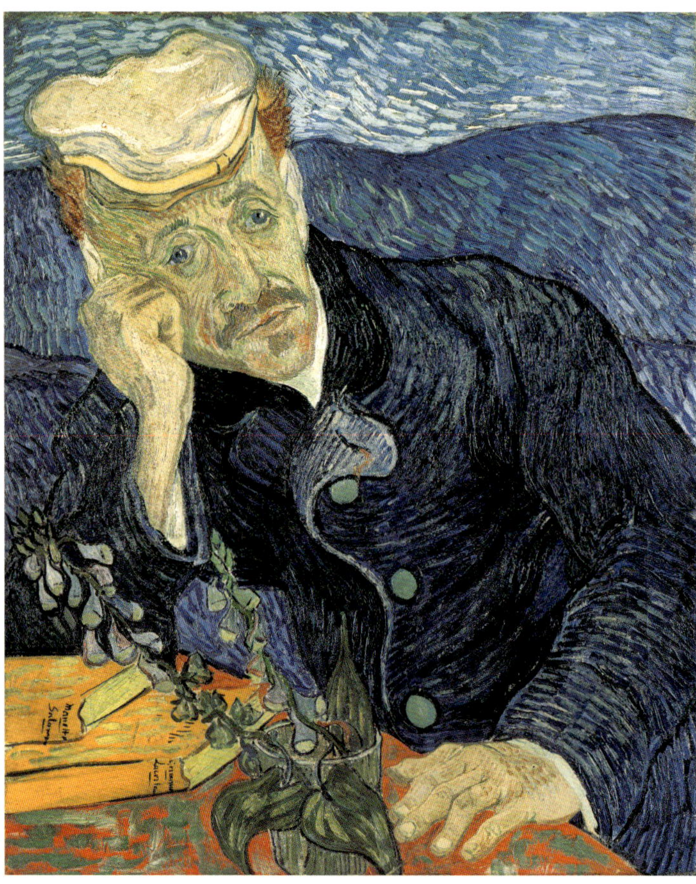

85 / Vincent van Gogh, *Doctor Paul Gachet*, 1890
Oil on canvas, 66 × 57 cm
Private collection

vivid through his creating such evocative images.[15] For attentive observers, art reveals the psychology of a society to itself, even to its artists.

Progressive painters of the Van Gogh–Munch era were supported by critics who lamented the pervasive social dysfunction among urban populations: the dulled sensibilities, the clichéd responses to intellectual and aesthetic stimulation, the emotional stagnation. Along with the loss of personally rewarding craft in an industrialized economy – academics refer to it as 'deskilling' – the general population seemed to be losing their skill at living itself.[16] Life continued but with tedium replacing its human interests and potential rewards. Symbolist writer Gustave Kahn commented caustically in 1886: 'Living is living only when creating or preparing for creation. Everything else is merely to exist like a stone or to vegetate like a plant.' Just as anomie deadened the bourgeoisie, the deskilled working class suffered from 'a diet of intoxicants [and] the depression resulting from the monotony and degradation of mechanized labour.'[17] In the same spirit Aurier, in 1890, having selected Van Gogh as a paradigm case of an individual isolated by his creative passions, tasked him with 'regenerating the decrepit state of our art and perhaps of our imbecilic industrialist society'.[18] And in 1905, Paul Cézanne's advocate Maurice Denis condemned conditions evident in the urban environment and its conformist order: 'Life loses each day a bit more of its character. Our streets are chillingly ugly, our [domestic] interiors banal [...] the police suppress every form of fantasy within social life.' The result: 'Our era prefers abstractions [in art] to reality.'[19] During the late nineteenth century, abstraction functioned as a double-edged concept, referring both to imaginative fantasies and to sensation reduced to its experiential essentials.[20]

Tirades against the social status quo marked the years around 1900, just as they do now, at least within the fully industrialized economies, where critics attribute social ills to the pernicious dependence on social media, as well as to the more general, unrelenting pressures of a capitalist system. The free practice of art, as Denis implied, restores character to life. Aesthetically heightened experience – the intensification of sensation and its abstraction – has traditionally offered escape for both artists and consumers of art. Or, if not complete release, then a position of reflection, where self-awareness becomes the antidote to stultification.

Imbalance

Melancholia has many psychological manifestations, corresponding to the range of its causes. Like other illnesses, whether of the body or mind, it is a condition of imbalance. Etymologically, the term refers to an excess of black bile, one of the four bodily humours. Societal or mass melancholia, the type to which Wong alluded, would be caused by collective excess. Of what? For the nineteenth-century critics, it was regulation, uniformity, standardization – all promoted politically for the sake of social order and harmony. Academic teaching of the craft of painting facilitated standardization by ensuring that a cadre of representational artists would generate ideologically acceptable imagery in a manner accessible and instructive to the general public. Van Gogh in his time and, to a degree, Wong in ours, addressed the public in other ways, without relying on a normative mode of presentation.

Both Van Gogh and Wong embodied Kahn's dictum, 'living is living only when creating'. As alive as one could be, Wong was executing his art even when he was not: 'Most of the work is done in idle moments when I am at home daydreaming, or watching movies and listening to music, drinking coffee or going out on walks that have no destination or purpose in mind. During these in-between moments I'll often have quick flashes of imagery appear in and out of my thoughts.'[21] The creativity of 'in-between moments' recalls Wong's metaphor of 'the flow from hand to surface'. He was not planning or plotting his compositions; his 'quick flashes of imagery' were themselves sensations and not – or not yet – elements of a conceptual order. His idle daydreams contributed to his hyperactive productivity, cure for the catatonia of a melancholic. 'Melancholy, if it can be overcome,' wrote Van Gogh, 'must be overcome by toil.'[22]

Wong's accelerated mode of creativity, extreme in its way, manifests imbalance. To a historian or critic seeking analogies, the case of Van Gogh casts a long shadow over Wong's practice. Aurier stressed Van Gogh's excessiveness even as the painter sought to represent his world as it was, labelling him both realist and neurasthenic – the latter was an all-purpose descriptor common at the time, alluding to a debilitating hypersensitivity associated with the stresses of modern life.[23] Octave Mirbeau – first owner of Van Gogh's *Irises* (1889, J. Paul Getty Museum, Los Angeles) – noted that Van Gogh's 'need to produce, to create, made for him a life without pause, without rest [...] It wasted him away little by little [until] it killed him'.[24] By Mirbeau's reasoning,

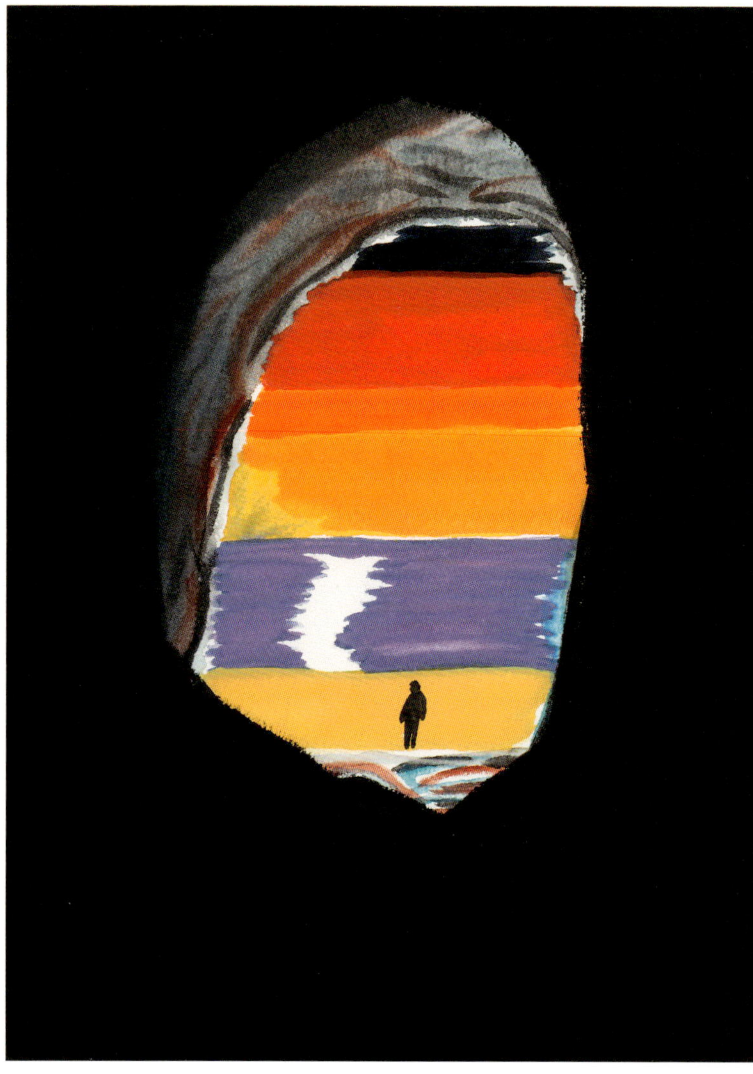

86 / Matthew Wong, *Origin*, 2017
Watercolour on paper, 30.8 × 22.9 cm
Collection of Shio Kusaka and Jonas Wood

suicide was no more than incidental to Van Gogh's death, a proximate cause; the final cause was his all-consuming practice of art.

Wong shared Van Gogh's hyper-productivity, compressing his aesthetic maturity into a brief career: 'Have come to realize traveling isn't my thing[,] need to just work all the time to feel a semblance of contentment in life.'[25] Though he took an interest in fashion, Wong experienced little that distracted him from concentrating exclusively on painting. In art, such imbalance can offer psychological advantages. We may feel that the imagination is all the more stimulated by a situation in which a quality exists in excess, lacking a compensating quality to offset it. Wong may have succeeded in reaching 'people across the spectrum' because he mastered an art of melancholic imbalance – openness without a promise of closure, movement without a causal foundation to orient it, compositions that, regardless of scale, seem to expand an imagined world without hinting at its limit. His title for a major work, *See You On the Other Side* (fig. 81), tempts a critic to explore the suggestion; the 'other side', an element of an innocuous idiom, may in Wong's case seem ominous and unreachable. His art was confirming what people already felt, causing them to become intensely aware *that they do feel* (that is, that they are alive, that existential dilemmas confront them, that the status quo raises doubts).

A modest example. The small watercolour *Origin* (fig. 86) features one of Wong's characteristically diminutive figures, who (as in *See You On the Other Side*) faces an expanse of water, here denoted by a band of blue-violet with a serrated swatch of white evoking surface reflectivity. Beyond the blue-violet – pictorially above it – bands of yellow, orange, red and black extend upwards as progressively darker chromatic values, indicating either gradations of atmospheric light or a deeply receding, elevated landscape. It could be a screen of dense vapour or an impenetrable wall of earth, as in high desert. The location of a horizon becomes uncertain. Wong's structuring of space typically presents such ambiguity. The isolation of the single figure is also typical,

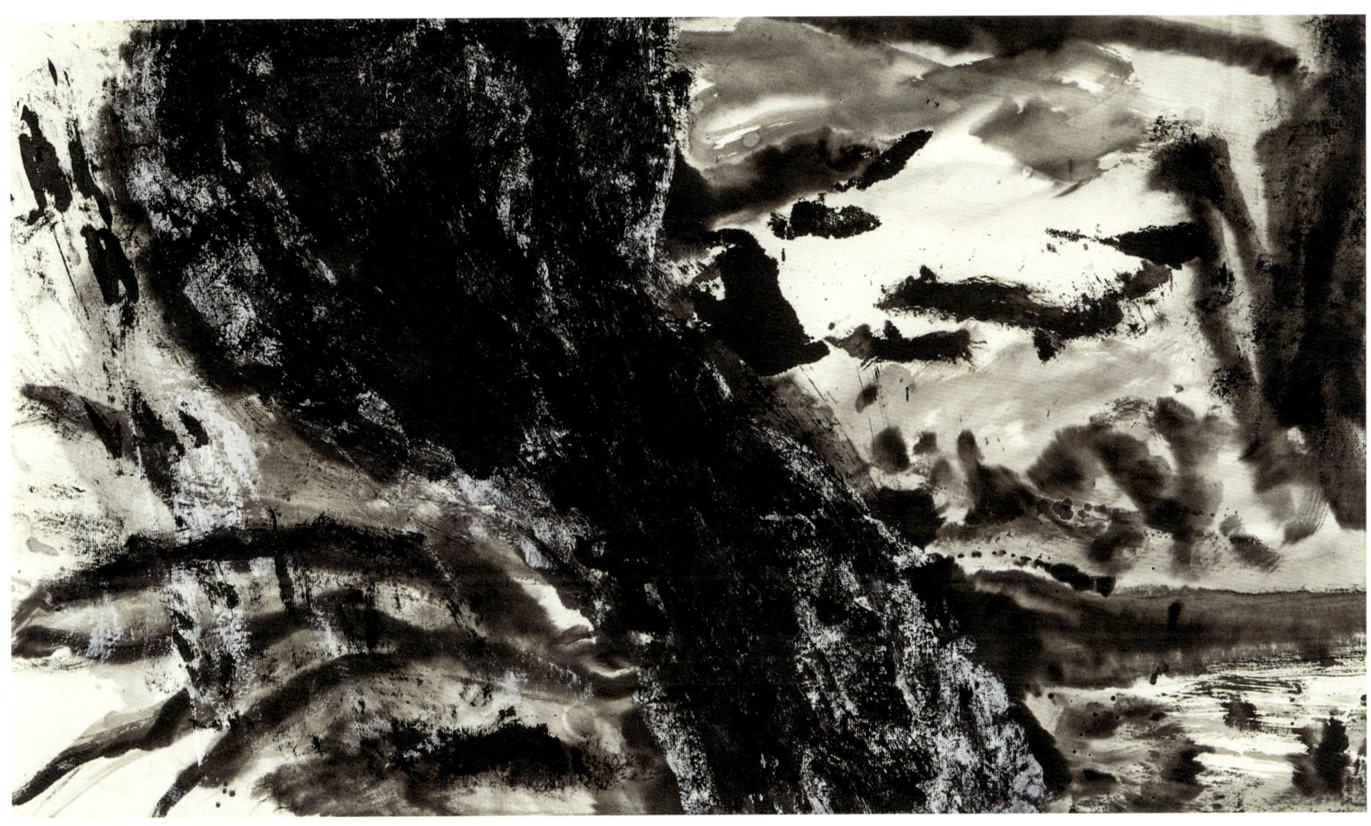

87 / Matthew Wong, *Untitled*, 2013
Ink on rice paper, 39.4 × 68.6 cm
Private collection

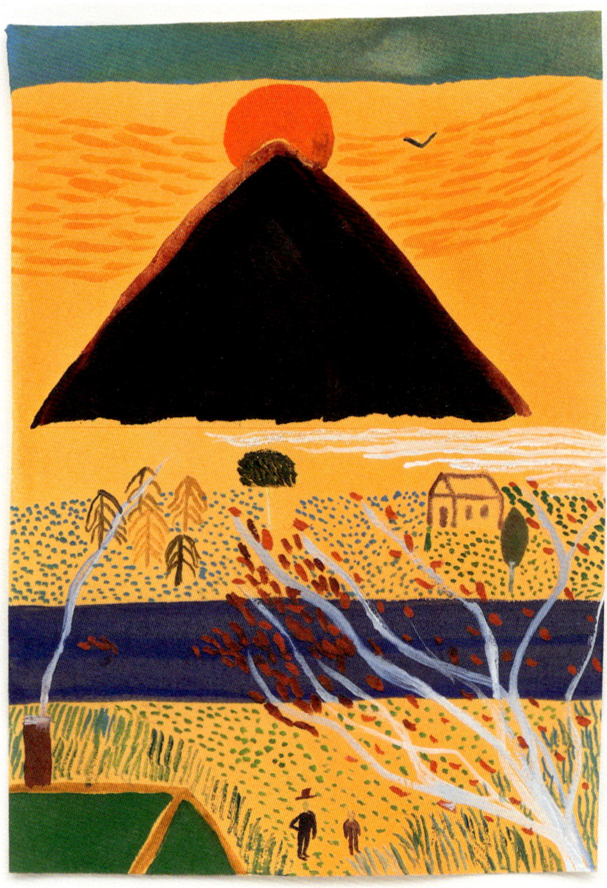

standing without direction, an emblem of loneliness, even melancholy.

The implied position of the viewer introduces further uncertainty and unease. Because black surrounds the bright bands of colour, the composition evokes an opening to light from within darkness. *Origin* sets its potential viewer within a cave, looking outwards through an articulated aperture or channel (like a volumetric *O*) and towards the figure within the illuminated scene. Given both the title and the arrangement, the suggestion of a birth canal is inescapable, a secure location to which the figure can never return. To stand before *Origin* is to be situated in a contained, encompassing world (cave, womb, womblike interior of a camera), while the depicted figure, Wong's alter ego, exists in a void that lacks measure. *Origin* is inherently disorienting for those who seek to identify with its perspective, to stabilize the communicative link of private artist to viewing public. The composition induces voyeurism, an illicit look at the figural surrogate for both artist and viewer. Somehow, this perspective fails to correspond to either. It offers no coherent standpoint, whether spatial or temporal. Potentially, the origin invoked by the title inaugurates all of human history (the lone figure as first human) or merely a single life (a modern melancholic). In a scene of such disequilibrium, the souls whom Wong observed around him might identify their melancholic condition.

'I think it's healthy', Wong said, 'to embrace two sides that are paradoxical to each other. It's an expanding of the consciousness.'[26] Paradoxes project the mind beyond its customary logic, beyond communal constraints. At the time of this statement, August 2012, Wong was distinguishing his representational interests in photography from the abstraction of the ink drawings that he was exploring simultaneously (see the somewhat later work in ink, *Untitled* (fig. 87)). More generally, he was alluding to irresolvable dualities that maintain a tension between conflicting concepts and sensations – a psychosomatic imbalance. He seems to have recognized that concepts, generated in language, and sensations, received physically, are inherently incommensurable. A picture never illustrates its culturally assigned meaning with complete precision, and critical interpretation remains open unless reductive rules are imposed.

88 / Matthew Wong, *Pastoral*, 2018
Watercolour on paper, 30.8 × 18.1 cm
Private collection

Every material representation – a painting, even a photograph – retains some degree of dumb materiality that speaks only of itself,

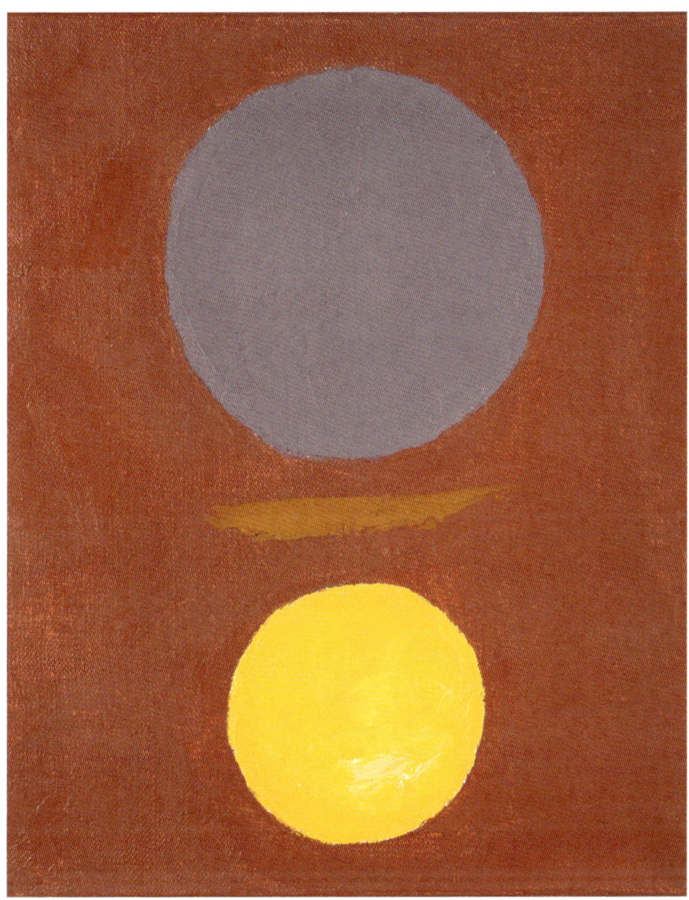

without reference elsewhere. There is always an extra, an element of abstraction that abstracts nothing. 'The process of markmaking tends to highlight paint's abstract reality', Wong stated, referring to the inescapable presence of base materiality.[27] A mark brings its reality to the image it configures. Yet cultural habit masks the reference-free, sensory qualities of a representational sign. This was Roland Barthes's warning when he wrote: 'Meaning sticks to man'.[28]

Perception that begins with meaning can nevertheless end in sensation. In 2015, Wong reviewed an exhibition of the Lebanese-American Etel Adnan, held at White Cube in Hong Kong, where Wong then lived. At a glance, he notes, Adnan's compositions evoke landscapes, though highly abstracted. With more studied observation, however, Wong's assessment shifts: 'Slowing down to look again, we notice that paradox and uncertainty begin to settle in: what is that brown dot looming directly over the sun?'[29] Here Wong appears to refer to Adnan's *Untitled*, 2014 (see, as comparable, fig. 89), in which the addition of a second circular form counteracts the obvious interpretation of a solar disc above the horizon. The mind reverts from determining meaning to open observation of shape and colour.

Wong created many analogous cases of 'paradox and uncertainty'. In his watercolour *Pastoral* (fig. 88), a 'sun' (red-orange circle) is positioned behind a 'mountain' (reddish-black triangle), and yet appears below a band of 'sea' or 'sky' (blue-green rectangle). We look and ask: When do geometry and colour ever become secure in representing something other than their materiality, extension and configuration? *Pastoral* consists of bands evoking different distances and perspectives, as if the concept of the scene were changing in the course of its realization. In the context of Adnan, Wong resorts to the general, impersonal pronoun 'one' as he concludes: 'The longer one looks, the more hesitant one becomes to name the object of looking, and all that one is left with is the act of looking itself – an act which is as necessary as reaching for the nature of the ground one is standing on.' Wong's conceptualization here, his self-criticism, is profound. His 'one' includes himself as both artist and art critic; he ventures to apply his understanding to everyone else, his melancholic confrères.

89 / Etel Adnan,
The Weight of the World 25
(*Le Poids du Monde 25*), 2016
Oil on canvas, 27 × 22 cm
Fondation Louis Vuitton, Paris

>> 90 /Matthew Wong, *Valley*, 2014
Oil on canvas, 100 × 157.5 cm
Private collection

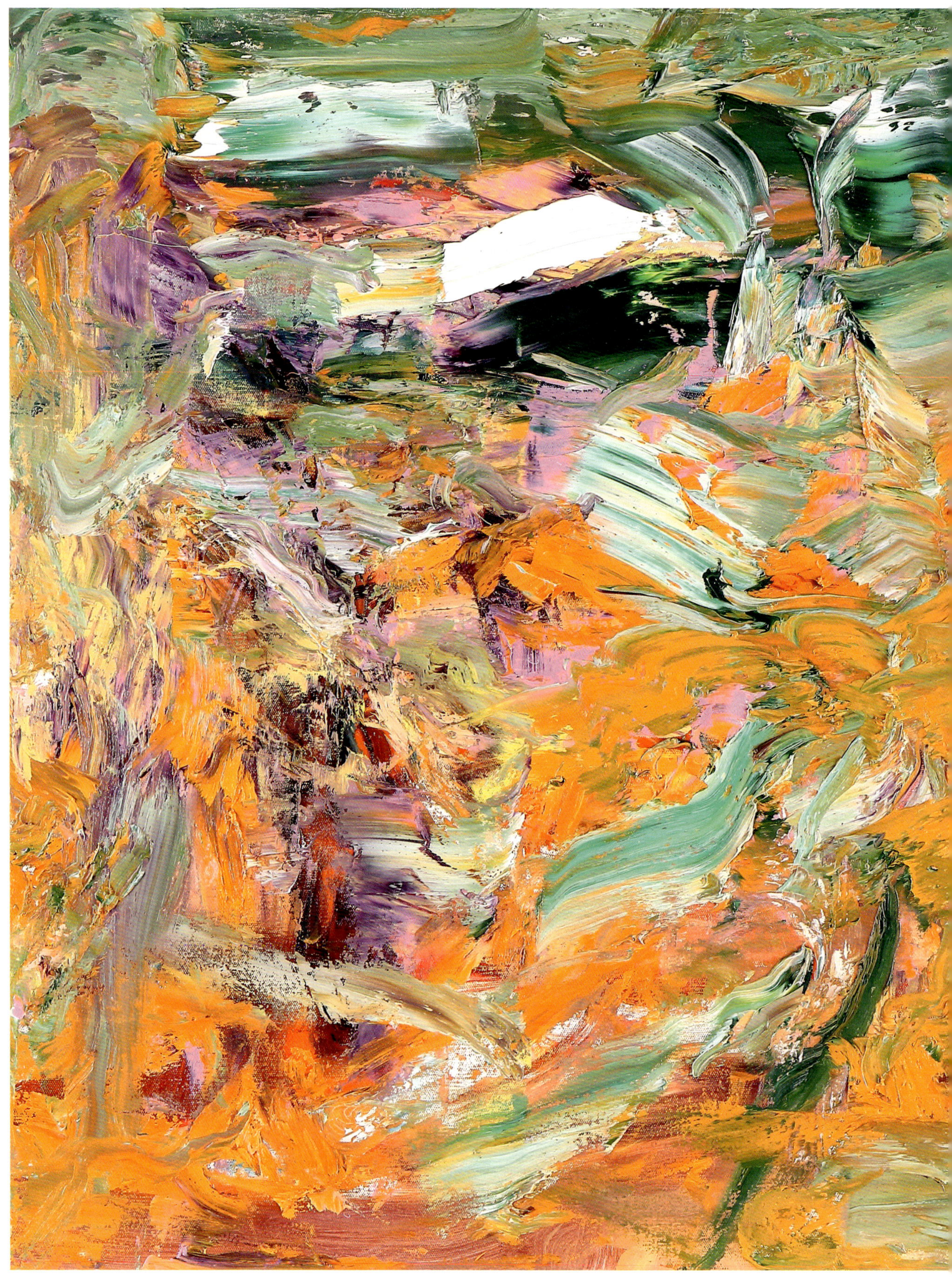

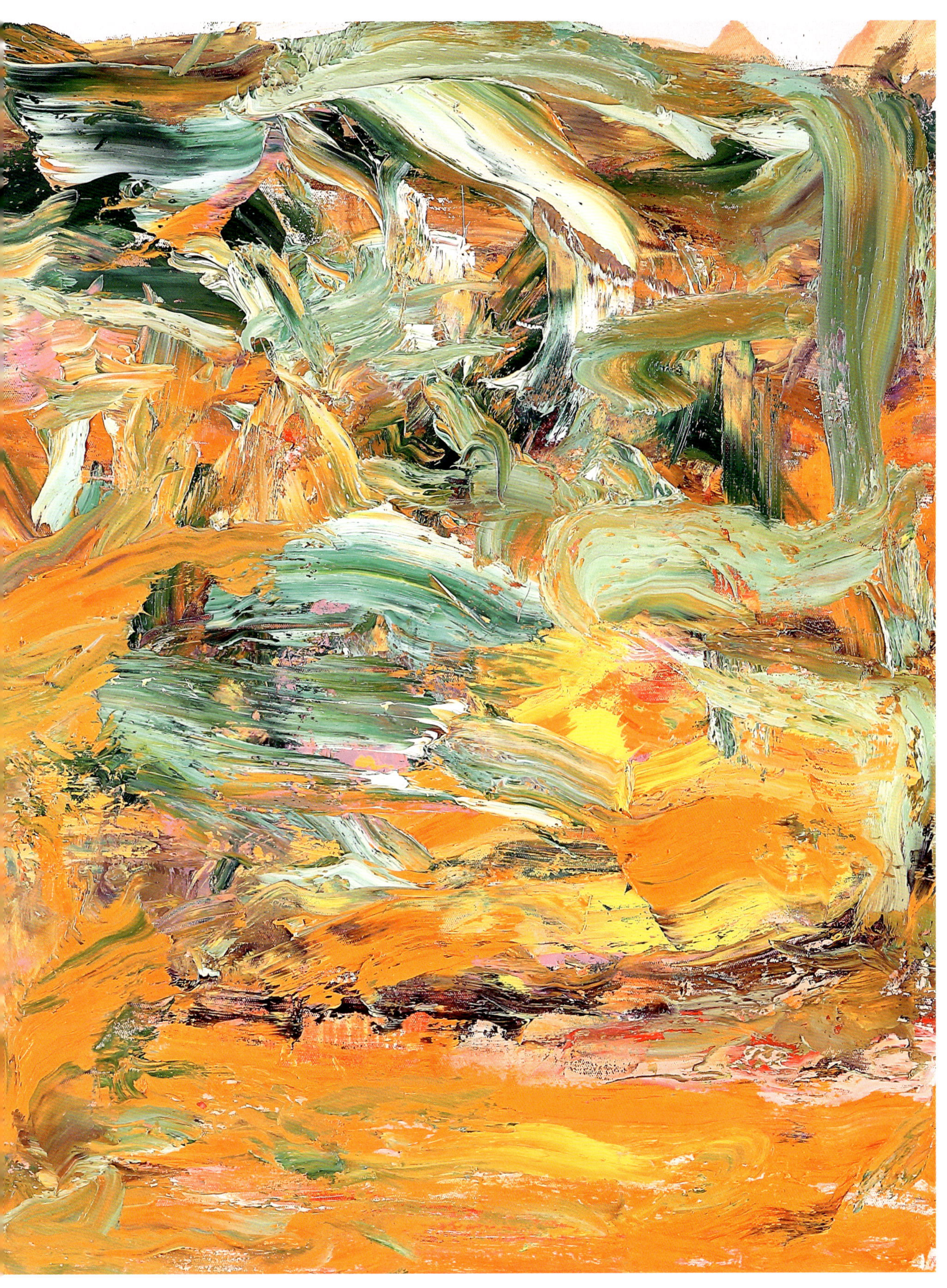

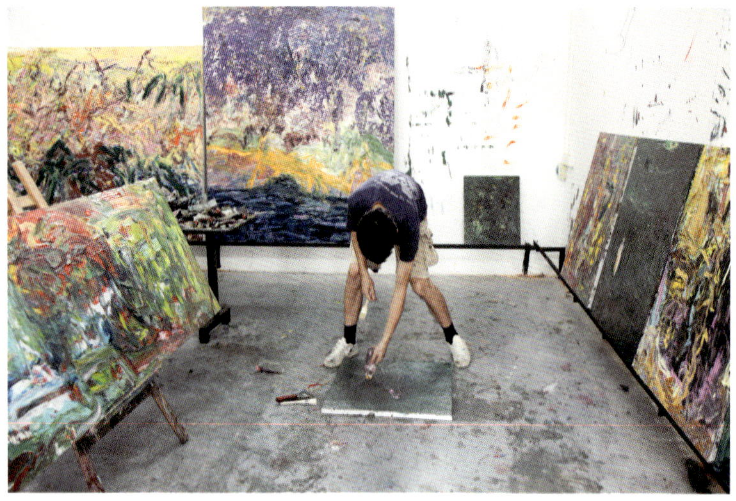

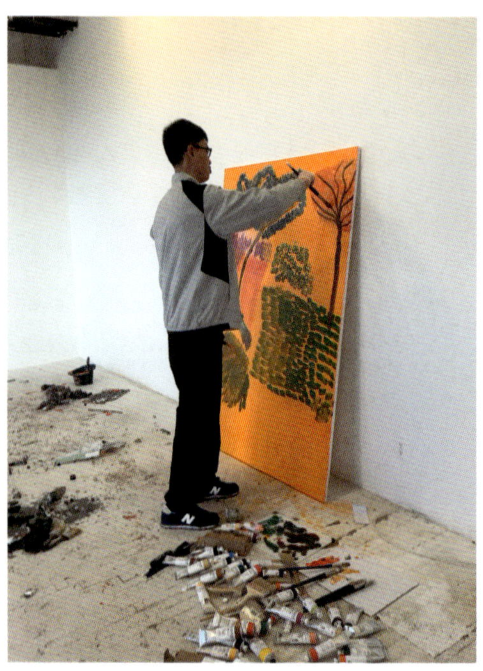

91 / Matthew Wong at work in his studio in Zhongshan, China

92 / Matthew Wong, at work on canvas *Untitled*, 2017, in his temporary studio in Brooklyn

He adds: 'Looking is never a passive act. It is always a political one, in its inexorable movement towards confirming a perceptive truth that ultimately may not be found.'[30] Having abandoned the security of ideology, Wong embraced the politics of doubt, an insecure grounding.

Wong's abstraction emerged from organic impulses rather than from knowledge of what the history of art was demanding. Historical determinism will not explain his choices. Self-taught as a painter, he had never learned to make conventional figuration and had no need to unlearn it through deskilling. To the extent that chance entered his painting process, this was not a strategy, such as Jean Arp's dropping forms cut from paper to the floor to create a composition or Cy Twombly's drawing in utter darkness. In an interview of 2014, Wong recounted his transition from photography to drawing and painting a year or two previously: 'I bought a sketch book, a bottle of ink, and made a mess every day randomly – pouring ink into the pages, hoping something interesting would happen.'[31] At times, the 'interesting' might well have occurred by resemblance to what the culture and Wong himself already accepted as art. Among his early paintings, *Valley* (fig. 90), has the diptych format, density of brushstroke and chromatic range that recall works by Joan Mitchell, such as *Two Sunflowers* (fig. 93).

Yet Wong's method was not imitative, for in 'the flow from hand to surface' the artist learns to look and to make by making and looking – looking at what is being made, whether a 'mess' or a pseudo-Mitchell. Wong's statements encourage this stress on happenstance: 'I've been right-handed my whole life, but when I paint I actually use both hands. *It isn't something I started doing consciously*, but sometime in 2014 I noticed that I was actually passing painting utensils back and forth between each hand while working.'[32] Wong's ambidextrous handling and choice of format realized his visceral will: 'I feel more comfortable and at ease on this [large] scale than [at] easel size [...] It could be because I'm tall and better when I can use [my] whole upper body.'[33] A photograph shows Wong bent over a large canvas on the studio floor, exercising his long reach, a posture to accommodate his physical being, not an art-world gambit (fig. 91).

Although Wong discovered that painting served his emotional needs better than his initial medium of photography, he recognized

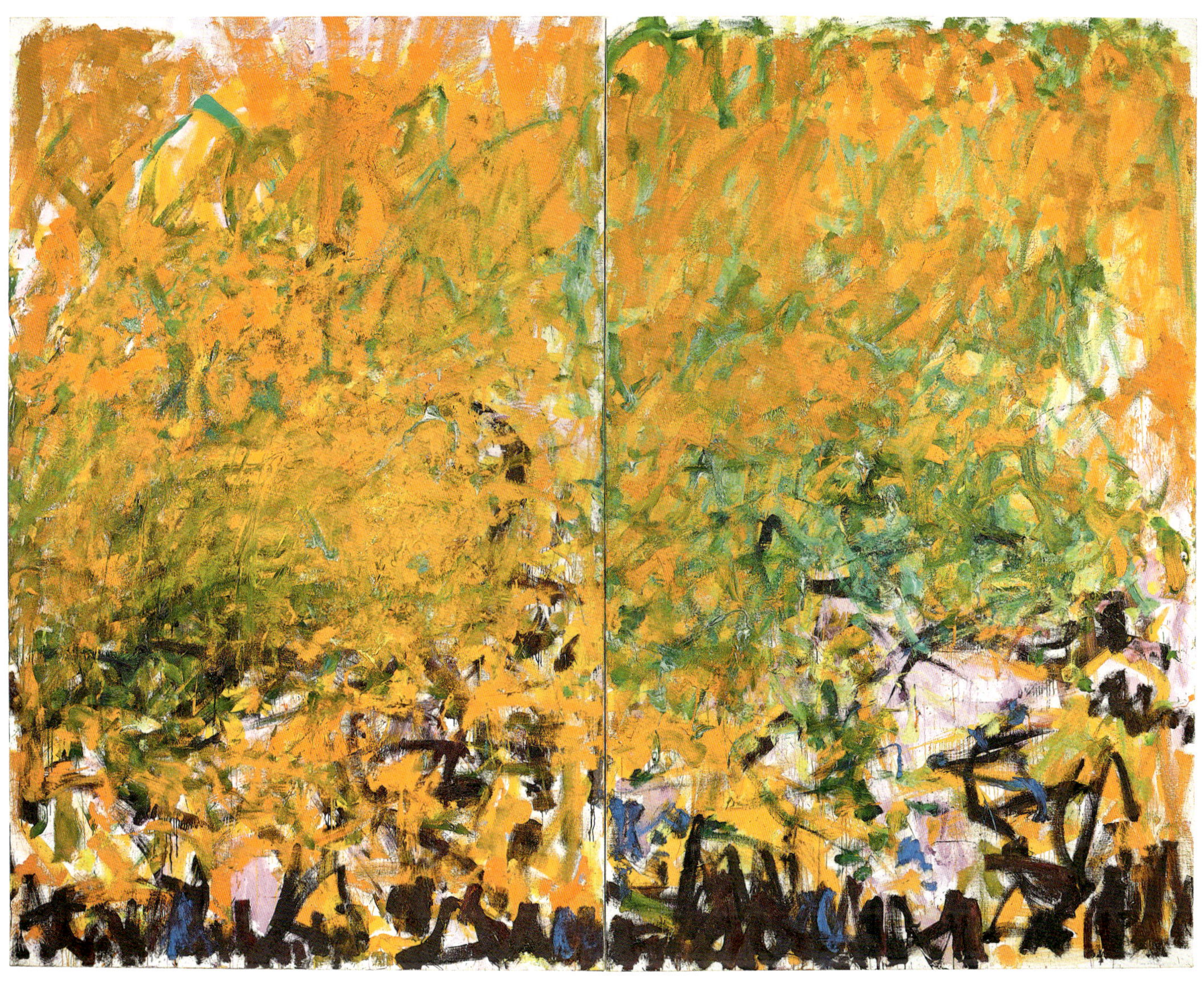

93 / Joan Mitchell, *Two Sunflowers*, 1980
Oil on canvas, 280.1 × 360.7 cm
Fondation Louis Vuitton, Paris

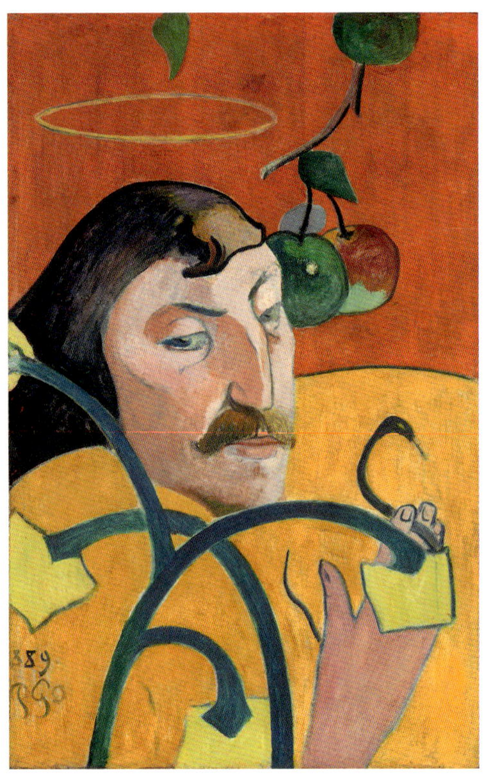

94 / Paul Gauguin, *Self-Portrait*, 1889
Oil on wood, 79.2 × 51.3 cm
National Gallery of Art, Washington. Chester Dale Collection

value in his photographic practice: 'My photography is as much about the act of seeing itself as it is [about] the subject matter in the images. [...] I take a picture of something because I see myself in it.'[34] Seeing becomes happenstance self-discovery – discovery by way of the other: 'Whenever I'm shooting people I don't look through the viewfinder; I adjust all the settings ahead of time and just walk by and take a photo.'[35] The succession of discrete images anticipated the painting technique that Wong developed, in which clusters of brushstrokes follow upon each other in somewhat separate areas of a pictorial surface (see in a studio in Brooklyn, May 2017, fig. 92). As photographer and painter, Wong developed a process to approach the spontaneity of unconscious acts of perception as they attain consciousness in perceptible representation. His imagery visualized its own pre-existing traces, the evidence of its maker's being. 'For me, to take photographs is a way of confirming that I exist, which is something I question all the time. When I can make an image I'm satisfied with, then that question goes away for a little while. [...] I don't spend much time looking at the images afterwards, it's really about existing very intensely in the present.'[36] To continue existing, Wong would continue creating.

Like Van Gogh, Wong may have experienced depression (melancholia) while perceiving that it belonged to his cultural environment as much as to him.[37] He spoke of observing conditions around him as a way of establishing his identity, as if he needed to project his self-image onto a physical object – a painting, a photograph – from which he could absorb his projection back into himself ('I see myself'). Such a psychological dynamic corresponds to an art that slips from material abstraction into representational fantasy. The former condition is more concrete, more 'real', than the latter, which is dreamlike. Wong perceived images emerging from his mark-making, in the very process of making the marks. The bands of colour in *Origin* begin as abstraction, only to become a representational motif that is at once a destination for the depicted figure and a barrier to it.

By contrast, Van Gogh's representational technique tended to slip from representation into abstraction (as did Cézanne's, as did Matisse's – this constitutes their 'modernism'). At one point, referring to *The Sower* (fig. 6), Van Gogh confessed that he 'could hardly give a damn about the *veracity* of the colour';[38] here, flecks of bluish violet, yellow and orange render muddy earth, while the disc of a setting sun spews golden rays. Having gradually allowed the chromatic intensity and the evident materiality of the paint to increase, Van Gogh worried that the image became too much of an abstraction: 'you fall into a whole metaphysics of colours [...] a mess from which it's damned awkward to escape with credit. And that makes you absent-minded [*abstrait*], like a

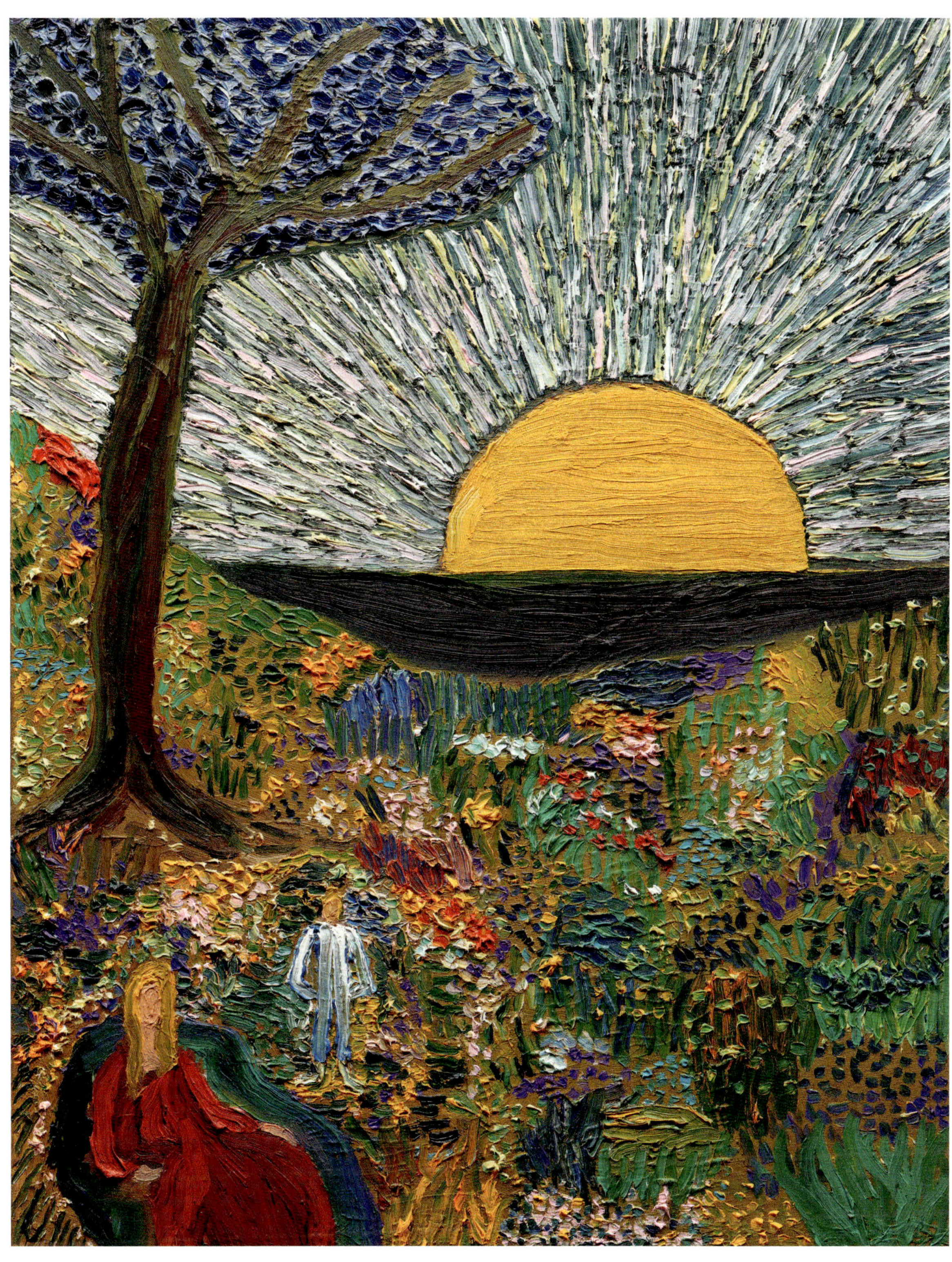

95 / Matthew Wong,
Landscape with Mother and Child, 2017
Oil on canvas, 71.1 × 55.9 cm
Brooker-Pardee Family Collection

sleep-walker.'[39] The concern seems to have been that instinctive feelings would obliterate rationality along with representational realism. But Wong's similar instances of intensified colour and brushwork – as in *The Sun* (fig. 31), and *Landscape with Mother and Child* (fig. 95) – do not appear to have yielded any misgivings. He admitted to being an abstract artist.

In 1888 and 1889, Van Gogh and Paul Gauguin argued over the proper balance between visual observation and pictorial abstraction in painting. Gauguin, presumably responding to Van Gogh's stress on working from nature, asserted that for him abstraction paralleled vision itself and was just as natural: 'I want to consult nature too [when working with an image of symbolic significance], but I don't want to take from it what I see there [...] where's the natural in a painting? *Everything* in paintings since the most distant ages has been completely conventional' – a product of mind. 'The truth is what one feels, in the state of mind one's in. [...] the dream always comes from the reality [experienced] in nature.'[40] Gauguin's 'dream' was his imaginative projection, an art rendered 'conventional' by the presence of its abstraction, which distinguished it from the putative, normative real – its optics having been affected by the painter's emotionally charged sensation (fig. 94). To every artist, their convention, endlessly personalized – theoretically, is a universal condition. This type of difference, if accepted as the socially equalizing, natural order, would obviate imbalance and relieve melancholia, too.

Universality

Like melancholy (but less disabling), doubt is a common psychological state. In 1945, Maurice Merleau-Ponty published 'Cézanne's Doubt', an ageless essay that continues to be consulted for its articulation of the modernity of modern artists. As a theorist of art, Merleau-Ponty is analogous to Van Gogh as a painter, his popularity perennial. His accessibility transcends generational difference and passes beyond the limits of Western culture.[41] The 'doubt' of his title belonged not only to Cézanne but to others. In the midst of his essay, Merleau-Ponty made a poignant assertion that collapses all of history. He suggested that centuries of aesthetic evolution in practice and theory had hardly affected the psychological equilibrium of artists: 'The artist launches his work just as a man once launched the first word, not knowing whether it will be anything more than a shout.'[42] Wherever art appears, there must be acceptance of doubt. Merleau-Ponty's 'artist' would seem to include everyone from mark-makers of the Ice Age to moderns like Cézanne and Matisse. If we read his text now, it relates to Gauguin's sense of 'the most distant ages' as well as to our contemporary Matthew Wong.

96 / Matthew Wong, *Good Morning*, 2018
Oil on canvas, 101.6 × 76.2 cm
Private European collection

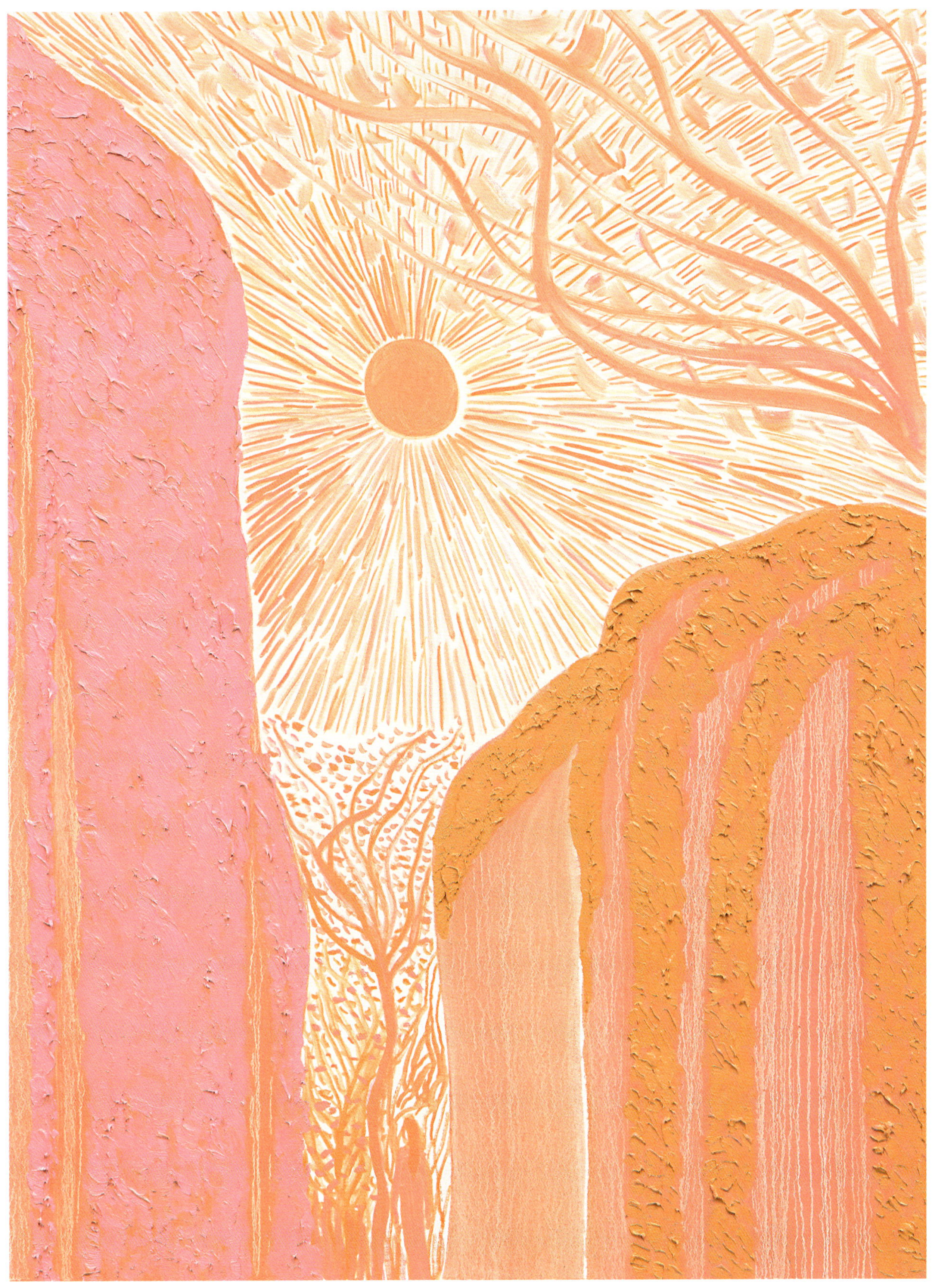

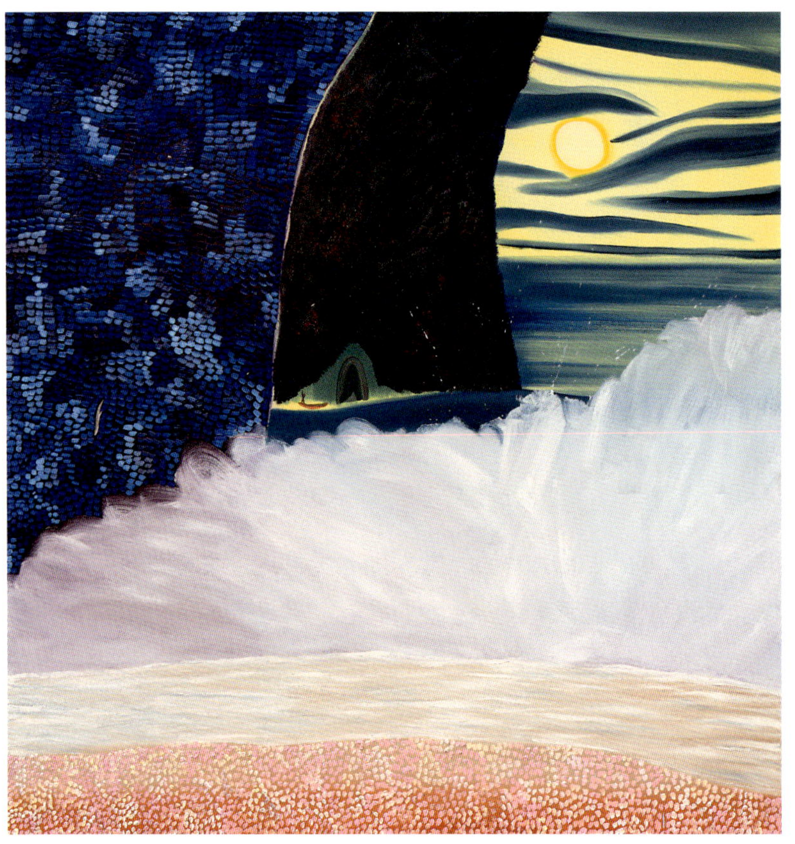

Wong probably suffered doubt no more than his peers. Doubt is a most human condition, experienced intensely, Merleau-Ponty implies, by those among us who are most human.[43] He was profiling the artist as a type, not an individual. Acting as the last in a line of painters – to be now is to be last – Wong (in Merleau-Ponty's sense) was the first in 'not knowing' the form his aesthetic message would assume when received. As a matter of principle, he denied himself a practice that would guarantee acceptance: 'I am just trying to see "what the paint does" [...] I must always keep in mind to prioritize constant movement and experimentation over the acquisition of virtuosity.'[44]

Radically experimental or predictably doctrinaire, all painting, Wong believed, constituted one and only one tradition, a single practice. An interviewer asked in 2018: 'Where do you think your work fits in dialogue with artists who came before you?' Wong's reply is direct, without nuance, yet searching, caught somewhere between modesty and grandiosity: 'I have not really thought much about my place in the histories and lineages of painting. This may sound a bit idealistic, but I really would like to think that anybody out there painting or drawing something at the moment is engaging in the same larger, perhaps infinitely vast conversation as I am about the craft.'[45] Accordingly, he spoke of his work acquiring 'a universal dimension'.[46] Craft, common and accessible, is not specific to an era, such as an age of melancholia. Wong, who composed poetry, cared about his words; his choice of the term *craft* must have been deliberate or at least the natural, unthinking option for him, consistent with his identity as a self-taught artist. Anyone who manipulates materials learns by doing, which amounts to self-instruction in a craft. Whether the results constitute 'art' becomes a separate question, adjudicated by historical and social framing. 'Craft' is an observation; 'art' is a value judgement.

With his reference to an 'infinitely vast conversation', Wong, confident of his own capability, might well have realized that he was assuming a minority position. In 2007 he earned an undergraduate degree in cultural anthropology from the University of Michigan. During his years as an exhibiting artist, his educated peers, at least in

97 / Matthew Wong, *Hideaway*, 2019
Oil on canvas, 182.8 × 177.8 cm
Matthew Wong Foundation

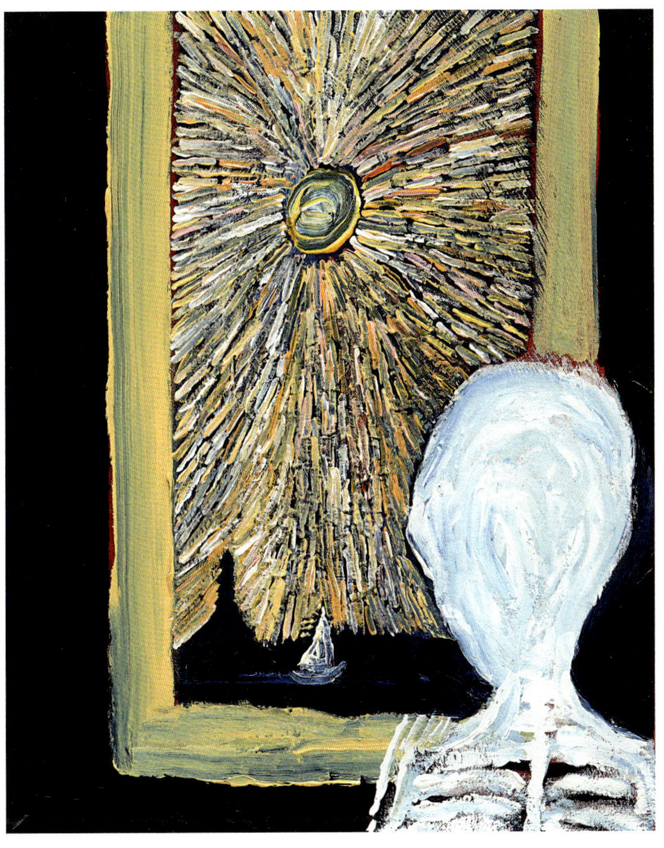

98 / Matthew Wong, *Nostalgia*, 2016
Acrylic on canvas, 50.8 × 40.6 cm
Private collection, Wilfram AG, St. Moritz

North America, were stressing the social reality of ethnic and gender differences; a person's choices and actions should be interpreted as a fluid product of the multiple identities that were determining each individual's sensibility. All was culturally coded. There could be no 'universal dimension' to social agency, no more so in aesthetic life than in political life. Ironically, while academic fashion dictated rejecting any claim to universal, timeless values, the intellectually outmoded became by default culturally countercultural. To attain universality in some form of human communication was to achieve a certain transcendence, contrary to the prevailing negativity, a way out of the contemporary social malaise. We may think that a 'universal dimension' must be higher, like the universally accepted truths of higher mathematics. But universality exists in low or common forms as well, as in ordinary visual and tactile sensations of the external environment, experience with which everyone identifies and, for most people, requires no explanation.[47]

Mark-making

To the extent that Wong's art spoke to his contemporaries by addressing their collective melancholia, he had an affinity with Van Gogh, who was also sensitive to social transformation and social malaise. But Wong's practice had the potential to transport him much further back in history, to ages so distant that analogies to contemporary social psychology lose all pragmatic value. The physicality of his art linked him not only to Van Gogh, Munch, Klimt and others of the early modernist moment, but to the entirety of humanity. The art of moderns who, like Wong, feature mark-making seems to connect naturally to the representational figuration found in the caves of Lascaux in France and Altamira in Spain, and now with the newly discovered linear engravings of *Homo naledi* in South Africa, incomparably older and lacking discernible reference.[48] Wong's manner of rendering landscape, figures and interiors will at times recall Matisse or Doig but is essentially elemental, as if in dialogue with, or coordinated with, tool-bearing hands of any era, including those of prehistoric populations only dimly imaginable. Graphic artist S.W. Hayter, addressing the centrality of line for human communication,

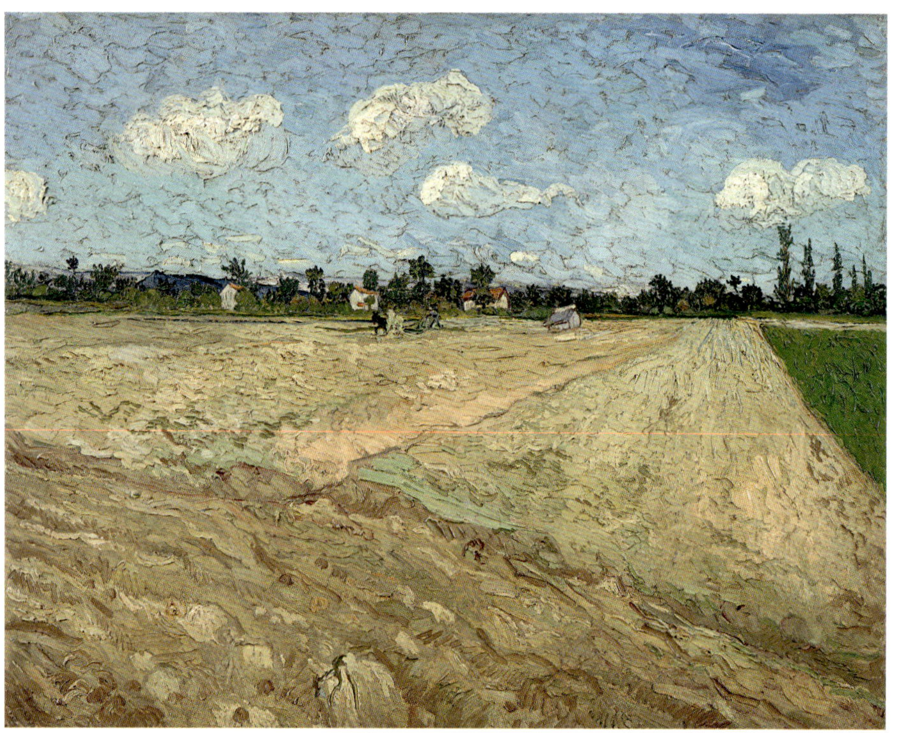

99 / Vincent van Gogh, *Ploughed Fields ('The Furrows')*, 1888
Oil on canvas, 72.5 × 92.5 cm
Van Gogh Museum, Amsterdam
(Vincent van Gogh Foundation)

wrote in 1949: 'In the phenomenal world around him prehistoric man could observe relatively few examples of true line to imitate except those he had made himself with such ease.'[49] Before representing anything, line signifies a human presence to other humans.

Numerous artists of recent decades have limited their range of graphic marks. Many have been inspired by, and even imitated, untutored drawings made by children, artworks created by psychologically alienated adults and the symbolic abstractions characteristic of isolated Indigenous populations. But most of the moderns differ from Wong in being self-consciously calculating about such associations, intending to achieve the expressive directness and sincerity attributed to individuals who, for one reason or another, remain unaffected by the cultural refinements of an advanced consumer economy. Wong appreciated the sophistications of modern art but did not appropriate them, including the strategy of elemental expression. His means of expression had no need to return to the look of the elemental, for this was his 'native' style.

Instinct is native. The human hand instinctively responds to the feel of materials. Wong's craft as a painter in oils or acrylics capitalized on the inherent malleability of his medium. He used viscous dabs of colour; smears of paint that compound two or more hues; pigment applied with irregular, mottled edging; loosely articulated forms offset by contrasting light or dark chromatic grounds; and strokes of halting fluidity (as if reacting to the movement as it occurred). Apparently, these methods accorded with Wong's impulses. Despite the distinctive character of his manner, all seems bound together by a commonplace sense of direct linearity. Whatever is not linear is often punctiform – a spot, a dab – a gesture that respects the physicality of paint as much as a linear deposit does. Lines and spots correspond to the two most natural tactile probes, as if the human body, as a way of negotiating its environment, had been designed to leave such traces, the signs (indices) of an inquisitive, exploratory presence. As the hand passes

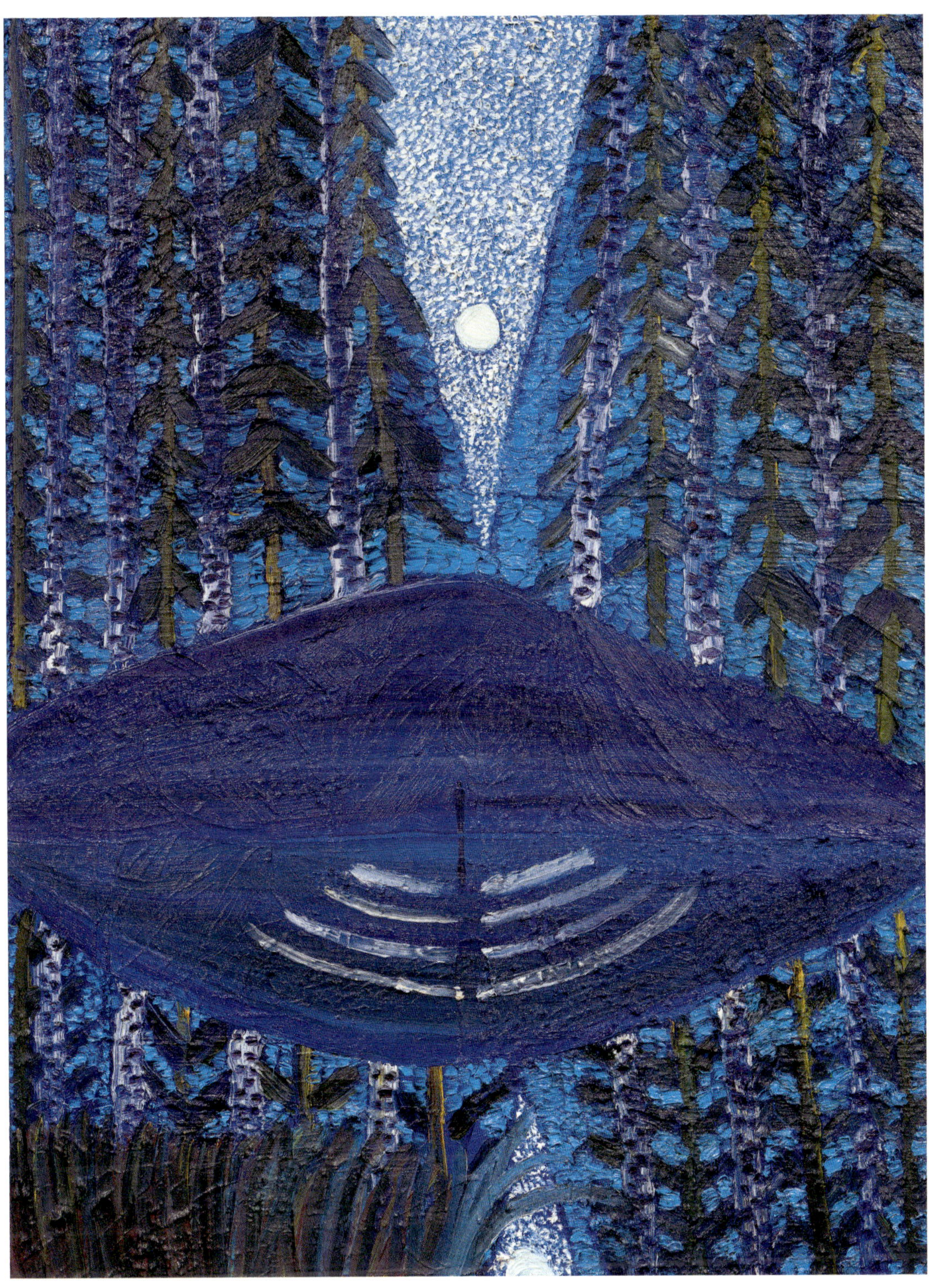

100 / Matthew Wong, *Ripple in the Night*, 2018
Oil on canvas, 101.6 × 76.2 cm
Matthew Wong Foundation

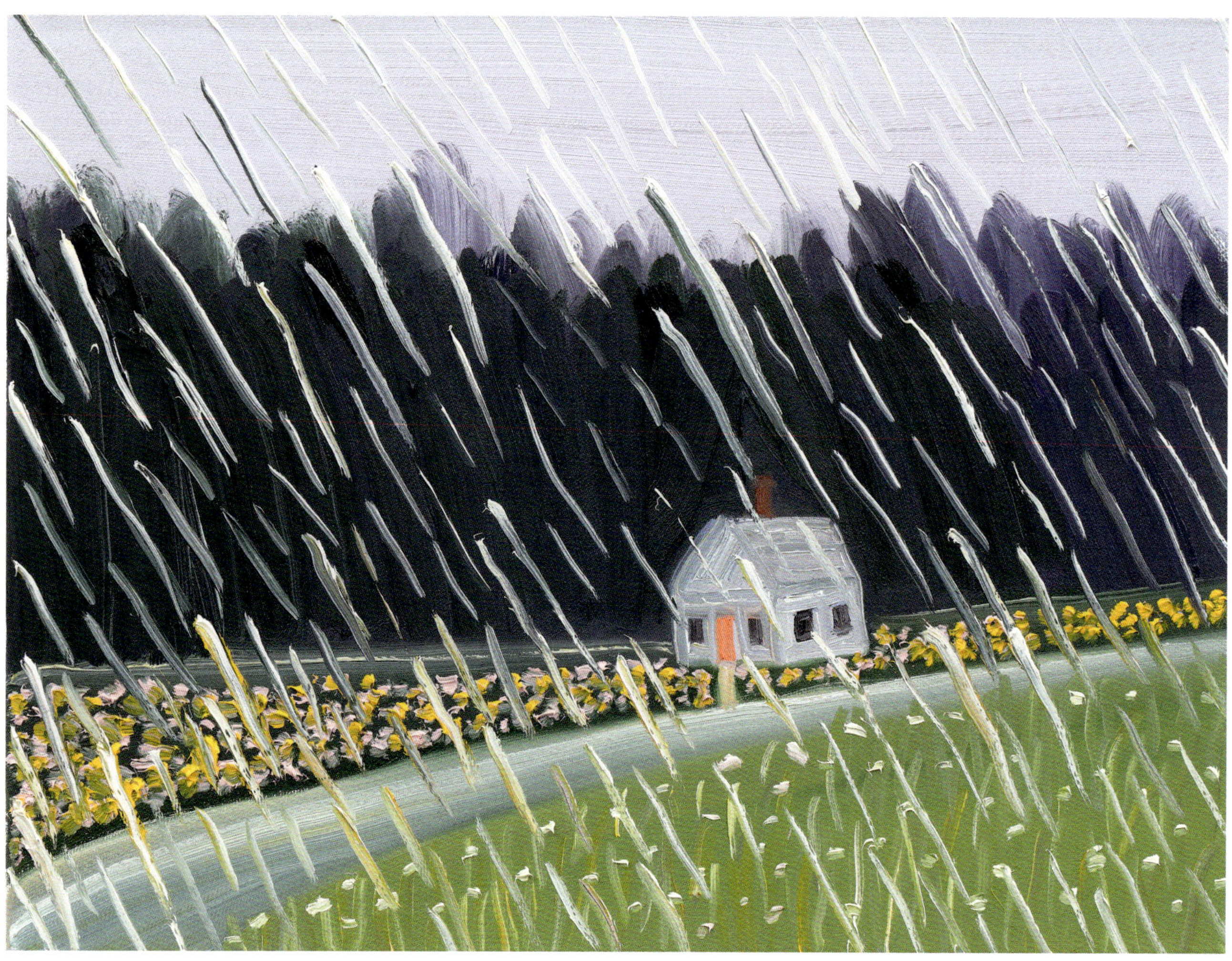

101 / Matthew Wong, *Spring*, 2018
Oil on canvas, 30.5 × 40.6 cm
Brendan Dugan

102 / Matthew Wong, *Blue Rain*, 2018
Oil on canvas, 182.9 × 121.9 cm
Collection of KAWS, promised gift to the Metropolitan Museum of Art, New York, inspired by Julia Chang

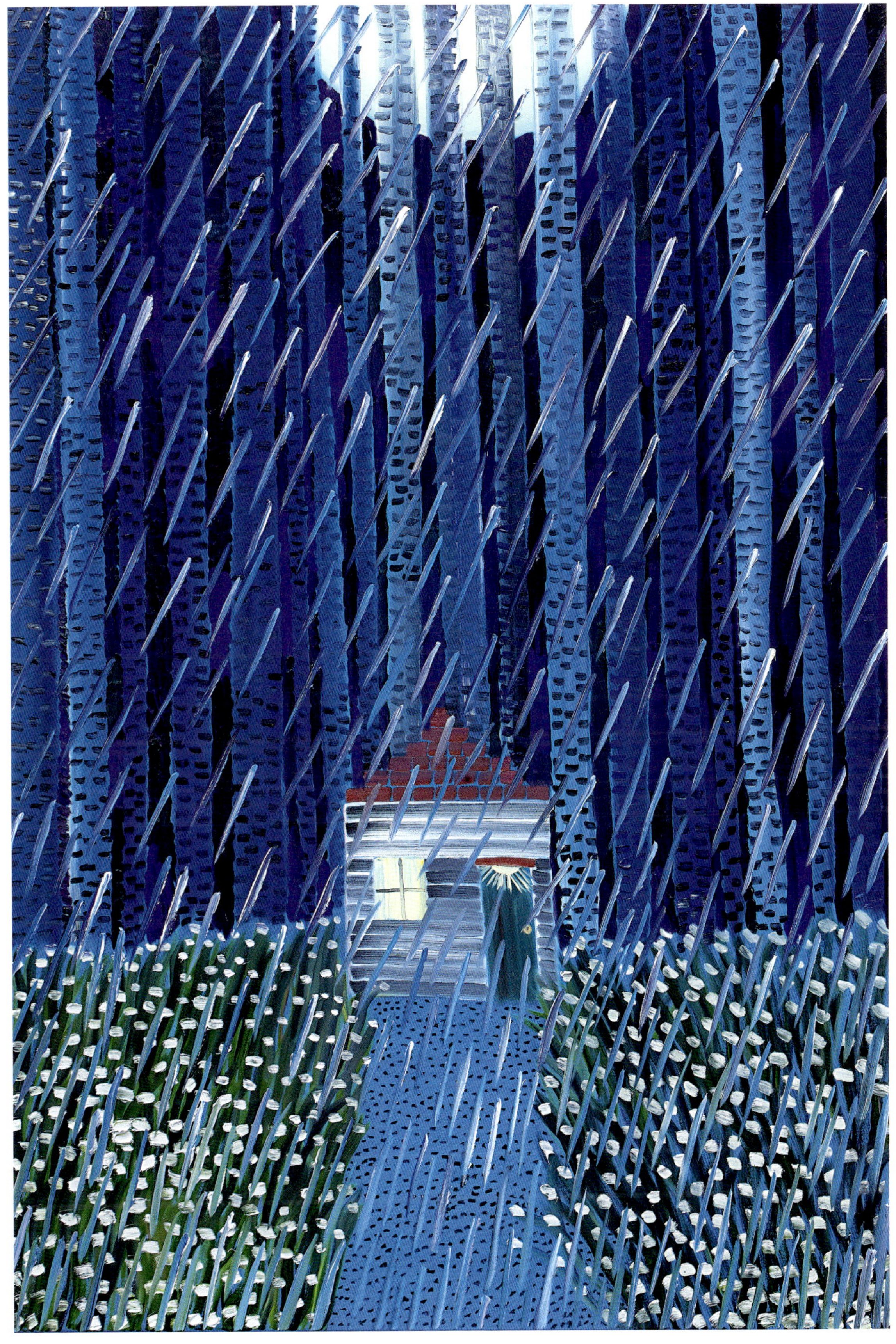

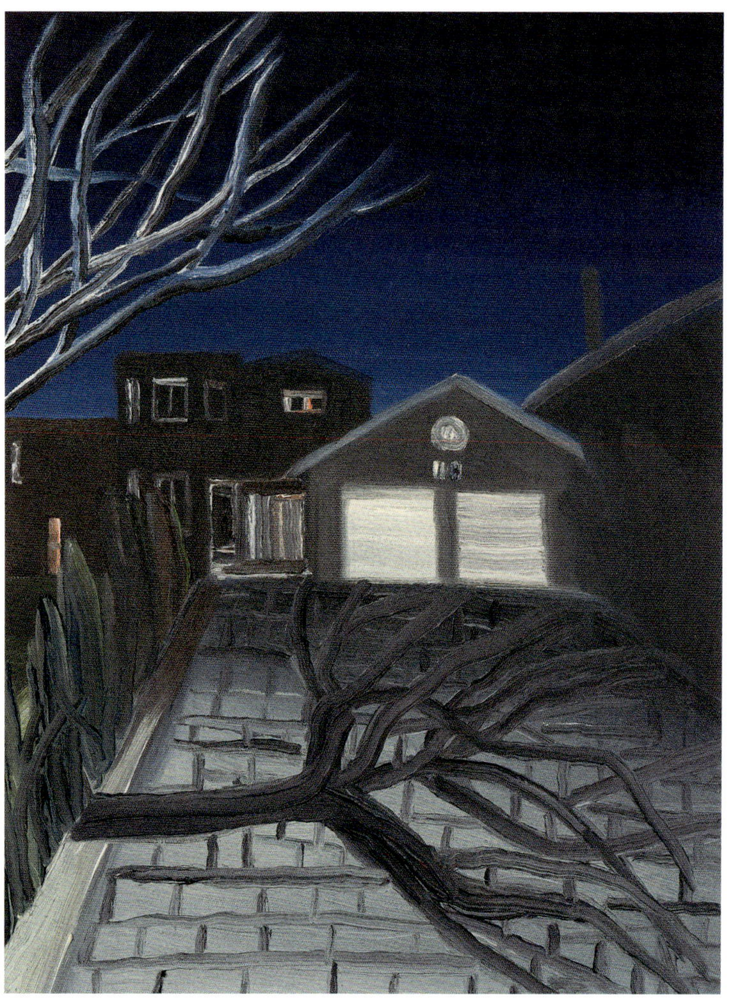

old, natural condition, its potential universality. Styles of representation, specific to a culture, have evolved within measures of historical time; the human hand has not.

Perhaps without intending it, Wong may have created a representational art that approaches the most instinctive forms of abstraction. Certain pictorial configurations communicate so directly that viewers never question their fidelity; they seem without a rhetoric and demand no analysis. Wong's notion of an 'infinitely vast conversation' resonates with the sense of a communicative network extending beyond the present to all of history. Line may be its founding element, a material trace, a ground, offering a more immediate, animalistic sense of self than could be gleaned from the social structures, the artifices, of an ideologically organized world.

In 2017, Wong painted *Old Town* (fig. 52), a work of imposing scale and chromatic brilliance. As if by sheer will, he conveyed the impression of a flowering tree in front of one of a different variety in full leaf; the two trees have branches that are similar in sinuousness but contrasting in thickness and colouration. It may be unwarranted to suggest with the word 'variety' that the two trees belong to distinct species, for the visual information Wong provides is vague and mimetically ambiguous. Here, pictorial imagination dominates pictorial reason, with fantasy overruling observation. Wong's characteristic markings – linear waves, compact daubs, extended streaks – indicate a changing 'flow from hand to surface' that may or may not respect an actual scene, such as *A Dream* (fig. 106). Noting this degree of abstraction in Etel Adnan's imagery led Wong to declare: 'All that one is left with is the act of looking itself.'[56]

Van Gogh's conflicted attitude towards the play of abstraction, already cited, is relevant. He complained that when he substituted expressive colours for the ones he observed, he became 'absent-minded [*abstrait*], like a sleep-walker'.[57] A sleep-walker sees without thinking.[58] Van Gogh yielded his rational control to a more instinctive, dreamlike reality that originated in himself. His painting, representational but abstract in a late nineteenth-century sense, was, in Wong's early twenty-first-century sense, intensifying sensation; and through the senses, it stretched the

105 / Matthew Wong, *Hazelmere*, 2019
Oil on canvas, 45.7 × 30.4 cm
Matthew Wong Foundation

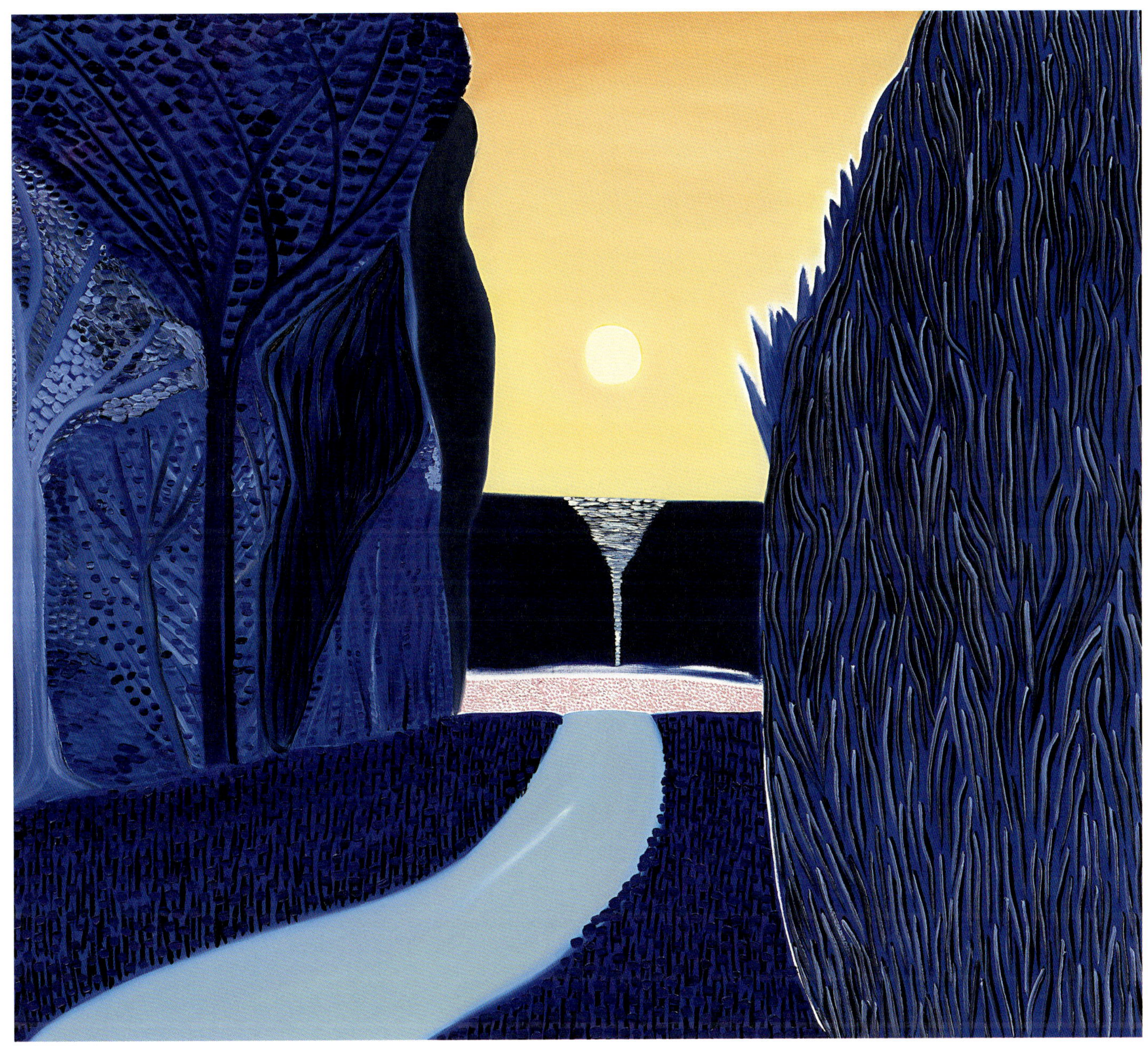

106 / Matthew Wong, *A Dream*, 2019
Oil on canvas, 177.8 × 203.2 cm
Matthew Wong Foundation

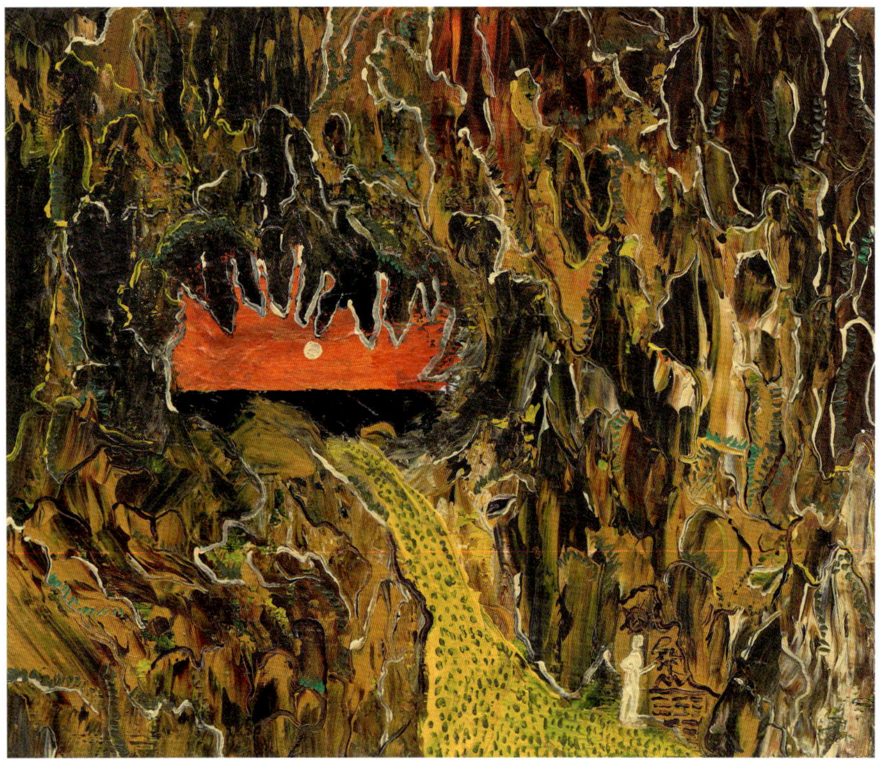

mind ('It's an expanding of the consciousness').[59]

What one sees and what one thinks one ought to see can diverge. Wong seems to have escaped the 'ought'. In his impulsiveness, he ignored commonplace concepts that regulate our understanding of a visual field and its proper representation. In *Hazelmere* (fig. 105), a visual recollection of his childhood Toronto home, his depiction of a shadow establishes a novel pictorial dimension existing between the illusion of volume and the illusion of flatness. Central to the painting, the shadow of a tree projects onto the plane of a residential driveway patterned with paving stones. It is easy to perceive the living, upright tree at the pictorial left as volumetric, in contrast to the receding planar driveway. But what of Wong's horizontal shadow? It introduces a dualistic paradox. The shadow illogically retains the volumetric character of its source by appearing dimly two-toned rather than flatly monochromatic. A shadow, defined by the absence of light, cannot have highlighting. Yet, at a diminished level, its subtly illuminated branching reproduces the brightly reflective branching of the living tree above (a night-time effect of moonlight or streetlight). The 'light' of Wong's shadow, dimmed but not absent, evokes no proper shadow but light *becoming* shadow (fading to shadow). The moment of Wong's image remains transitional, caught in time, as if he were proposing, absent-mindedly, that when a shadow is cast, it only gradually loses the light of its source. This insight might arise in the 'flow from hand to surface', which leaves time and space for sleepwalking to enter reality.

A shadow that represents both volume and plane evokes fantasies of an era when representation had not yet become codified like a fully differentiated language. Wong's 'shadow' – a creation of painting – contains all dimensions in embryo. It suggests that the origin of painting, of which the tree-shadow becomes an index or remembrance, occurred before the development of organized society and its codes. Perhaps the craft of painting began in a dreamlike state of

107 / Matthew Wong, *The Painter*, 2016
Acrylic on canvas, 50.2 × 80.6 cm
Private collection

consciousness, just before social awakening. Examples of Wong's art, especially *The Painter* (fig. 107), inspire such speculation. Like *Origin*, *The Painter* situates its prospective viewer inside an enclosure looking out. Here, the inside is illuminated eerily by linear flows of pigment, both light and dark. An environment presumably of solid rock seems to be transitioning to viscous ooze, constituting a primordial state in which the elemental phases of matter blend. Nothing settles into fixed identity. The exterior of the cave, seen through a narrow, irregular aperture, reveals a white sun or moon against a red sky above a black expanse, perhaps a sea. One of Wong's characteristic pathways, yellow with green flecks (or a blue that turns green in contact with fluid yellow), leads toward this glimpse of primeval landscape. But birth, the birth of painting, may have occurred before the 'painter' located at the base of the pathway has considered exiting this womblike interior, an aesthetic paradise.

Wong's surrogate artist (probably male) draws a linear figure (with splayed legs, probably female) that is one grade more elemental than the brushed figure of the painter. This display of comparative dimensionality anticipates the illuminated tree in *Hazelmere*, which casts a dim yet still illuminated shadow – a two-dimensional projection also perceptible as a three-dimensional version of the physical tree in a fallen state. In both *Hazelmere* and *The Painter*, one phase of being seems able to pass into another. Wong deploys his craft to depict a painter who deploys *his* craft to represent the primordial condition of what an evolving culture will come to regard as art. When in the distant past this awakening to art – or dreaming to art – first occurred, we do not know.

As a student of anthropology, Wong would have been familiar with mythologies and morphologies of origin. Within the composition of *The Painter*, the painting being created represents a phase or dimension of reality already in transition, a stick-figure with painterly substance, accessible to the senses while conceptually deceptive. Like all representation, this figure changes as it appears, yielding multiple lines of interpretation. Wong's mark-making, elemental yet chimerical, enacts (in his phrasing) 'an expanding of the consciousness'.[60] He stimulates the viewer to entertain paradoxes of sensation. I learn that figures imagined are as real as figures observed. Rain rising is both. —

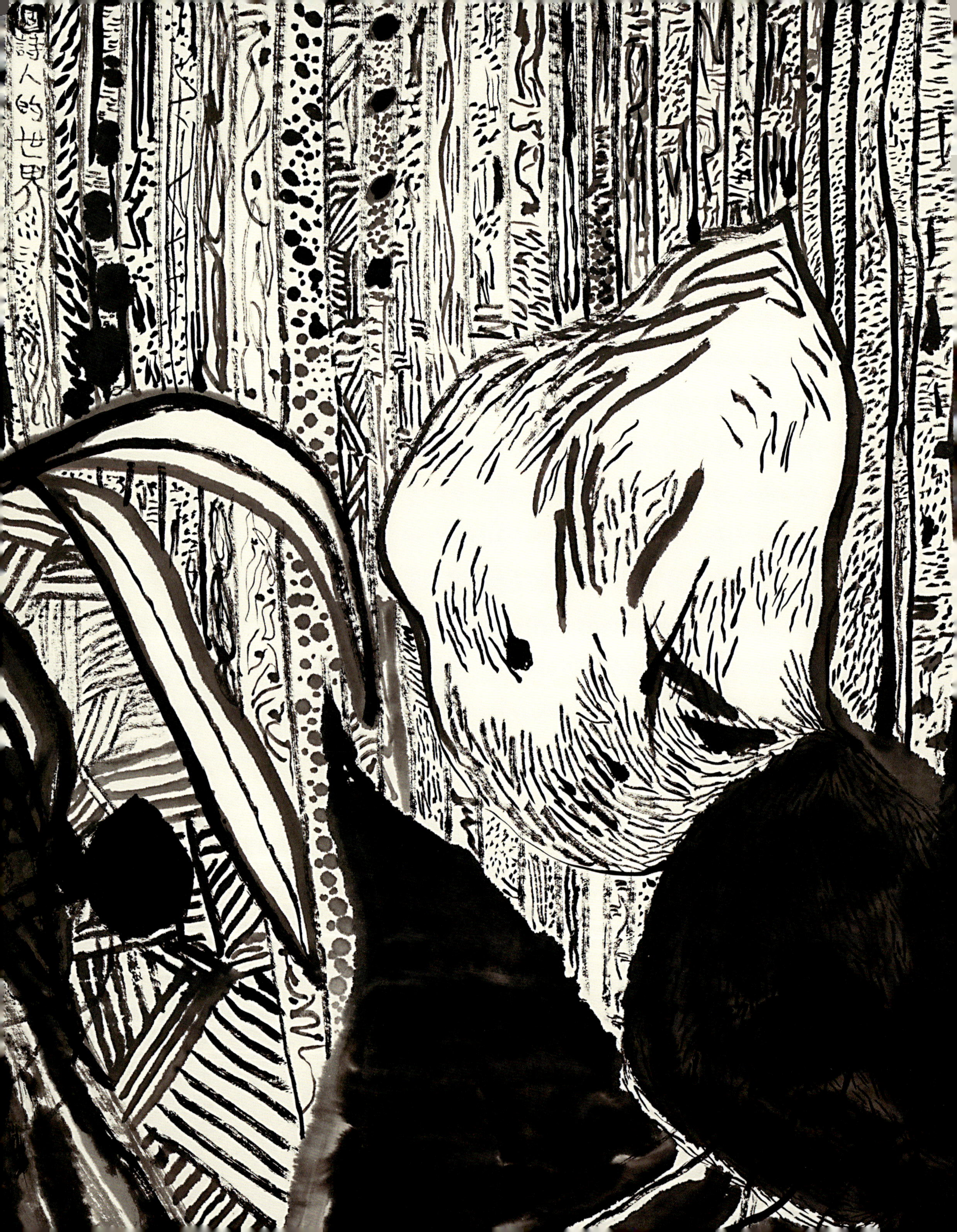
詩人的世界

John Yau

A Poet's World

It is remarkable how much art history Matthew Wong was able to internalize and reconfigure in such a brief period, as his career spanned little more than seven years (2012–19). Ambitious and brimming with energy, he had become increasingly dissatisfied with the medium he had initially studied. In 2012, shortly after graduating from the City University of Hong Kong School of Creative Media with an MFA in photography, he began drawing in ink. Known in the artistic community in Hong Kong, Wong had by the time of his graduation published three groups of thematically related photographs in *Cha: An Asian Literary Journal*, as well as contributing exhibition reviews to *South China Morning Post*, *Time Out Hong Kong* and *Ran Dian*.[1] His decision to change mediums did not go unnoticed. By 2014, he had gained enough attention to be interviewed by the online magazine *Altermodernists*, where he stated that he initially started with a sketchbook and a bottle of ink and made 'a mess every day randomly'. In that same interview, he also stated: 'Art is all-encompassing in my daily life. When I'm not working, I'm at the library doing research into the history of art, figuring out where I can fit into the greater dialogue between artists throughout time, or on the

Matthew Wong, *A Poet's World*, 2015 (detail fig. 120)

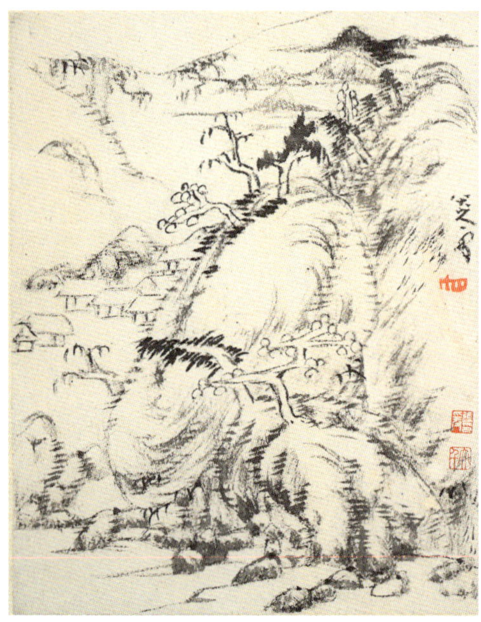

108 / Bada Shanren, Landscape album, leaf a, 1699
Album of twelve leaves; ink and colour on paper, 23.2 × 18.7 cm
The Metropolitan Museum of Art. Bequest of John M. Crawford Jr., 1988

internet looking at art-related websites and engaging in dialogue on social media with artists and art-world figures around the world.'[2] In order to recognize what Wong achieved in a short time, it is crucial that we understand how he brought together mark-making and a focused study of art history from different periods and parts of the world, including the present.

With impressive rapidity and astuteness, Wong was able to synthesize his cultural background as someone who studied calligraphy at school with his aspiration to make art that speaks to audiences far beyond his roots. In order to reconcile these two driving forces, Wong had to find precedents. The basis of this accord can be traced back to his decision to move from using a sketchbook to the unforgiving medium of rice paper. The cultural significance of this paper, which was evident to Wong, became one of the prominent threads of his work.

Black and white

Rice paper was invented in China at the beginning of the Tang dynasty (618–907 CE). Initially used to write on, it was not until the Yuan dynasty (1271–1368) that artists who wanted to break away from previous generations began painting in ink on rice paper, which interacts with ink differently than silk. It is unimaginable that Wong did not know this history. It seems that consciously being a Chinese artist was the foundation upon which he began and from which he never wavered, even as he absorbed a wide range of references and influences. 'I may really be a black and white ink painter at the core of my project.'[3] Familiar with two distinct cultures and languages (China and Canada, where he was born, spent significant periods of his formative years and later had a studio), Wong had a transcultural understanding of art. Yet the foundation of his work was Chinese.

Two prominent figures in Chinese art history were among those that captured Wong's interest most: Shitao (1642–1707) and Bada Shanren (1626–1705). These so-called 'Literati-painters', both of whom worked during the late Ming and early Qing dynasties, are renowned for their expressive and intuitive approach to traditional ink painting (figs. 7, 108 and 109)[4] Champions of their style valued its spontaneity and felt that awkwardness was a sign of the artist's sincerity. Wong's work is often compared to the scroll paintings or albums of Shitao and Bada Shanren, and the extent of their influence can hardly be overstated.

While many of Wong's commentators viewed him as a self-taught Chinese artist gesturing towards the work of European and American artists such as Vincent van Gogh, Lois Dodd and Julian Schnabel for

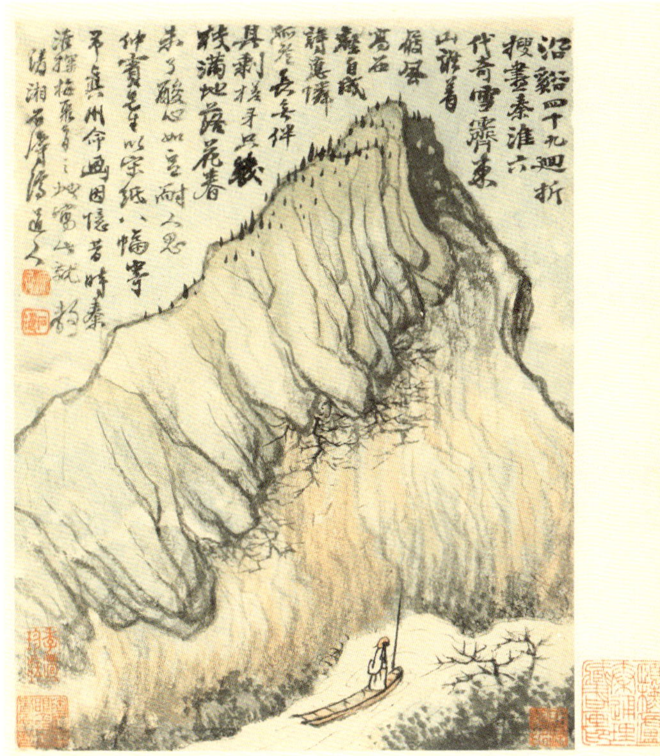

109 / Shitao, *Reminiscences of Qinhuai River*, probably 1695
Album leaf, ink and colour on Song paper, 25.5 × 20.2 cm
The Cleveland Museum of Art. John L. Severance Fund

inspiration and guidance, he was in fact absorbing their work through the lens of Chinese ink painting. Wong never moved on from using ink. Both the beginning and the end of each day were marked by the creation of an ink painting, a ritual that structured his life throughout his brief career as an artist. His works in oil and acrylic can be regarded as additions to his daily practice of ink drawing, rather than the main focus of his work.

Early experiments

In the early work, *Untitled* (2013, fig. 87) – which Wong made soon after he started experimenting with ink in 2011 and 2012 – we sense how far he has travelled in a short time. Wong stained the absorbent rice paper with different densities of ink, ranging from deep black to washy grey, essentially eschewing the calligraphic line, to evoke a non-perspectival space. It is, of course, calligraphy that most appealed to European and American artists interested in line, from Van Gogh to Mark Tobey, Robert Motherwell and Brice Marden. Wong, however, already understood calligraphy; it was, as mentioned, part of his education while growing up in Hong Kong. He knew that working in ink on rice paper connected him to China's primary art form, just as oil painting originated in Europe. 'China is such a hermetically sealed culture. I don't know if I relate totally to it, and yet there are parts of me that can't quite escape those roots by default.'[5]

By staining the paper with irrevocable shapes and marks, Wong undercut any evidence of tentativeness that he might have felt. What is remarkable about *Untitled* (2013) is the degree of confidence with which Wong evokes a complex, atmospheric space of near and far. Spatially, the orientation of the forms (vertical or horizontal), the density of ink (washy grey to black) and the size of the forms, and their relationship to each other, evoke an abstract landscape dominated by what seems to be a tree trunk on the drawing's left side, rising from the bottom edge to the top edge. The forms sit on the cusp between abstraction and representation. The layered black tree-like form on the left has bits of white and pale blue peeking though, giving it a gnarled and textured feel. The appearance of this early work beautifully resonates with a remark Wong made in 2019, during a panel discussion at the Whitney Museum of American Art: 'The way ink paintings proceed is that it is very much intuitive and improvised. One puts down rudimentary

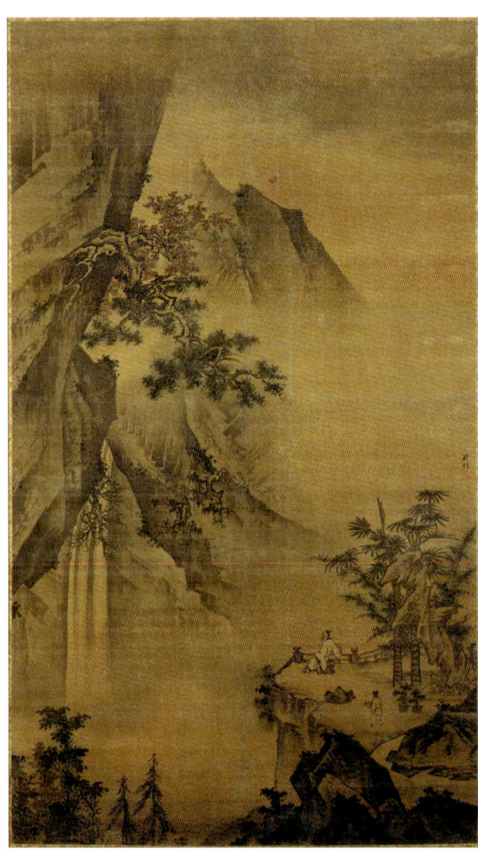

110 / Zhong Li, *Li Bai Gazing at the Waterfall on Mount Lu*, late 15th century
Hanging scroll; ink and colour on silk, 177.8 × 103.2 cm
The Metropolitan Museum of Art. From the P. Y. and Kinmay W. Tang Family Collection, Gift of Oscar L. Tang, 1991

strokes, different washes, to kind of feel the way across the landscape.'[6]

The grey horizontal forms to the right of the tree trunk, which vary in density, suggest that Wong's process was incremental, with both accident and control playing a part. This combination is also evident in *Untitled* (2014, fig. 111), in which an irregular grid, composed of ragged and swaying bands, criss-crosses the entire surface. Wong made each band by pouring ink. In many areas the ink has spread, forming dried black puddles connecting adjacent bands.

In the two works, *Untitled* (2013) and *Untitled* (2014), Wong is restless and open to experimenting with his medium, what he called 'messing around'. From the very beginning he seems to have been guided by the possibility of discovering something new, authentic and expressive, without seeking refuge in a style. Furthermore, while the earlier work evokes a landscape, the later ink on paper is abstract and non-spatial. Culturally speaking, the former can be traced back to Chinese landscape painting, while the latter has its origins in Euro-American abstraction and the use of the grid. In these two works Wong recognizes that he has access to two traditions.

Closer to tradition

By 2015 – a scant three years after he devoted himself to art – Wong has assembled a flexible, abstract vocabulary consisting of small calligraphic marks, puddles of dried ink and bands of varying widths. Using this vocabulary, titling of the works became more central to his practice, framing how we are supposed to read them. 'Is giving a title part of studio time? U bet ur ass it is.'[7] It was in 2015 that Wong deepened his connection to the Literati tradition of Chinese ink painting, which valued subjectivity and the depiction of inner realities, rather than objectivity and the description of outward appearances.

One of the recurring subjects in Literati painting is that of a solitary individual alone in nature, contemplating a particular phenomenon, such as a waterfall (fig. 110). These observers are surrogates for both the artist and the viewer. In Wong's *Stargazing* (fig. 113), we see different ways he elevated the motif of the lone traveller into an enigmatic individual whose presence animates the drawing. There seem to be two figures in the foreground, with two of them rising from the bottom edge. The vertical black form on the far-left side is cropped by the left edge and appears to be contemplating the landscape, which can be roughly divided into three areas, each distinguished by the kinds of marks Wong has made inside them.

The second figure, which appears to be stooped over and faces from right to left, has a black snake-like form extending from the top or neck area. The marks Wong made inside its silhouetted body differentiates

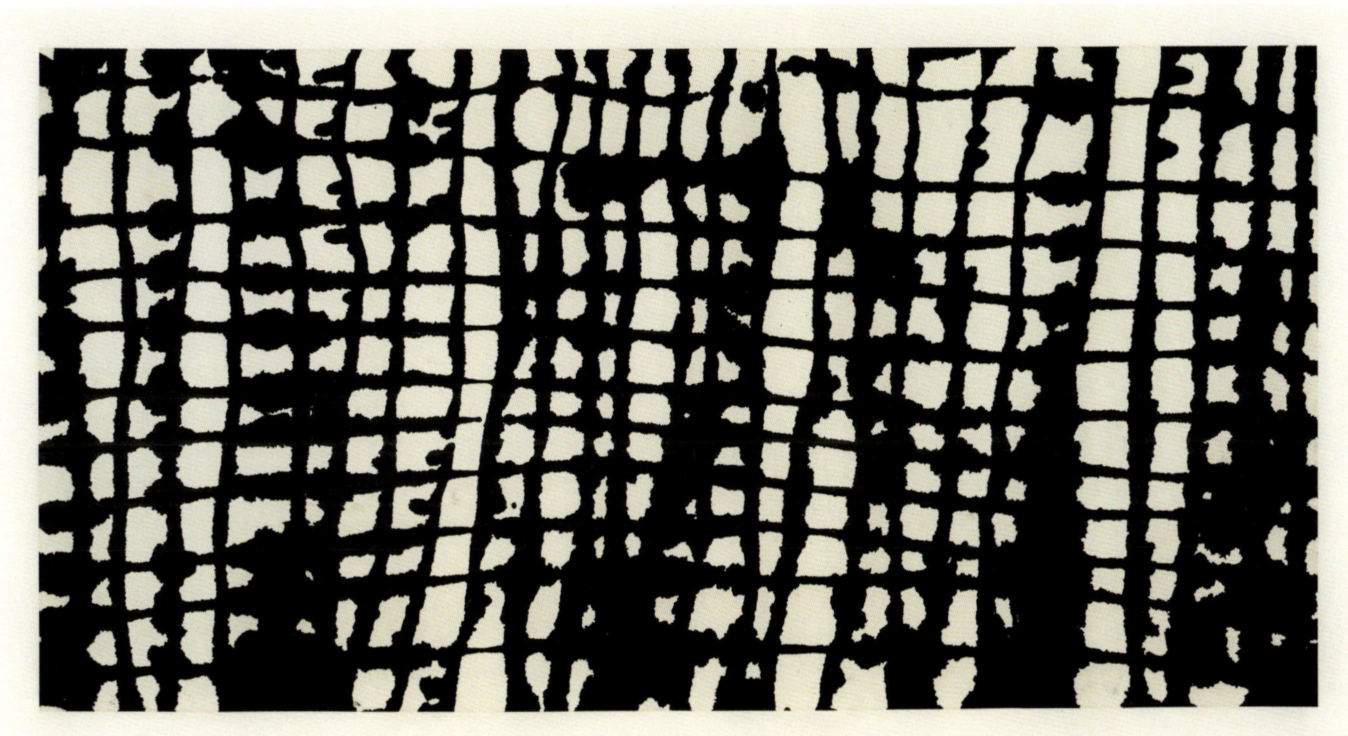

111 / Matthew Wong, *Untitled*, 2014
Ink on rice paper, 78.1 × 145.4 cm
Matthew Wong Foundation

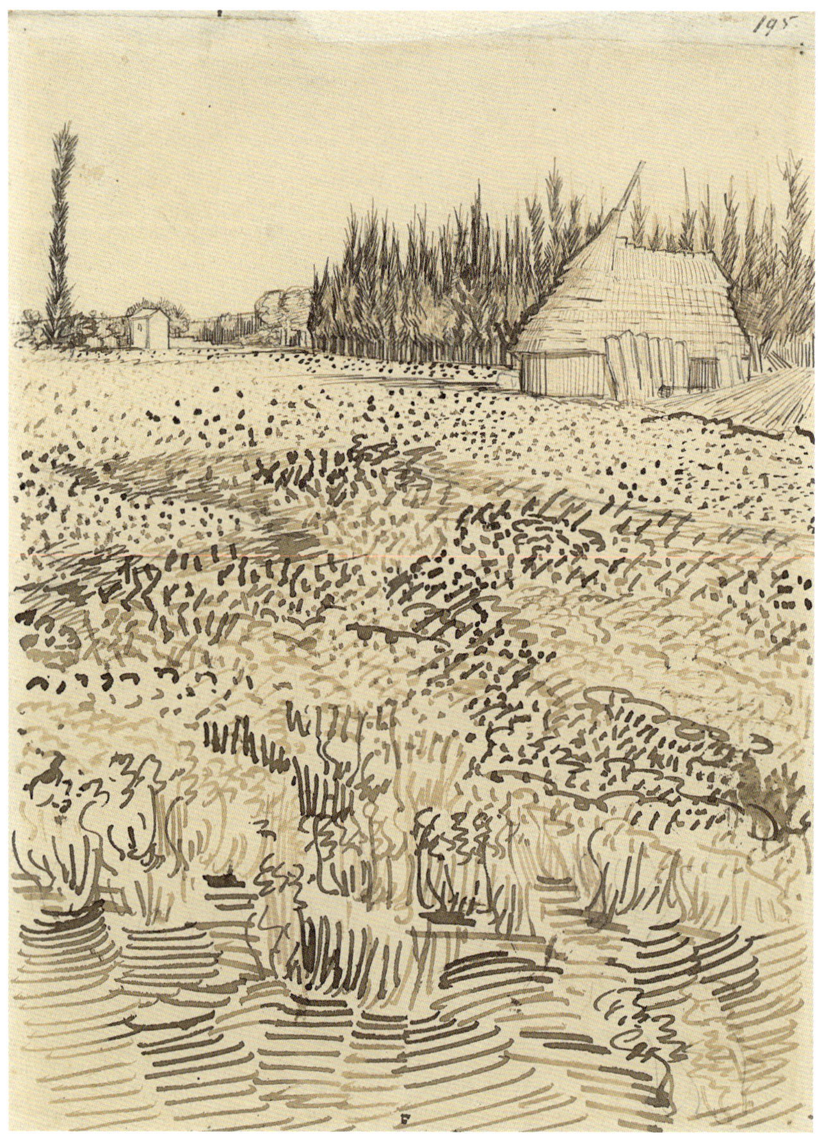

112 / Vincent van Gogh, *Landscape with Hut*, 1888
Pencil, pen and reed pen and ink on paper, 34.8 × 25.7 cm
Van Gogh Museum, Amsterdam (Vincent van Gogh Foundation)

it from its surroundings. Who is this creature and where does it come from? If we take our cue from the work's title, we are likely to read the marks in the upper left-hand corner as stars, while interpreting the two descending areas as mountain and field.

The use of a specific type of calligraphic mark to distinguish one area or thing from another in his drawings is something that Wong shares with Van Gogh. Yet the purposes of their strikingly comparable styles are very different. The self-contained, enigmatic world in *Stargazing* is subjectively expressive, evoking the interior worlds of both artist and traveller. Wong's mark-making underscores the imaginary character of his worlds. Van Gogh's views of cottages and fields, however, were based on direct observation. The differing 'calligraphic' marks he combined in *Landscape with Hut* (fig. 112), for example, evoke the varying of terrain and vegetation in his landscape.

Not only was the purpose of Wong's and Van Gogh's calligraphic marks dissimilar. The technique they used to achieve the effect also differed. Where Wong used a brush to apply his ink, Van Gogh preferred a reed pen, which he made by cutting a reed at an angle so its point could hold ink. Van Gogh was able to control the thickness of his lines by adjusting the sharpness of the points.[8] He had learned his technique from a French guide to various drawing techniques, while Wong's practice was steeped in Chinese traditions: the difference in their cultural backgrounds in a nutshell.

Another notable example of Wong's subjective and personal approach to landscape and his close reading of Literati painting is *Landscape of the Longing* (fig. 115). The steep mountain and the focus on verticality vividly recall Shitao's mountainous landscapes (fig. 114). Mountains are considered sacred in China; they are the places where the gods reside and are closest to heaven. They offer a respite from

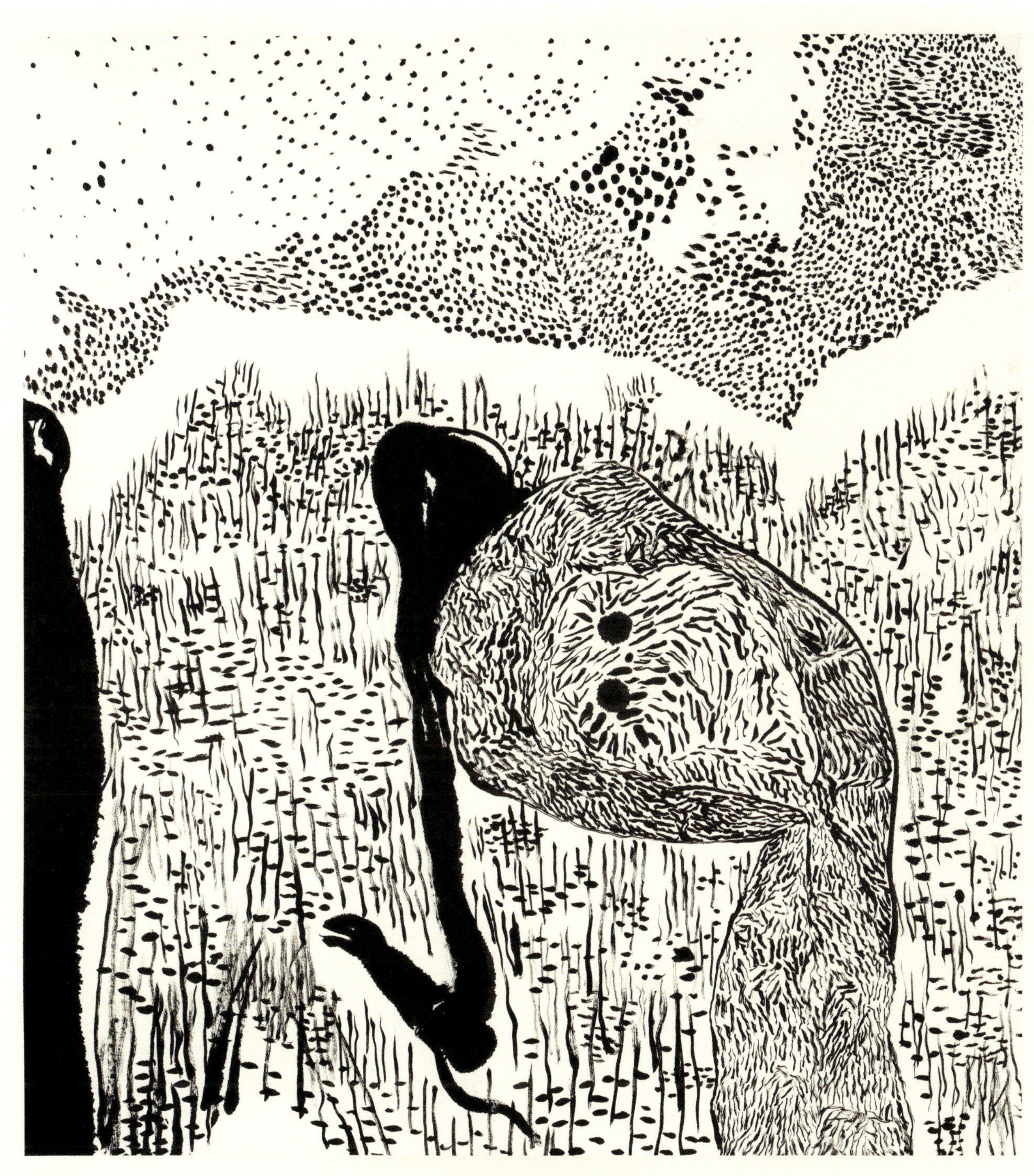

113 / Matthew Wong, *Stargazing*, 2015
Ink on rice paper, 113 × 94.6 cm
Matthew Wong Foundation

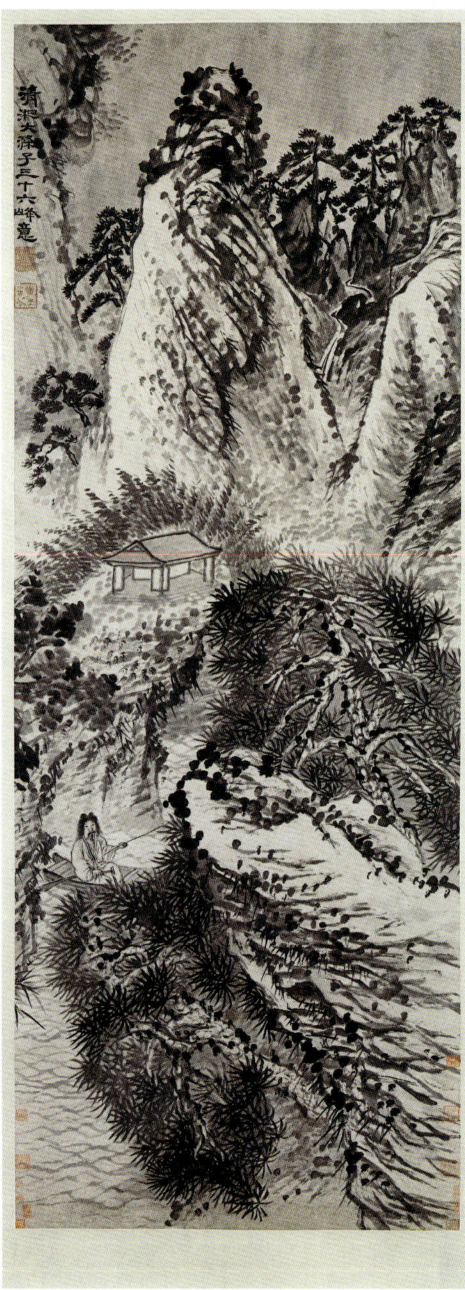

114 / Shitao, *Thirty-Six Peaks of Mount Huang Recollected*, c. 1705
Hanging scroll; ink on paper, 205.9 × 78.7 cm
The Metropolitan Museum of Art, New York. Gift of Douglas Dillon, 1976

the everyday world. By having his imaginary mountain, with its steep grades and plunging sides, dominate the composition, Wong evokes a summit that appears nearly impossible to ascend. The unidentifiable orb in the upper right confirms that it is a mountainous landscape with a looming sun that we are looking at, not an abstract form. As the title suggests, Wong depicts a world where what is longed for is never attained.

This feeling of impossible fulfilment animates many of Wong's ink drawings, watercolours and paintings. Beginning on the lower left side of *Footprints in the Wind* (fig. 121), an ever-narrowing path horizontally traverses almost the entire drawing before vanishing on the right side. There are abstract footprints marking the entire pathway. Who preceded us? What happened to the lone traveller, whose footprints we see? Above the path is a dense wall of black marks, a visual barrier. Does the path ascend, go through, or go around this section? Are those the only possibilities? Wong has depicted another barrier between the viewer and the path. Six vertical tree-trunk-like forms rise from the bottom edge. Although there are spaces between them, they become a kind of obstacle to the path. There is an unmistakable feeling of darkness and isolation running through Wong's art, which, in the case of the paintings, he offsets with bright colours. That synthesis of opposites is one of the hallmarks of Wong's work that holds the attention, because it deters us from reaching a conclusion.

Tree trunks

In *Untitled* (2015, fig. 24) and *A Poet's World* (fig. 120), the compositions are dominated by a silhouetted form set against a landscape of tightly packed tree trunks with a variety of abstract marks buzzing between them. In each work, Wong both complicates and heightens their claustrophobic settings by obscuring the figure's face. In *Untitled*, he superimposes a black, cage-like mask on a creased face that leaves the eyes visible. To this viewer, at least, the mask looks like something that might have been used during the Spanish Inquisition to get a sinner to confess. In *A Poet's World*, Wong encloses the head in what resembles a white cloth with one eyehole visible. The placement of the eyehole suggests that the figure is seen in profile, moving from right to left, a position that is parallel to the one in *Stargazing*. At the very least, the mask and hood suggest the figures can see but cannot be seen. That irreconcilable space between observing and being seen (or, more accurately, being recognized) adds an emotional depth to Wong's work.

In the upper part of a tree trunk near the left edge of *A Poet's World*, Wong has written the work's title ideogrammatically. By writing in Chinese, Wong consciously identifies himself with the Literati tradition,

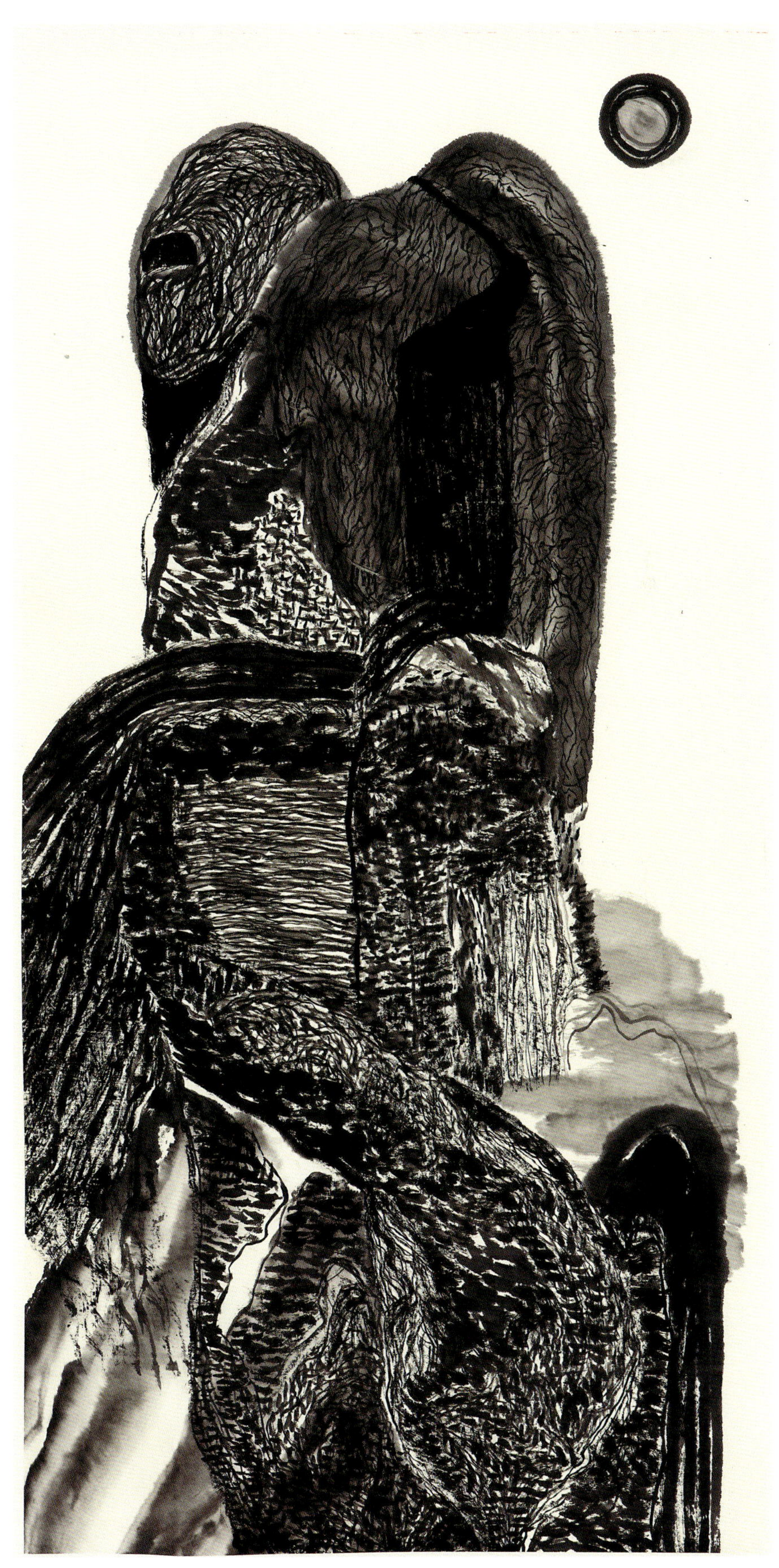

115 / Matthew Wong,
Landscape of the Longing, 2016
Ink on rice paper, 138.4 × 70.2 cm
Matthew Wong Foundation

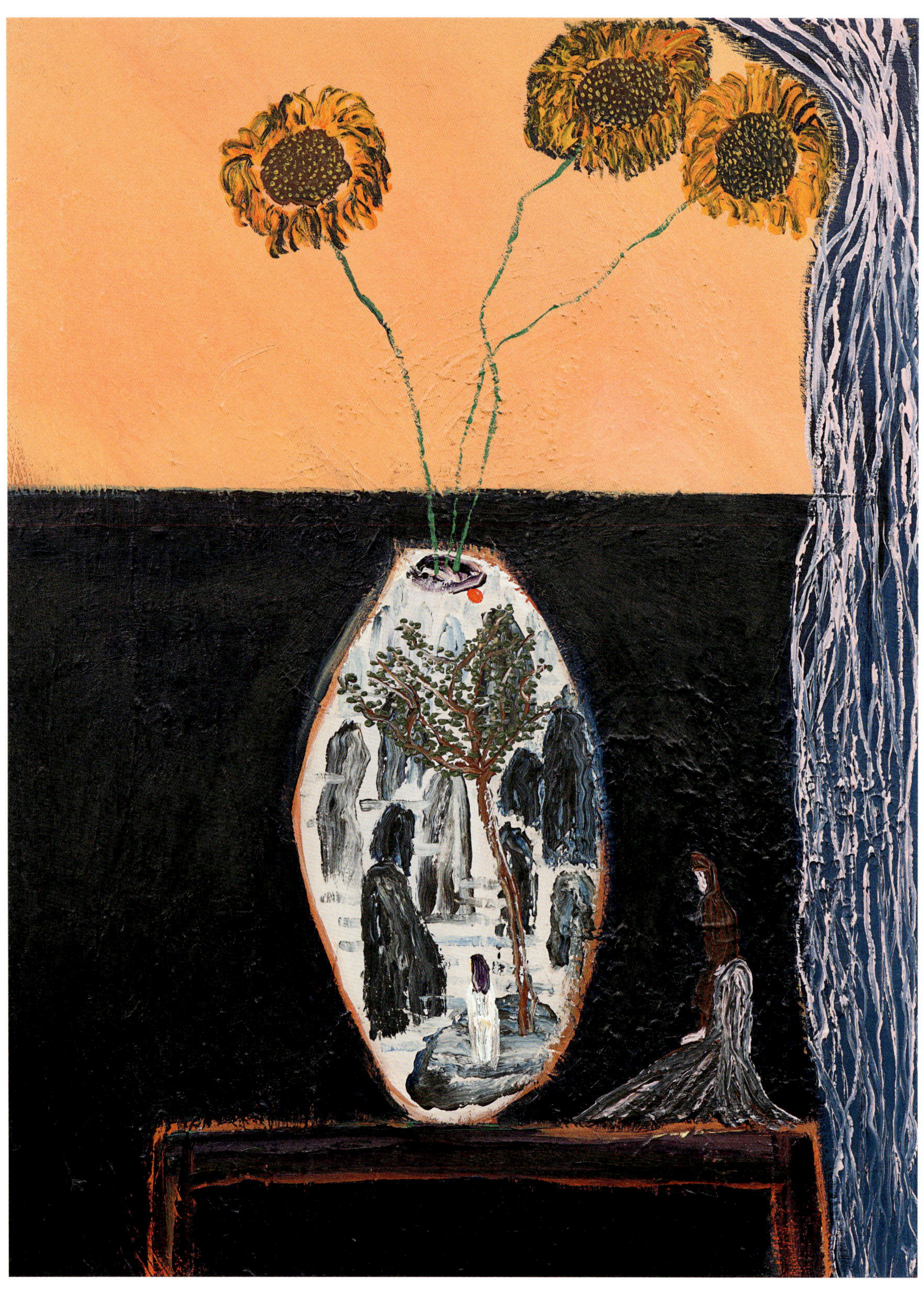

116 / Matthew Wong, *The Realm of Appearances*, 2017
Acrylic on canvas, 101.6 × 76.2 cm
Matthew Wong Foundation

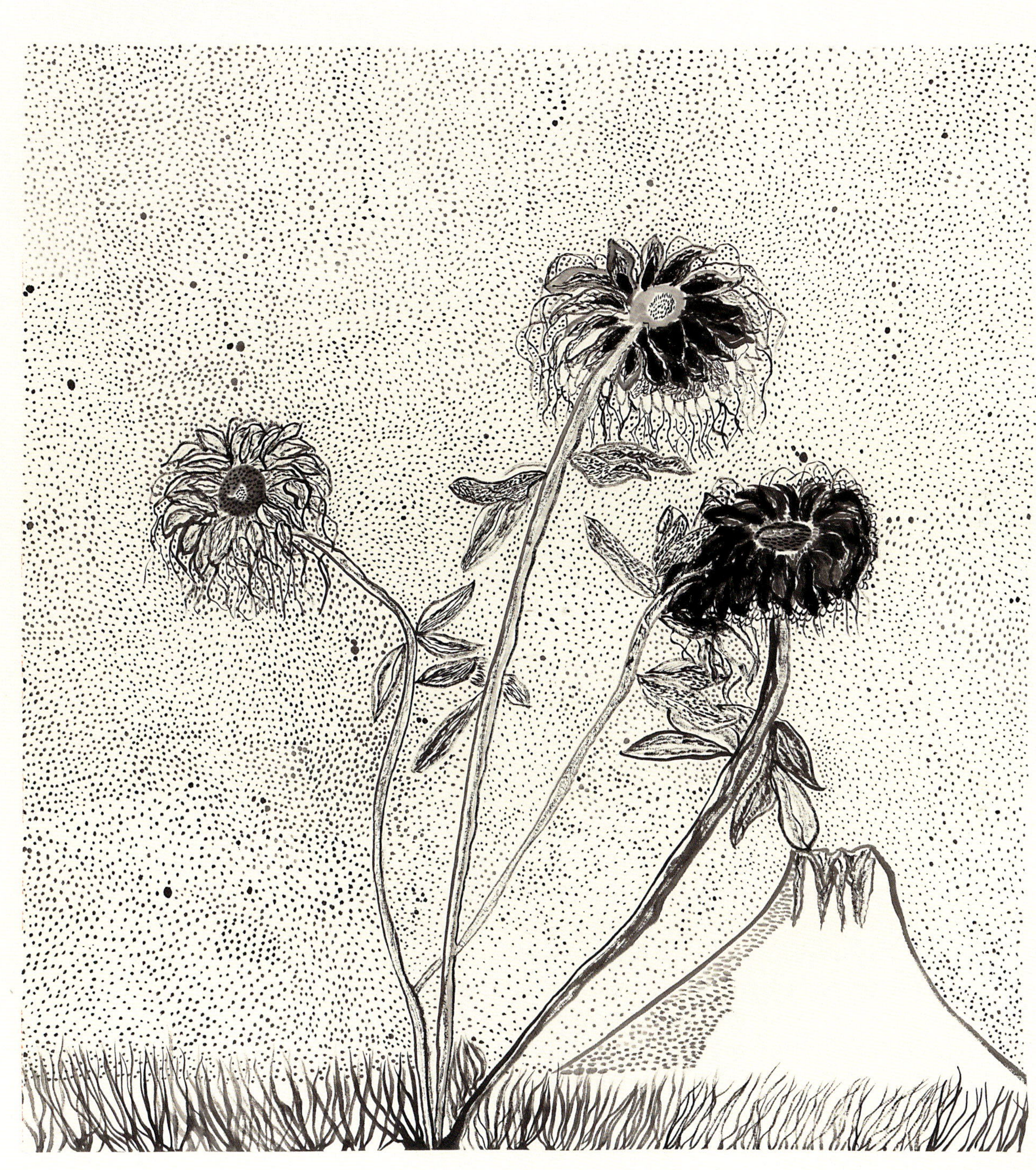

117 / Matthew Wong, *Flowers in a Starlit Landscape*, 2017
Ink on rice paper, 107 × 101 cm
Matthew Wong Foundation and Cheim & Read, New York

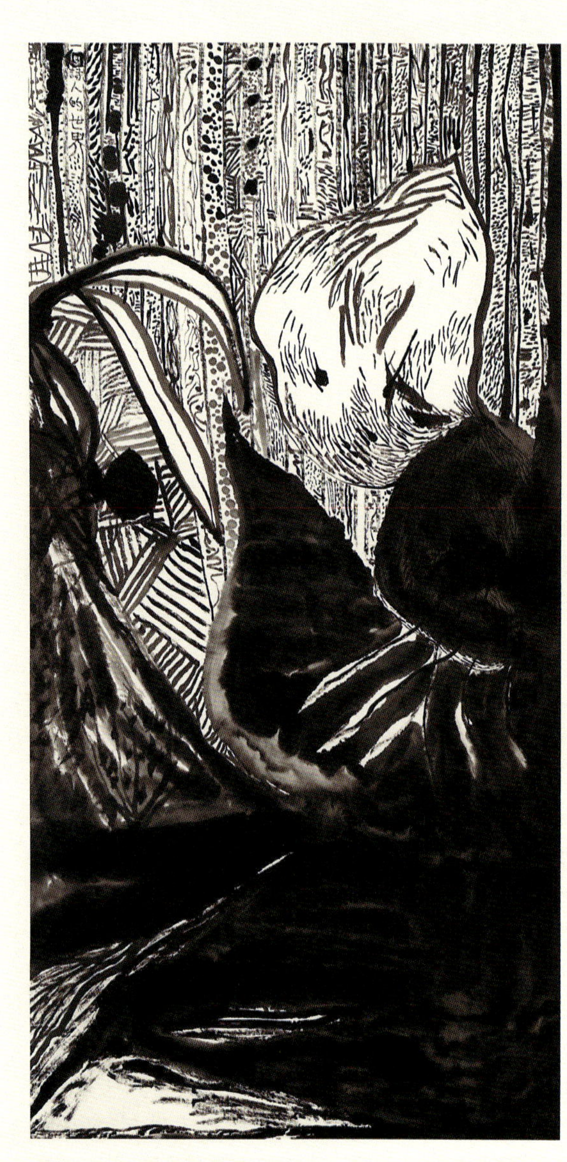

120 / Matthew Wong, *A Poet's World*, 2015
Ink on rice paper, 159.4 × 80.1 cm
Matthew Wong Foundation

In the middle panel, the boat is brown and floats on a sea made up of short, curving brushstrokes in different colours (dirty pinks, various shades of orange, off-white, a few browns and blacks). The sun is an impasto orange-red orb and its white rays are laid over an orange sky. Those rays, and the other marks we see in the other two panels, build upon what Wong does in the two drawings, with one difference. The paint, with its different hues, allows him to achieve a streaked field of partly blended colour, as in the orange, yellow and pink ocean in the left panel.

In the right-hand panel, the yellow sun sinking below the horizon line, and the jade blue rays are set against a pale orange sky. The grey-black boat is in the jade green path signifying the sun's reflection, cut off from the darker blue, pink inflected ocean. Small black silhouettes are visible on the path running along the crest of the large, hill-like shape (or island) in the right-hand corner. How are we to read the change the sail undergoes from white in the left-hand panel, to black here, especially in conjunction with the setting sun?

In this group of thematically connected paintings, Wong transcended his own feelings of displacement (was he Canadian or Chinese, a North American or Asian painter) by restating the well-known motif of the solo sojourner. The triptych is both direct and nuanced, visual and tactile. With each of his small brushstrokes, Wong felt his way across the canvas, concocting a world in which he felt alone and full of yearning, perhaps dread.

Like Wong, Van Gogh depicted similar motifs both in ink and oil paint. However, a striking difference in their seemingly comparable practice is that a considerable number of Van Gogh's ink drawings made in the south of France were usually done after his paintings, whereas Wong's drawings preceded the paintings, without being studies in a strict sense. His ink drawings were always at the forefront of his practice, as they were his means of internalizing the lessons and examples of Literati painting. In a way, they functioned as a gateway between one of the most important sources of inspiration for Wong and his paintings. Working in ink can, in fact, be seen as the main thread of Wong's short and intense career, enabling him to bridge the gap between the two traditions in which he was brought up and fuelling his celebrated vocabulary in paint. —

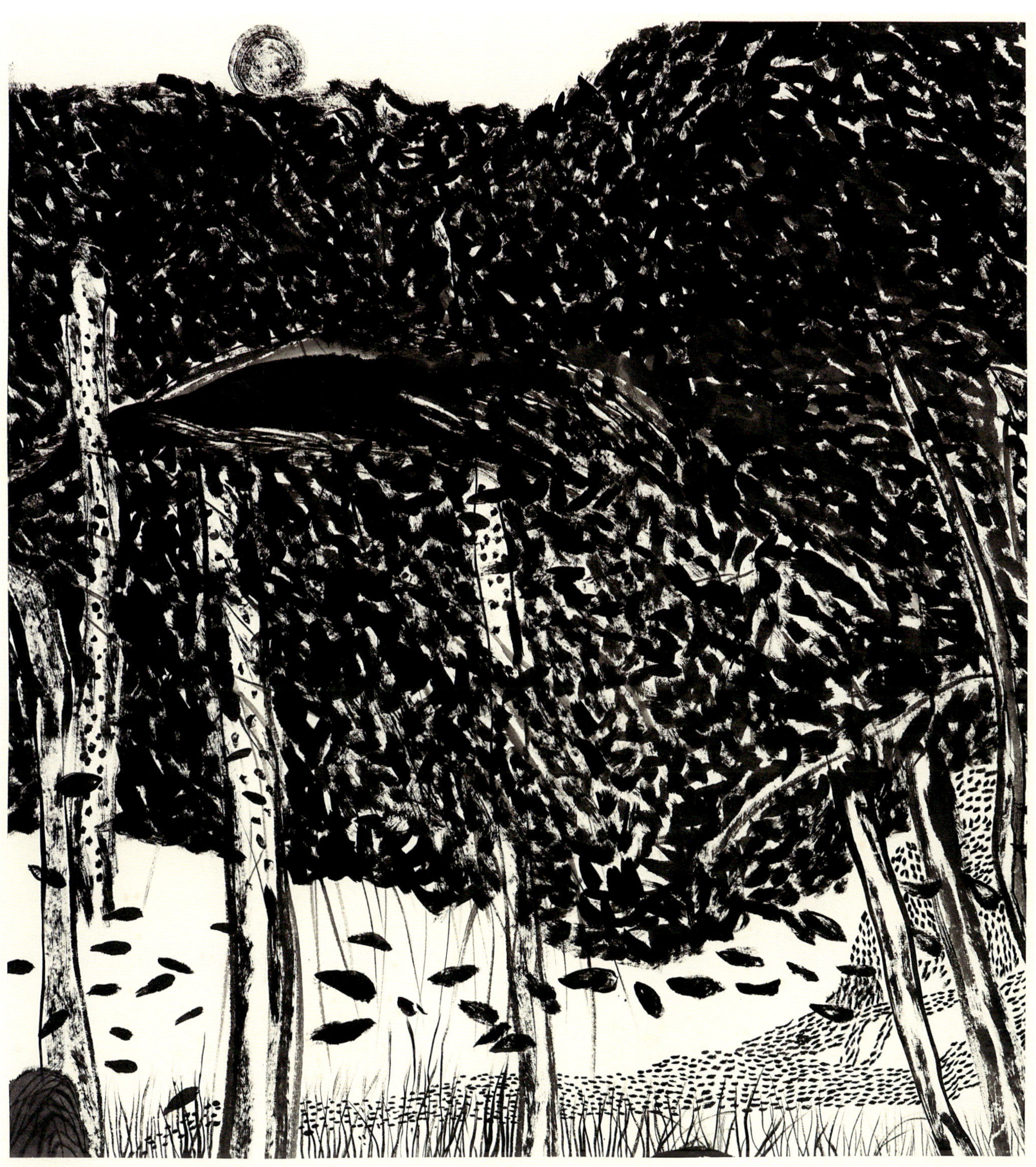

121 / Matthew Wong,
Footprints in the Wind, 2016
Ink on rice paper, 96.5 × 88.9 cm
Matthew Wong Foundation

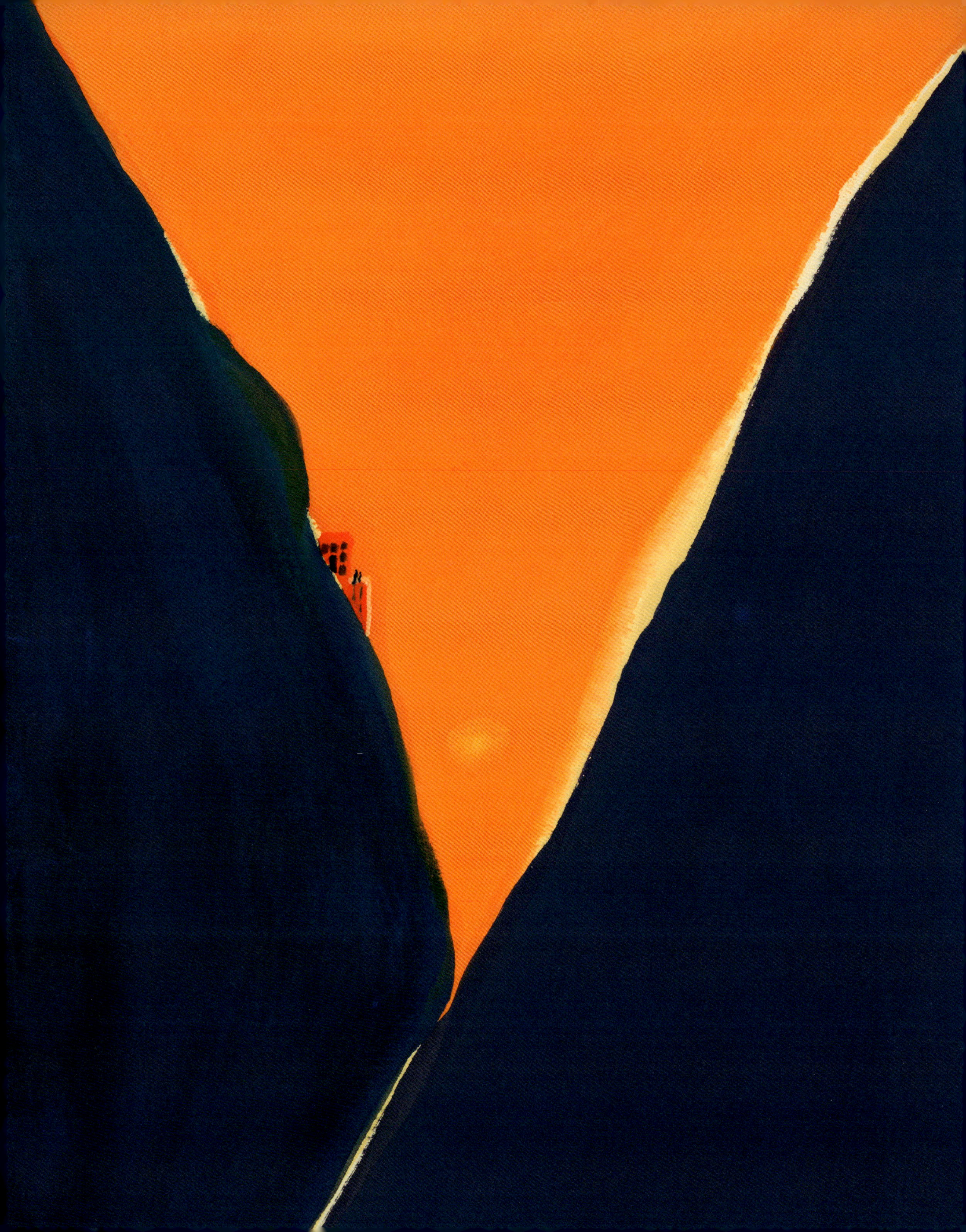

Living the Past in the Present

Joost van der Hoeven in conversation with Sofia Silva

During his brief career as a painter, Matthew Wong was in touch with numerous artists around the world through social media. The artist and essayist Sofia Silva, who lives and works in Padua, Italy, was one of them. Even though she never met Wong personally, her correspondence with him was very comprehensive and profound. Silva and Wong found mutual support as they tried to navigate the art world. As a result they knew each other well. In this interview Silva reflects on topics that were vital to Wong's life and work, such as social media and its impact on art, nostalgia for the past and Wong's self-proclaimed status as an 'outsider artist'. In this last aspect of Wong's career she recognizes a striking parallel with Vincent van Gogh.

To begin where it all started: how and when did you meet Matthew Wong?
In 2017 I had a Facebook account open to few people on which I posted images of my work and that of other artists. I was registered with a nom de plume, Betty de La Cabane. Matthew realised who I really was and wrote to me 'Sofia!' From there a long conversation started in which we detailed each other's lives at length: our most recent paintings, trends in contemporary painting, sleepless nights, his perplexities and difficulties in dealing with the art world, mine in making ends meet. We were both without filters. With variable regularity, written or by telephone, the conversations continued for three years.

At what stage of his career was Wong when you two were corresponding?
When he began writing to me, Matthew was thirty-three years old, my age now. Those were the months leading up to the group exhibition *The Horizontal* at Cheim and Read [6 July – 31 August 2017], as well as those of his first major sales. He knew that that exhibition, in which he was represented with one work, would be an excellent platform, almost unthinkable for a painter who started only five years earlier. Matthew should have been glad, but other emotions were lurking. He called painting 'my last resort'. Anyone familiar with the mechanisms of the art world would have called Matthew's a meteoric recognition, with a very short waiting time. But waiting times are subjective. The feeling I sensed in Matthew was not contingency-related anxiety but existential haste. He was in a hurry, as if there were a train to catch, the departure time of which only he knew. There was a sense of fever, to use a word much loved by Van Gogh's earliest critics. Those months, those years, were feverish. When I met Matthew, I also met all this.

Matthew Wong, *Red House*, 2018
(detail of fig. 74)

How did Wong reflect on social media as a factor in the current art world?

For Matthew, social media was more than a showcase and it was the visitors to this display who were giving him grief: painters who mirrored themselves in his work; opportunistic connoisseurs who praised him on a daily basis; characters who rose to more or less temporary fame (whom Matthew deeply analysed). And then there were us, the pen pals. If any of his friends – Peter Shear or I or who knows how many others – doubted themselves or their own work, or was particularly weary of poverty, Matthew would first heartily encourage them and then be greatly troubled by the melancholy of the friend in question. If you doubt yourself, one whom I do not doubt, should I doubt myself? With Matthew it was best not to doubt. He was an *anima in pena*, a 'soul in distress', and this restlessness, this youthfulness by which he felt perpetually late, was also an element of his greatness.

The issues related to art on social networks are not only self-curatorial or relational but can also be regarded from a wider historical vantage point. In an art system where movements, groups or currents no longer exist, an artist who paints almost identically to another is a plagiarist rather than a comrade. However, instead of identifying overly derivative artists, the system uncritically includes them by distributing their supply among several galleries. Within this perspective, where does the artist who exhibits their paintings online before showing them in a real exhibition venue end up? Their paintings, not yet validated by the system, become a visual source from which anyone can draw, even the fellow painter living on the other side of the world whose derivativeness will never be identified. Such thoughts were also occupying Matthew's mind, and it is useful to take this into account in order not to think that the art-historical issues of sharing art on the internet are as virtual as the medium that conveys them, because they are not.

Studying the life of Matthew Wong opens numerous issues; one is that of the isolated artist in the era of the globally shared artwork. Matthew did call himself an outsider but put this term in quotation marks. Outsider in inverted commas, perhaps that was his real positioning. To comprehend Matthew's ideas about himself, one would have to understand how Matthew engaged with the artists that came before him, in which he saw an example.

So, how did he engage with his examples?

Matthew thought of himself as an outsider in the company of giants. For Matthew, other artists, from any time or place, be it Shitao [the Chinese calligrapher and artist of the early Qing dynasty] or Van Gogh, were companions, closely connected to a feeling of lack, of nostalgia – secret friends who prevented him from being alone, who stood by him in solitude. To understand this kind of feeling I find it useful to go back to Rilke. In 1898, Rainer Maria Rilke, a poet Matthew would frequently return to, travelled to Italy and wrote *Das Florenzer Tagebuch*. The *Diary* shows Rilke's peculiar form of aesthetic and emotional enjoyment of the past, especially when manifested through works of art. This specific feeling also belonged almost identically to Matthew.

In a passage from the *Dairy*, Rilke unites his own feeling with the beauty of a cloister by activating the power of his imagination to project himself into the past and goes back to the image of the Capuchins who once tended its gardens. He nostalgically evokes 'the memory of the plenty' no longer offered. He tries to reconstruct what the Old Masters 'felt'. In other words, for every work or architecture he sees, he resurrects the persona of the artist behind it, as if it were a hologram. The past belongs to us only insofar as we are able to establish communication with its ghosts.

For Matthew, as for Rilke, it was extremely important to experience the work of art by creating a *sympatheia* [bond] with the – often deceased – artist who had created it. He considered himself a painter of ideas and his paintings were 'an exploration of past precedents in both Chinese and Western culture, as there are bodies of work that seem to be about a kind of projection into someone who has walked the earth in various periods and styles.' Both in the realm of art history and in his personal sphere, Matthew thought

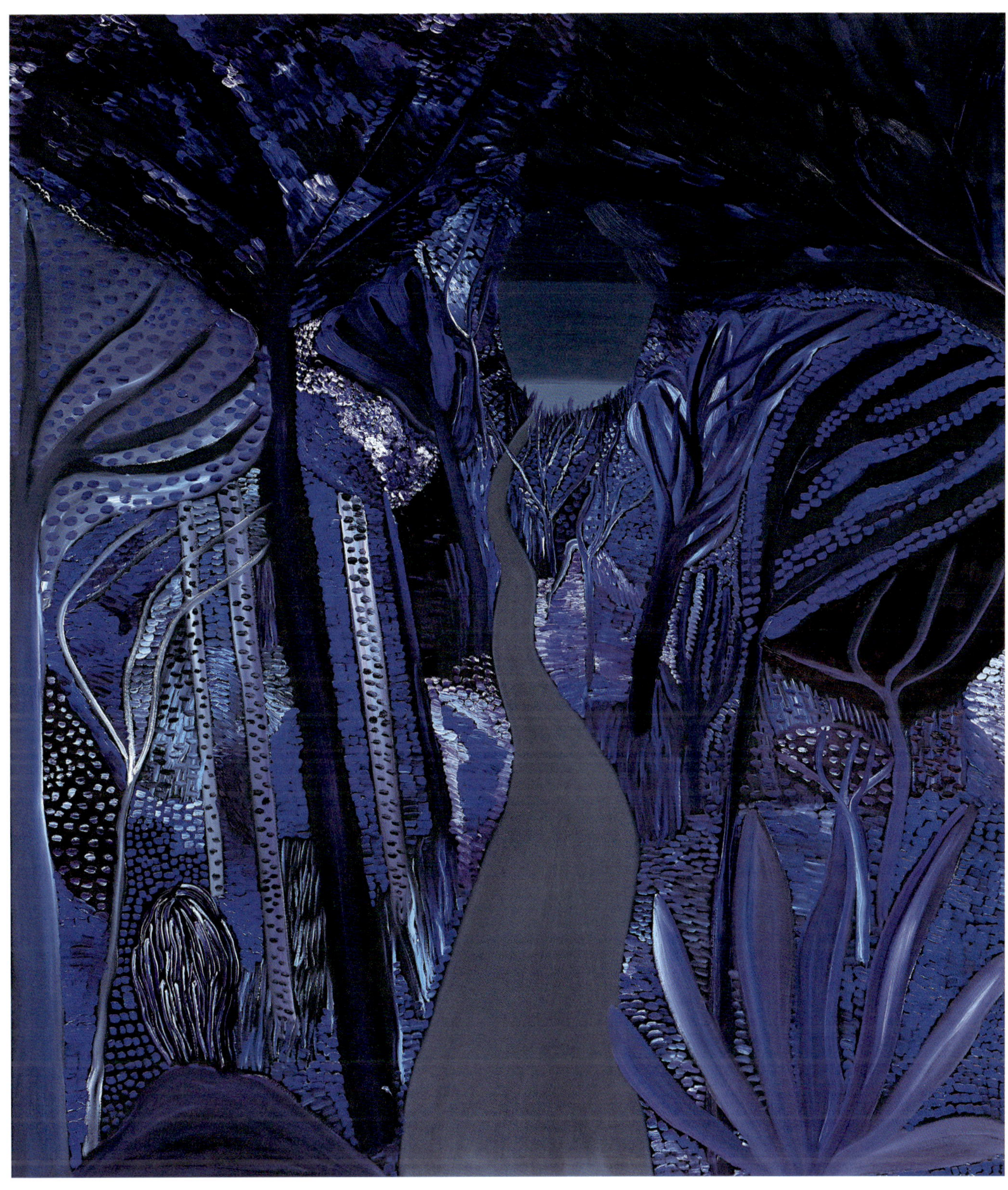

122 / Matthew Wong, *Path to the Sea*, 2019
Oil on canvas, 203.2 × 177.8 cm
Matthew Wong Foundation

'experience was necessarily suffering'. As such it could only be analysed aesthetically when the lens of the past was placed between it and the subject: 'but memory is always positive.'

In the *Diary*, Rilke wrote that the artist 'has no place for his past, and therefore in his works, he gives it an independent existence of its own.' Matthew took onboard this kind of thinking; each artwork was evidence of a reworking of his own personal past and that of others. History is not a repository of styles or techniques to draw upon but a repository of lives. Not without pain and fatigue, Matthew perceived the presence of what Rilke calls 'the thousand other historical worlds'. As Shitao wrote: 'Authentic work is that which is based on one's own being there.' For Matthew, that 'being there' was not an automatic action like breathing, but a factor to be analysed seriously, using the exempla of other painters.

So in fact Wong was more attuned to the past than to the present?

From his earliest statements as a street photographer, Matthew spoke elaborately about his difficulty in experiencing the present time. Photography is the first and most suitable medium to crystallize it, a 'tool of memory' to eternalize 'the brush of contact'. The first image I had of Matthew was that of one of those predators who, before eating their catch, bring it back to their lair in order to be able to enjoy it calmly. He was an 'image hunter', but he could not consume them on the spot: he had to get them home or to the studio, in order to filter them through the dual lens of time and feeling, following the tempo of his own conscience. Matthew lived the past in the present and archived the present experience to analyse it in the future. A process applied to images of life and to the fruition of art history, understood as an archive of the lives of those artists who came before. When critics present the image of Matthew Wong in the library, absorbed in research among his stacks of illustrated and non-illustrated books, the painter-researcher unleashed, it is useful to bear in mind that this artist did not think he was looking at encyclopaedias of artworks but rather at encyclopaedias of lives. What for a connoisseur or academic might be study, for Matthew Wong was nostalgia. The lives and works of artists are the object of Matthew's nostalgia.

You mentioned Wong was aware of his outsider status. Before focusing on what the term meant to him, could you indicate where the term originated from and how it has been used. How much validity does it hold for you as an artist?

Terms like 'outsider' and 'self-taught' in relation to an artist, just like 'naive' and 'visionary' in relation to an artwork, are nowadays 'summary' words in my opinion, used by certain members of the art world ever more for purposes of strategic vagueness, for commercial motivations or ones of (over)simplification. Words have their own history, and those from art history often prolong their use by inertia, yet without being accompanied by any real development. Think of 'surrealist': of course, Apollinaire [Guillaume Apollinaire, who first coined the term in 1917] could not have imagined the thousands of connotations with which – a hundred years later in the context of decadent capitalism – 'his' word would have been used to excuse the chaos of semantic laziness of certain artists or critics. So too the words 'outsider' and 'naive', 'amateur' and 'self-taught', 'folk', 'popular', 'primitive', 'instinctive'– each with its own nuances and origin – have taken on various meanings and varying degrees of legitimacy over the decades.

The label 'Outsider Art' was first coined by the critic Roger Cardinal in 1972, but the notion had preceded the term. 'Outsider' (literally: outside the community) and some of its quasi-synonyms mentioned above indicate artists who for various reasons were marginalized and ignored: those who could not gain access to art academies due to racial or economic constraints; artists who were disabled or who experienced mental illness; those who were neurodivergent or who had non-normative sexualities; or those who were deemed eccentric or isolated – even geographically – from society to some significant degree. Personally, I try to use other words or periphrases to indicate the 'categories' listed. I believe the issue at the basis of the term 'outsider'

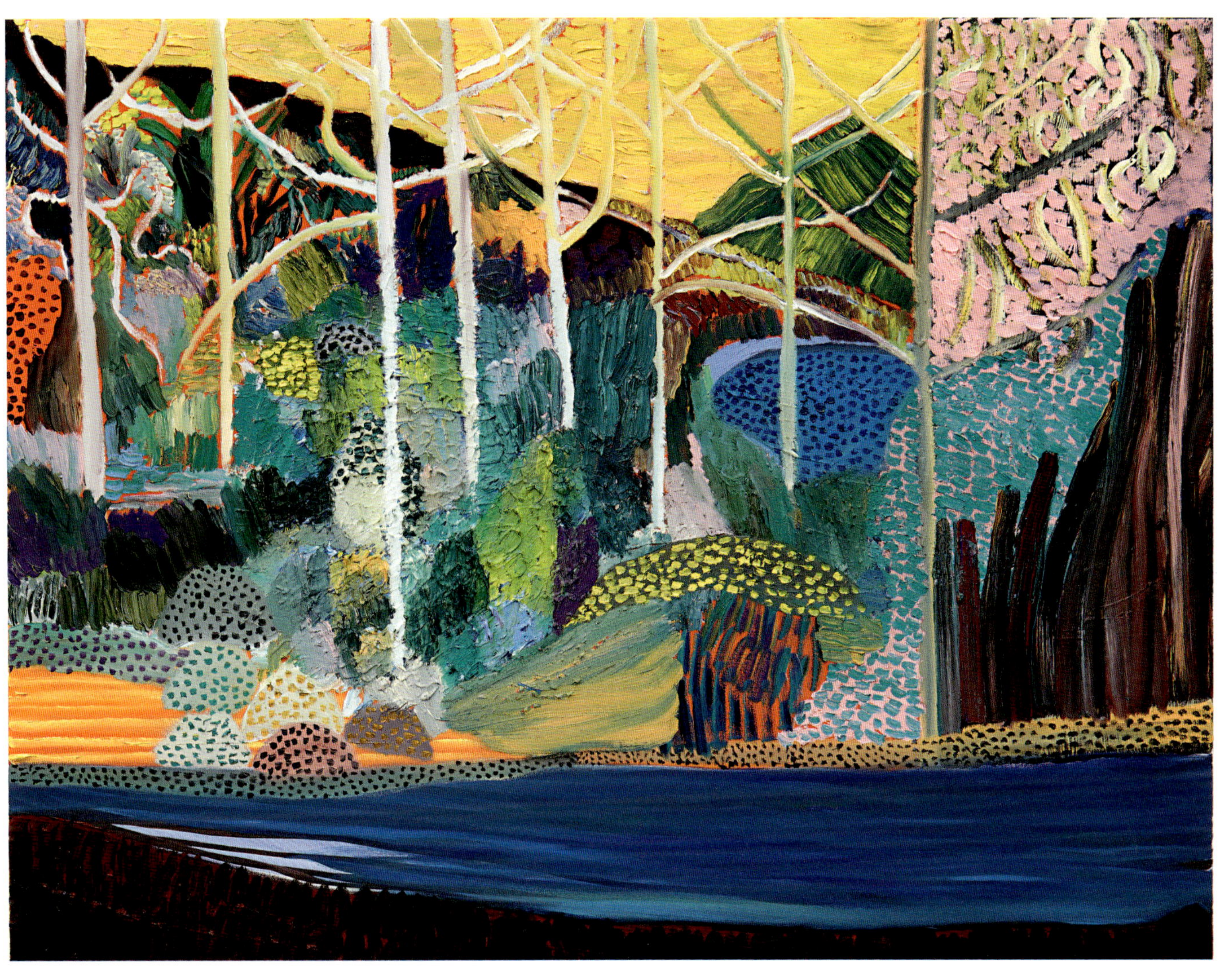

123 / Matthew Wong,
Morning Landscape, 2017
Oil on canvas, 91.4 × 121.9 cm
Cindy and Armond Schwartz

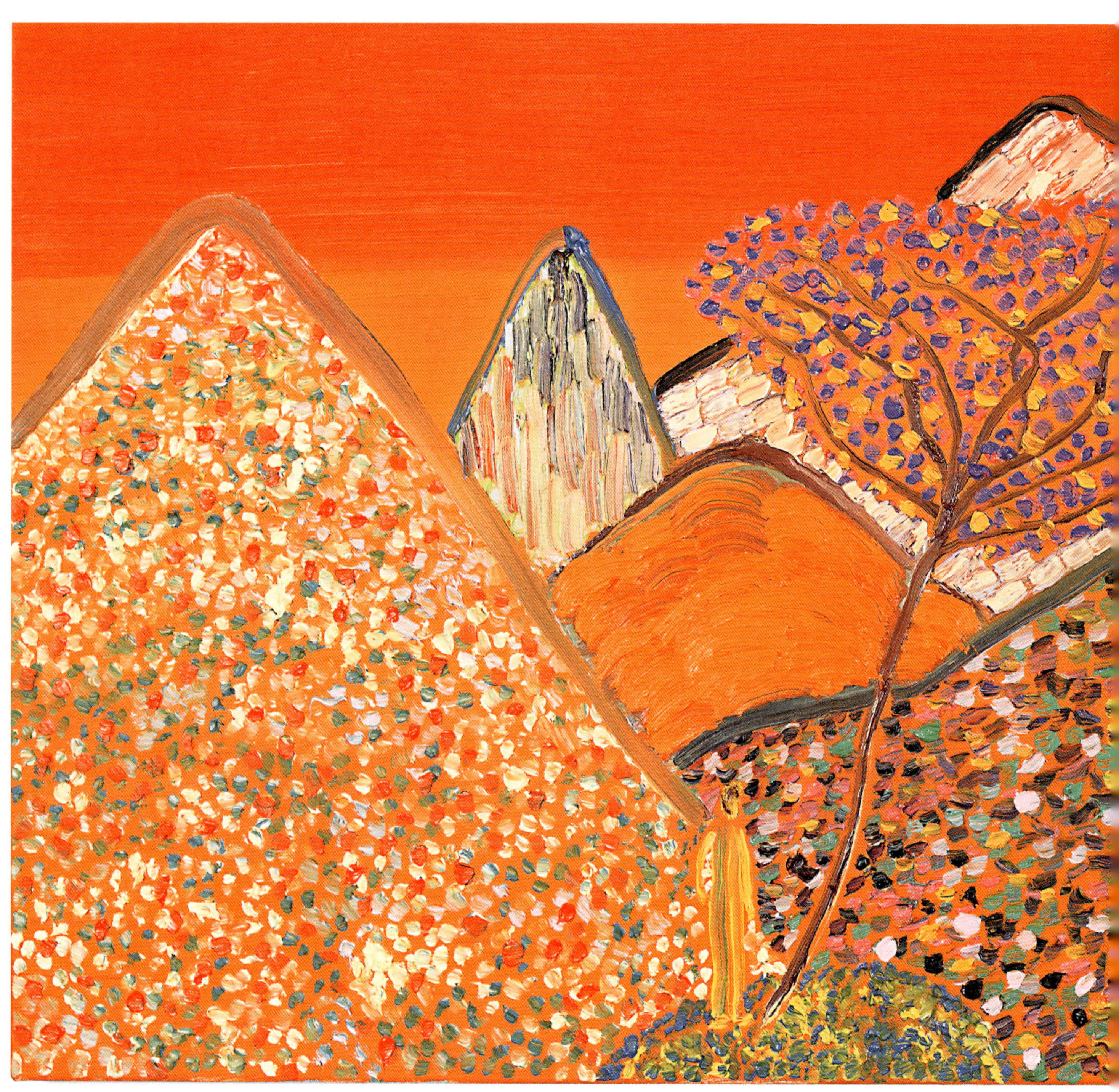

124 / Matthew Wong,
Far Away Eyes, 2017
Oil on canvas, 66 × 147.5 cm
Private collection

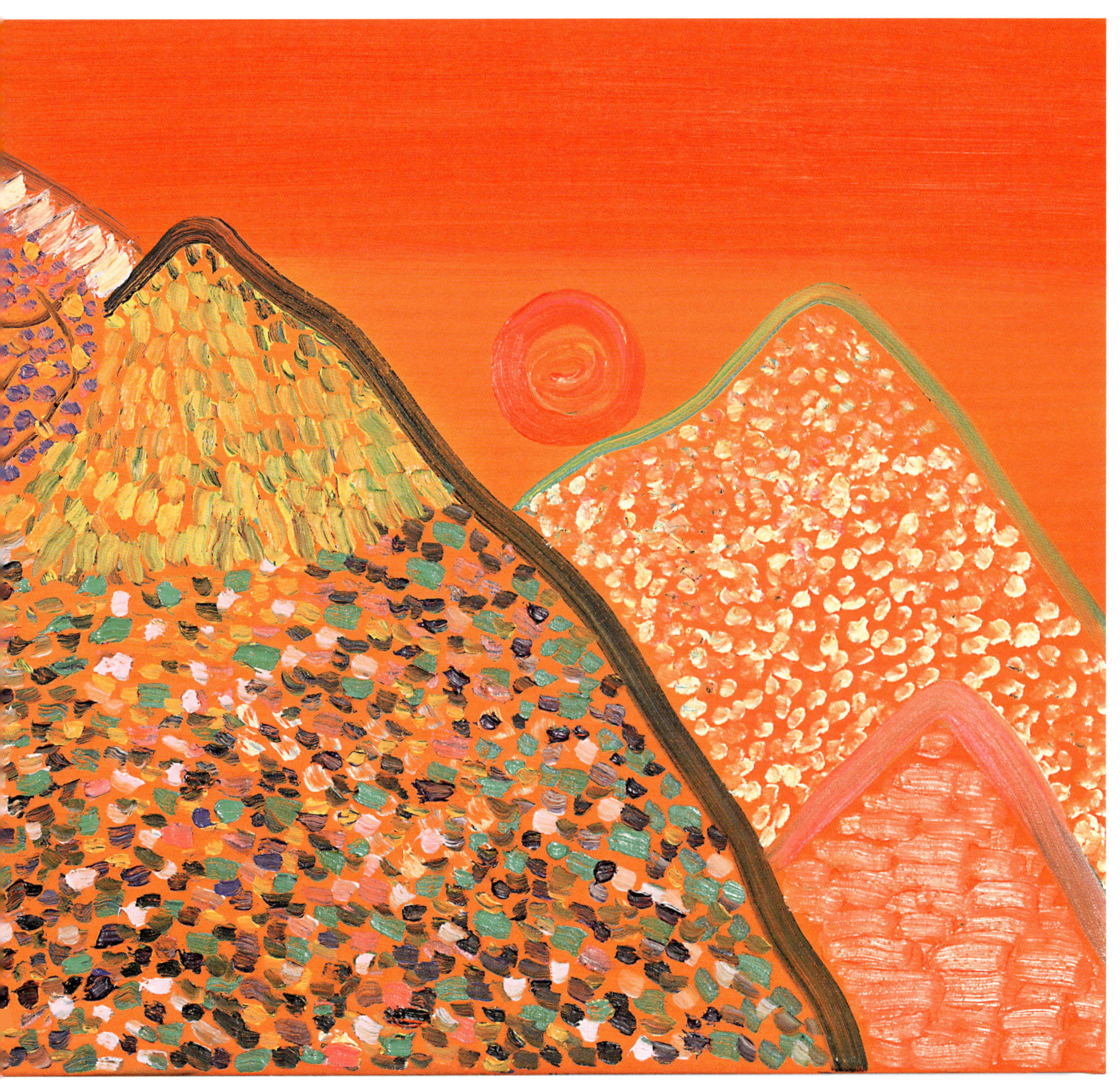

is above all that it refers to the individual and not to the work of art ('outsider' is the opposite of 'insider'), and I do not believe in anything that leaves the artwork aside.

And how much validity do you think the term holds for Matthew Wong?

As I said, Matthew called himself an 'outsider' and insisted on being a self-taught painter. I think it would be helpful if his future researchers did not focus exclusively on these concepts which might be too open to a certain kind of storytelling. Is a painter who has studied Visual Arts to BA or MA level without ever dealing with painting technique in an academic setting (as is frequently the case today) 'self-taught'? Is a photographer who apprenticed in a painter's studio an 'autodidact'? Does having an art master mean learning to use the eye or the hand? Is learning art from a book, be it a catalogue or a biography, less valuable than learning in the classroom? Is an artist living with a clinically certified mental illness but perfectly capable of understanding, analysing and using the art system an outsider? For some psychiatrists and neurologists, Van Gogh's art is 'sane' art, free of classification, but for others and above all for the artist's contemporary physicians, his was an example of 'insane' art. If twentieth-century Western painting cannot disregard Van Gogh's work, can 'the sane' be said to have appropriated 'the insane'? And what happens when the stylistic features of the outsider become aesthetically manageable by an insider artist?

The questions do not end here, for there are as many questions as responsibilities, especially since to this day, against an increasingly self-conscious cultural landscape, some continue to profit from and glamorize what was once ruthlessly known as 'art and madness': perhaps they still think 'madness' is more akin to freedom than to prison, to instinct than to repetition. However, the person I got to know as a pen pal, Matthew Wong, would have given ironic and romantic answers to each of these questions.

How do the most common interpretations of the term 'outsider art' compare with Wong's understanding of it? What were the main facets of his outsider status in your opinion?

For Matthew, the term 'outsider' firstly defined the conditions of his neurodiversity and psychiatric diagnosis, which made him 'unable to integrate into society,' as he used to say. Then he was an 'outsider' in terms of schooling, a circumstance he summed up in the term 'self-taught'. As I have already tried to express, we are all self-taught to a certain degree, and Matthew knew that his education was not unlike that of many other artists who entered painting by complex routes. He then juxtaposed a third and more properly artistic meaning of 'outsider': belonging neither to the painting community of Hong Kong nor that of New York, the latter the place where his art was exhibited and received. Finally, Matthew cultivated a fourth meaning of the term, an aesthetic one, closely bound up in the category he coined: 'neo-sincere' art.

'Sincerity' is one of the key words used by the art critic Albert Aurier in his 1890 article on Van Gogh, suggesting he was unencumbered by education or too much 'rationality' and therefore earnest and direct in his work. But to Matthew the notion of sincerity included elements from a more up-to-date definition of 'outsider'. Matthew explained that by sincerity he was referring to a characteristic of a certain type of contemporary painting that 'tends towards markers of authenticity [as] a kind of naïveté and twee quality.' The neo-sincere painters, Matthew added, were not contradictory on a psychological level, a detail that would have 'saved' them, but they were adept at hiding the absence of this contradiction on an aesthetic level.' They lacked: 'the psychological navigation that lends the appearance of the work its gravity.' Put it in more brutal terms, the 'neo-sincere' were painters who had learnt what naivety is and had found stylistic and aesthetic solutions to use it without becoming naive artists. Matthew presented his art as aesthetically lying on a razor's edge: 'Always walking a tightrope or flirting with a dangerous line into pastiche or sentiment but somehow not quite arriving into that area like much "sincere" work today.' His paintings displayed visual elements of sentimentalist art, but stopped short of being classed as 'neo-sincere'.

And here is Matthew's checkmate: Wong, a neurodiverse individual, identifies the features of outsider painting, and then identifies the features of a pretend-outsider painting current, carefully dividing the stylistic features of the former from the latter. He then introjects into his own work – legitimized by his status as a 'true outsider' – that subsection of stylistic features (of the former) that are rather risky and that will make his own work – imbued with notions and tradition – seem 'naive'. A bit like having a glass of Amarone red wine from Valpolicella and pouring a drop of milk into it, deliberately spoiling it with that drop, which the sommelier will then sense, realizing something is amiss.

The way I see it, Matthew was an 'outsider' who was more intuitive than any insider and who knew how to play on the concept of outsider.

Vincent van Gogh was also labelled an outsider during his life, only a different term was used. In his otherwise glowing article, Aurier called Van Gogh 'the isolated one'. How does the positioning of Van Gogh in this article relate to reviews of Wong's work in your opinion?

Today as yesterday, artists are taught that words are precious, fearsome and must be calibrated like quicksilver so as not to undermine the work. Van Gogh and Wong, on the other hand, were willing to speak freely, overcoming taboos; they were crystalline, vulnerable. Van Gogh's most moving letters are those in which he unmasks his self-consciousness towards the reasons why others [his contemporaries] did not exhibit him, did not buy him, at the cost of self-humiliation. He had no qualms about telling the truth even if it made him look like a complete loser, he had no masculinity to defend. The great link between Van Gogh and Wong is vulnerability, not isolation; some critics have sensed this connection but have not explored it yet. I hope it is this exhibition that opens up the subject more analytically. From their isolated positions, Van Gogh and Wong managed to create communities, whether they were made up of rural citizens or online painters. They believed in community, not in isolation on a poetic level, and harboured a deep, genuine interest in the art produced by their peers.

Do you think the popular story of Van Gogh as an outsider affected commentators in their assessment of Wong's work?

I think there is a serious issue with the distinction between art criticism and storytelling. Simply describing a painting is not art criticism, but neither is telling biographical anecdotes about the artist without relating them to their formal translation in the work of art.

Critics might have appropriated some of the shreds of Matthew's self-narrative – especially the one related to his compulsive use of social networks in a state of personal isolation – at the risk of turning them into branding. If I were a detached viewer of Matthew Wong's work, I would want to know why his hyper-saturated colours are more relevant than that of many of his contemporaries, why his unprocessed and sometimes 'bad' surfaces are unique in today's landscape. So yes, I think that even where he has not been named, the popular story of Van Gogh has opened the way to turn artists into cases, neglecting a true non-individualist critical approach.

We know Wong identified with Van Gogh, and that this identification was mainly based on the popular image of Van Gogh as an outsider. Do you think such an identification helped him much?

One day in 2017, when Peter and Matthew were debating who had been most unfortunate in life between Cézanne and Van Gogh, Matthew wrote: 'Man, that must've sucked to be Van Gogh.' I think that says a lot.

As I have already explained in reference to Rilke's feeling shared by Matthew, I think Matthew Wong felt Van Gogh's presence in the form of an exemplum. Van Gogh for Matthew was a father, a friend, an encouragement. To explicitly quote Van Gogh, who is both unique and printed on any T-shirt, napkin or mug, takes a certain amount of daring or naivety, but Matthew thought of him as a friend, so he did not question the issue.

Let's end on a personal note: what does Wong's work mean for you?

I think of Matthew and mourn him very often. With respect to his work, sometimes I have clear ideas, sometimes I am confused. In six years, he summed up all the successes and failures that a painter makes in thirty. Matthew was at the same time a painter in training, mid-career and senile; he collected all times in one and will remain an open question. He chose not to witness the pandemic or the disastrous outcomes of turbo-figuration, so his work represents for me a circumscribed moment in the world of contemporary painting. I would say that the *quid* of his years was denoted by the gradual re-appropriation by international painting of a colourist figuration open to the formless.

Just as Van Gogh's story taught Matthew, Matthew's story teaches his friends.

Painting lives on the places where it is created. However hard we try to keep images alive in our minds, to live from memory, a painting made in Edmonton will have the light of Edmonton and one made in Hong Kong the light of Hong Kong. Painting bears witness to the places of the world, and to think that there are so many artists who have moved to the metropolises is beautiful on one hand, because they write the history of the community, but on the other it is also rather paradoxical, because if a thousand versions of the same story are a thousand different stories, then other stories – the alien ones of those who have steered clear of the world – will no longer be written. The tension that bound Van Gogh to the Parisian cultural milieu, the sense of exclusion, the rapid passages through the city from Provence or on the way to the Oise Valley [Auvers-sur-Oise] were important and, like any tension, deformed the substance. But Paris was just like one of the women who had rejected him throughout his life, and when it finally welcomed him, he did not mind, because his poetics had been based on idealization and exclusion, on the sun that scorches down upon us, not on the sunset that looks us in the eye with its embrace.

The history of art will increasingly be studied in relation to urban growth and gentrification. How often do we hear of artists who, once they have consolidated their careers, having the earnings to afford a studio in highly speculative real estate environments, move from the provinces to New York, Paris or Milan? We should start to ask ourselves what the renunciation suffered by this choice is, not where the gain lies. Not to mention the non-emerging or semi-emerging artists who move to the big cities despite not having the financial clout to rent an adequate studio, just in order to be easily studio-visitable. In the era of inexhaustible availability, at least artists should ask their audience to pass through the biblical narrow gate, or take two planes and five buses. Today, to cheer Matthew up, I would recite a line to him by the Italian writer and poet Cristina Campo: 'Two worlds – and I come from the other one.'

In an 1889 letter to his sister-in-law Johanna [van Gogh-Bonger], Van Gogh wrote: 'It's quite odd perhaps that the result of this terrible attack is that in my mind there's hardly any really clear desire or hope left, and I'm wondering if it is thus that one thinks when, with the passions somewhat extinguished, one comes down the mountain instead of climbing it' [772]. I always thought that was it, the mountain painted by Matthew, the mountain that 'expresses what remains implicit' as Shitao wrote. Matthew's work can be summed up for me in the triad of mountain, portal and glass, in an interior view. Depression, so opaque, dusty and slow, belongs to the metropolis; but pain, the pain of living flesh, burns far from the centre, out in the provinces, and to be in the condition of being truly alone with it, and not alone in the multitude, is indeed tragic, but also beautiful. Hurray for the excluded, the half-empty glasses, the mountains that can only be descended, and may the motherlands that cannot serve as mothers rest in peace.

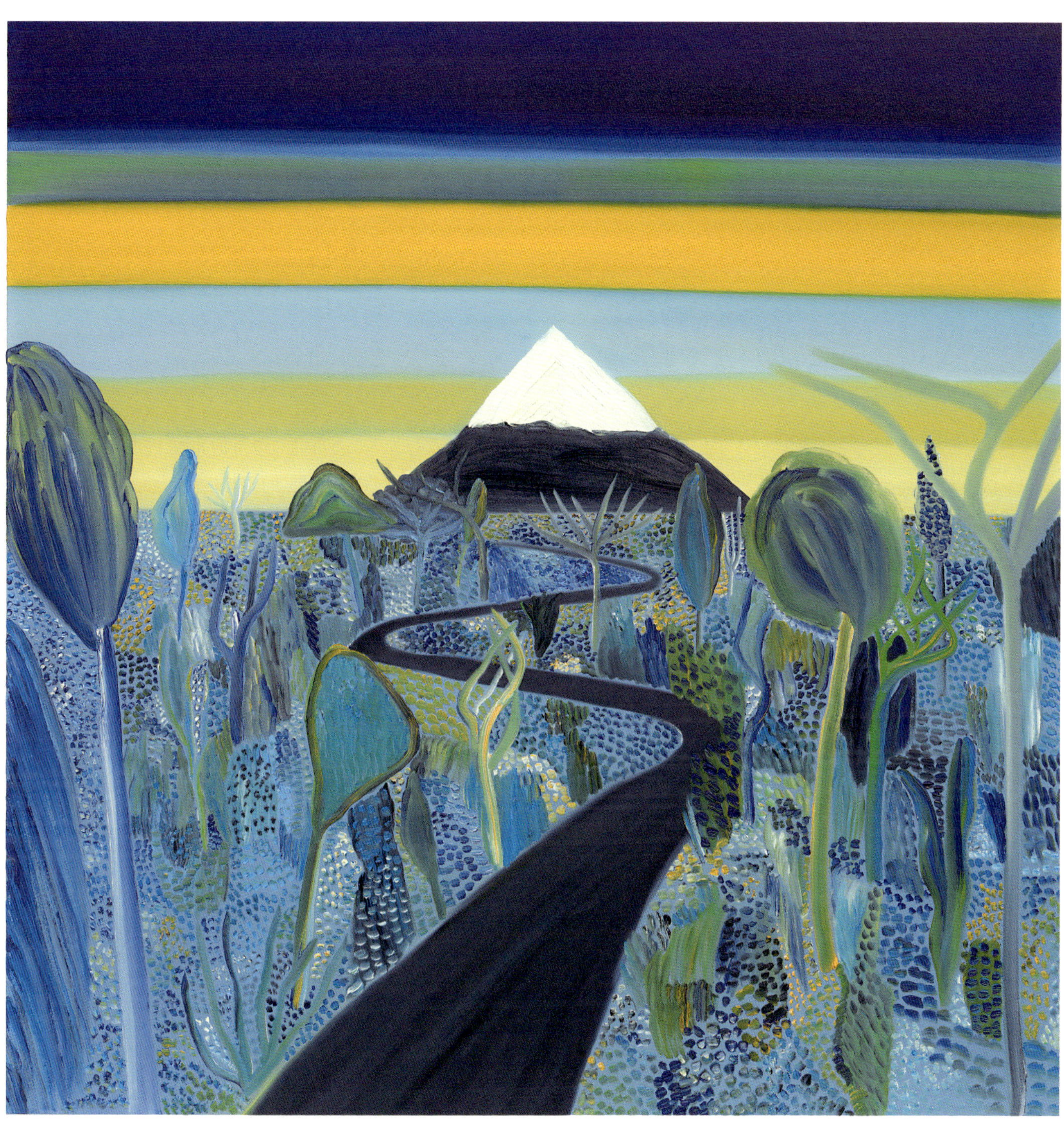

125 / Matthew Wong, *Unknown Pleasures*, 2019
Oil on canvas, 165.1 × 165.1 cm
The Museum of Modern Art, New York.
Gift of Monita and Raymond Wong in memory
of their son Matthew Wong, 2020

JUNE

I am that which is idle on a summer day.
I am the mouth that does not move.
I am the dish that parts the beef like a sea.
I am the wind's last legs at dusk.
I am six feet short of the moon,
Watching you as you sleep, and you,
Who came to my breath, perhaps expecting me
To turn up around the corner in the rain,
Like a memory of Paris, so I close my eyes
And kiss you as if I was there.

Matthew Wong, date unknown

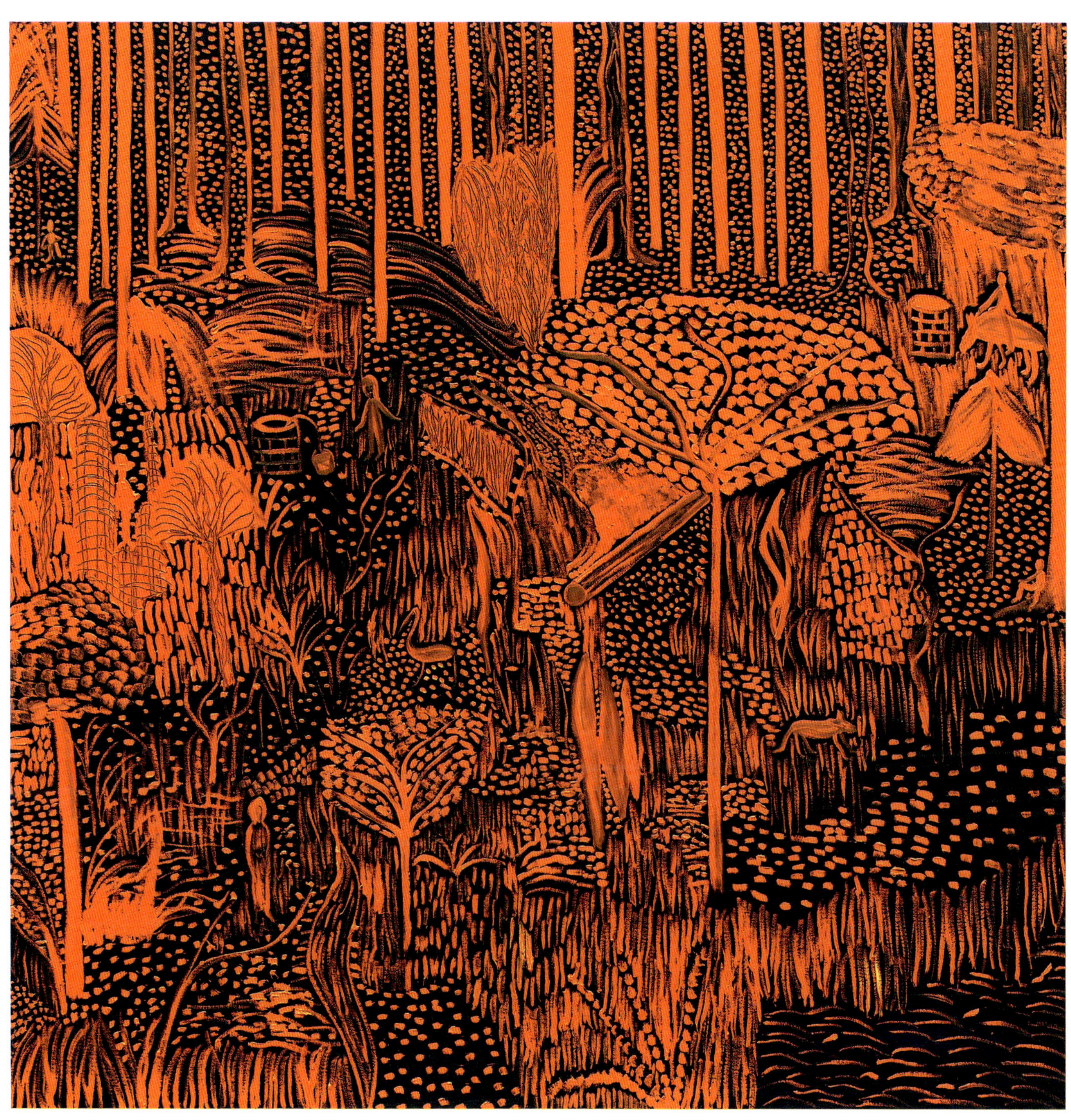

126 / Matthew Wong, *Somewhere*, 2018
Oil on canvas, 152.4 × 152.4 cm
Brendan Dugan

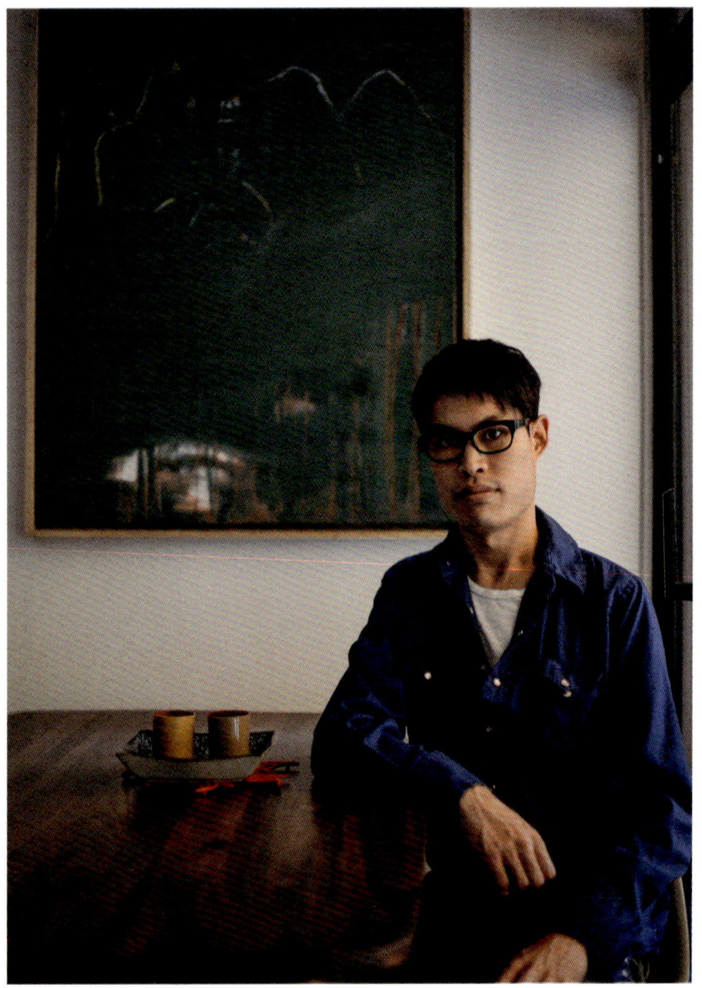

A. / Matthew Wong, 2 November 2015.

B. / Solo exhibition *Pulse of the Land* at the Hong Kong Visual Arts Centre, 19-23 October 2015.

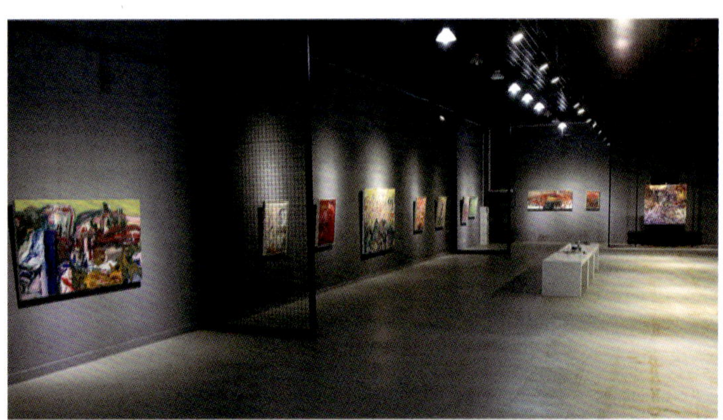

C. / Solo exhibition *Chapter One* at the Cuiheng Art Museum, Zhongshan, 30 August–20 September 2014.

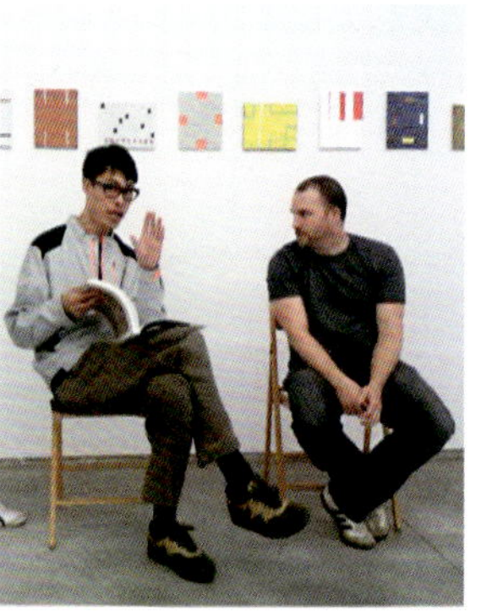

D. / Matthew Wong in conversation with Brian Cypher at the opening of *Good Bad Brush*, 16 July 2016. Work by Peter Shear hangs in the background.

Chronology Matthew Wong (1984–2019)

1984 Born 8 March in Toronto, Canada.

1991 Moves to Hong Kong at the age of seven with his parents Raymond and Monita Wong.

1999 Wong family returns to Toronto.

2003 Receives his high school diploma at York School in Toronto and begins a bachelor's degree in Cultural Anthropology at the University of Michigan, Ann Arbor.

2007 Receives his bachelor's degree from the University of Michigan and moves to Hong Kong. Follows various internships and traineeships there. He also works remotely for a publisher in the United States.

2008 Wong begins to recite his poems at poetry clubs in Hong Kong, including Peel Street Poetry and Joyce is Not Here.

2009 Takes photographs of his grandfather's properties, which he views as his first creative expression.

2010 Enrols on a master's course in photography at the City University of Hong Kong's School of Creative Media.

2011 Wong interns in November at the Hong Kong pavilion of the 54th Venice Biennale. The show includes work by the artist Kwok Mang-ho, better known as Frog King. Sees work by Julian Schnabel and Christopher Wool in Venice and is inspired to make his first drawings. That same month, Wong's photographs are published for the first time in *Cha: An Asian Literary Journal*. The series is titled *Grandma's Things*.

2012 Receives his master's degree in photography and publishes his photographic work a few more times while increasingly concentrating on drawing and painting. Works as project assistant for the Asia Art Archive from March to December.

2013 Secures his first studio space in a complex for creative professionals at Cuiheng in Zhongshan, mainland China. Comes into contact via Facebook with Peter Shear, John Cheim and many others in the art world.

31 October–10 November: Takes part in the eighth Song Zhuang Art Festival in Beijing.

2014 Continues to work on his abstract ink drawings and paintings and tries out different techniques.

30 August–20 September: Organizes his first solo exhibition, titled *Matthew Wong: Chapter One*, at Cuiheng Art Museum. It encompasses 30 works (fig. c).

2015 First experiments with figurative compositions. Sends a roll of drawings to John Cheim.

8 July: Posts one of his own works on Facebook alongside a Van Gogh.

19–23 October: Organizes his second solo exhibition, *Pulse of the Land*, at the Hong Kong Visual Arts Centre. Wong shows 39 works (fig. b).

2016 Wong and his mother set off in February on a long journey through the United States and Canada. They start out in New York where they meet John Cheim and others before moving on in March to Michigan and then Los Angeles, where they stay for two months. The trip ends in June in Edmonton, where Wong and his mother move into a vacant apartment belonging to friends.

16 July–7 August: *Good Bad Brush*: joint exhibition with Peter Shear at the Occasional Gallery in Burlington, Washington. It is Wong's first show in the United States (fig. d).

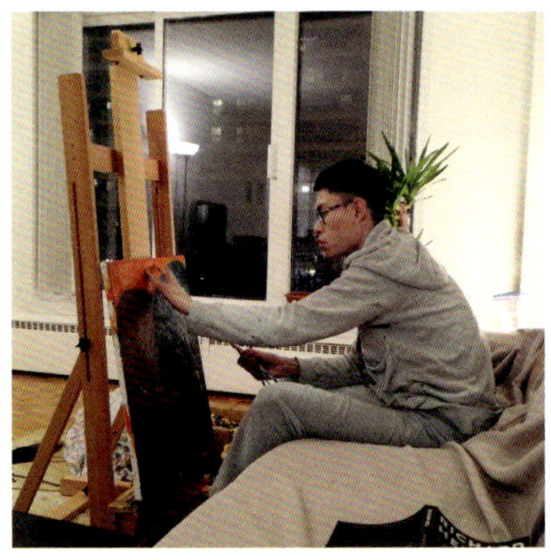

E. / Matthew Wong working at home in Edmonton, January 2017.

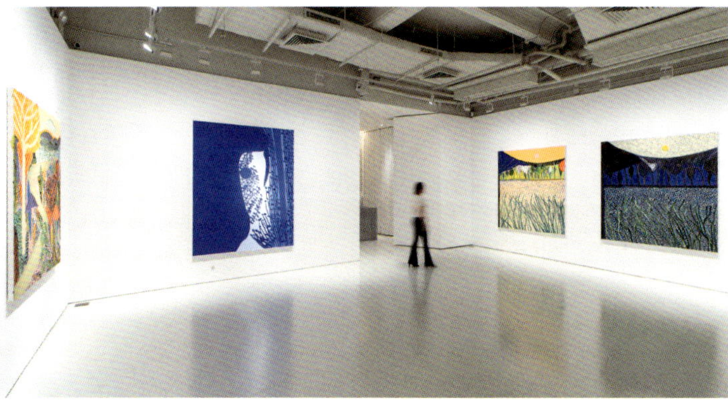

F. / Solo exhibition *Day by Night* at Massimo De Carlo, Hong Kong, 10 January–16 March 2019.

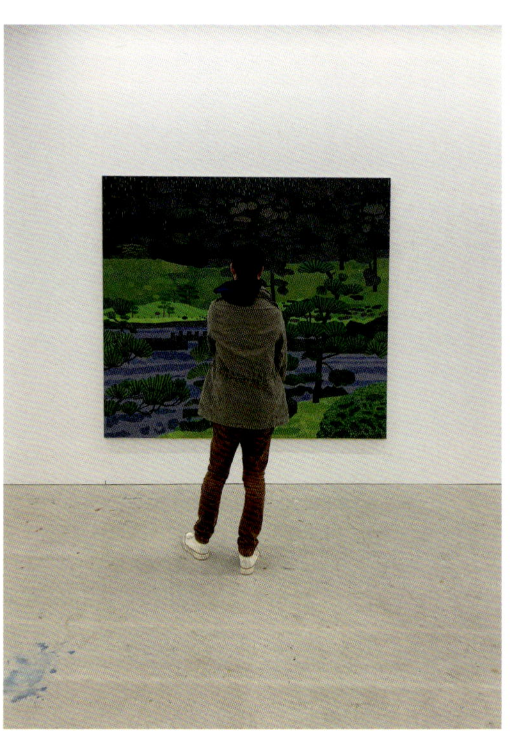

H. / Matthew Wong looking at *Japanese Garden 3* by Jonas Wood in the latter's studio, 13 February 2019. See also fig. 33 in this publication.

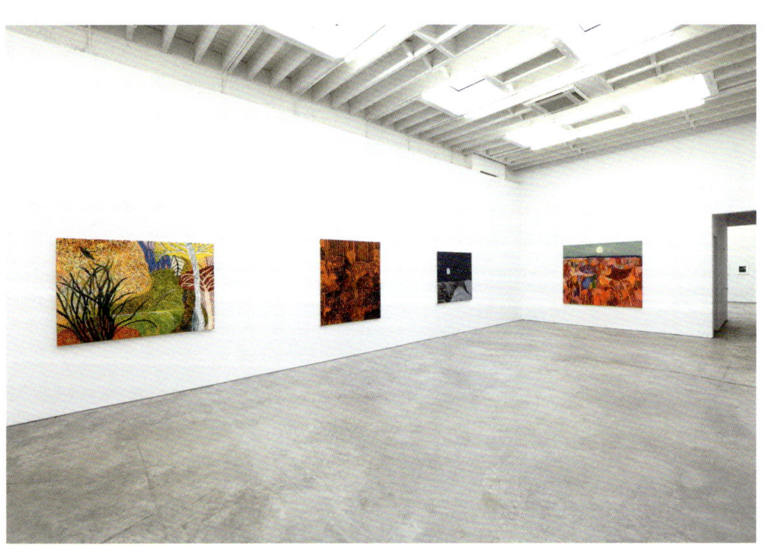

G. / Matthew Wong's debut exhibition at Karma, 22 March–29 April 2018.

2016 (continued) 3–25 September: The curator Matthew Higgs selects Wong for the group exhibition *Outside*, held at a temporary branch of the Karma gallery in Amagansett, New York. Wong sells a work and meets Karma owner Brendan Dugan.

20–23 October: Wong's work is shown in Paris at the Karma stand at the independent FIAC contemporary art fair.

2017 Wong begins to paint in what would become his signature style. Settles permanently in Edmonton. He is formally represented by Karma and not long thereafter by Frank Elbaz, who is based in Paris and Dallas.

6–9 April: Wong's latest works, including *The Other Side of the Moon* and *The West*, are shown at the Karma stand at the Dallas Art Fair. *The West* is purchased by the Dallas Museum of Art.

5–7 May: Wong's work is shown at Frieze New York, where it draws the attention of the critics Jerry Saltz (*New York* magazine) and Roberta Smith (*The New York Times*).

2 July: Moves into his studio in Edmonton, where he will continue to work until his death.

6 July–31 August: A work by Wong is included in the group exhibition *The Horizontal* at Cheim & Read in New York.

2 November 2017–13 January 2018: Wong takes part in the exhibition *Plastic Surgery, to look like you* at Frank Elbaz's gallery in Dallas. Work by Andy Coolquitt and Guillaume Leblon is also featured.

7–10 December: Wong's work is shown at Art Basel Miami at Frank Elbaz's stand.

2018 Wong continues to work in his familiar style, while simultaneously trying to instil more calm in his work. He exhibits at art fairs throughout the year and takes part in various group exhibitions and does multiple studio visits.

22 March–29 April: Wong's debut exhibition at Karma. He shows nine paintings and sixteen gouaches (fig. G).

22 October 2018–30 September 2019: Wong's work is selected for *Trance* at the Aïshti Foundation in Beirut. The exhibition is curated by the artist Albert Oehlen.

15 November: Interview with Maria Vogel for the online art platform *Art of Choice*, in which Wong mentions Van Gogh as one of his principal sources of inspiration.

21 November: Declares in a WhatsApp message to Dugan that he recognizes himself in Van Gogh: 'I see myself in him. The impossibility of belonging in this world.'

2019 Wong works primarily in blue tones and paints three works in which he refers directly to Van Gogh: *Starry Night*, *Untitled* and *The Space Between Trees*. He exhibits continuously at art fairs and group exhibitions.

10 January–16 March: *Day By Night* solo exhibition at the Hong Kong branch of Massimo De Carlo. It consists of four pairs of matching paintings; each with a day and a night version (fig. F).

17 April: Takes part in a panel discussion marking the launch of the publication *Landscape Painting Now: From Pop Abstraction to New Romanticism* by Barry Schwabsky. The interview, moderated by Schwabsky, also includes Verne Dawson, Lois Dodd, Enrique Martinez Celaya and Alison Elizabeth Taylor. Wong's work features in the publication too.

2 October: Wong dies in Edmonton at the age of 35.

8 November 2019–5 January 2020: The exhibition *Blue*, with the series of blue works that Wong made in 2019, is held posthumously at Karma in New York. It includes sixteen paintings.

Notes

Painting as a Last Resort: An Introduction

Joost van der Hoeven

1 M. Wong 2012, p. 3.
2 Vogel 2018: 'My first memorable encounter with painting was in 2011, when I was an intern for the Hong Kong pavilion of the Venice Biennale that year. Coming across works by two artists in particular caused a radical shift in my thinking – the Julian Schnabel retrospective at the Museo Correr, and a series of 8 large Christopher Wool silk screened Rorschach blots in the main pavilion. It hasn't occurred to me that painting could take these forms beyond realistic depiction.'
3 Wong bought the sketchbook while still in Venice. He visited the same store again to buy artists' materials during his final visit to the Italian city in 2019. Conversation with Matthew Wong's mother, Monita Wong, 26 May 2023.
4 Wong 2012, pp. 9–12.
5 Guzman 2012.
6 Khatchadourian 2022, pp. 36–37.
7 Matthew Wong, quoted in a conversation with his mother Monita, 9 October 2022.
8 Matthew Wong, Facebook message to his artist friend Peter Shear, 28 February 2014: 'I actually did an MFA in digital and new media. At the end of it got nowhere decided to turn to painting as a last resort with no prior skill or experience.'
9 Conversation with his friend Fedor Deichmann, 17 January 2023.
10 Yau 2018. The exhibition was simply titled *Matthew Wong* and ran from 22 March to 29 April 2018.
11 Saltz 2018: 'Matthew Wong's show at Karma is one of the most impressive solo New York debuts I've seen in a while.'
12 Smith 2019: 'He was 35, had Tourette's syndrome and depression, and was one of the most talented painters of his generation.'
13 The painting was *The West*, which was purchased in 2017.
14 Conversation with Monita Wong, 9 October 2022.
15 The list is drawn from the names Wong cited in the interview with art advisor Maria Vogel in 2018 and from his Facebook correspondence with Peter Shear (2013–17). David Milne was mentioned in a conversation with Wong's artist friend Brad Phillips, 4 May 2023.
16 Matthew Wong, Facebook message to Peter Shear, 8 July 2015: 'I just posted one of my own paintings next to a Van Gogh.' Wong later deleted the post, so it is no longer possible to identify the works.
17 Vogel 2018.
18 Matthew Wong, WhatsApp message to the art dealer Brendan Dugan, 21 November 2018.
19 Vincent van Gogh, letter to Theo van Gogh, 24 September 1880 [158].
20 Guzman 2012.
21 Matthew Wong, *On Photography*, artist statement emailed from Matthew Wong to Dena Rash Guzman, 26 June 2012 (Matthew Wong Foundation Archive): 'Typically operating in the manner of Baudelaire's flaneur, I go about much of daily life simply walking, sometimes with a purpose (i.e. going from one practical destination to another and in the middle taking a picture if I come across one), but mostly not.'
22 Miss Wong 2014: 'I paint on a daily basis, and none of the works are planned in advance, but rather worked out through an intuitive engagement with the pigment and surface, therefore my work can be seen as an existential meditation on the act of painting, painting as a marker of time.'
23 Guzman 2012: 'For me, to take photographs is a way of confirming that I exist, which is something I question all the time. [...] It's the clicking of the shutter that means everything for me.'
24 M. Wong 2013: 'Painting is a mysterious, often frustrating, but ultimately compulsive activity for me; working on a daily basis is basically a way for me to keep track of my life, like a diary.'
25 Vincent van Gogh, letter to Theo van Gogh, 28 January 1889 [743]: 'At the bottom of our hearts good old Gauguin and I understand each other, and if we're a bit mad, so be it, aren't we also a little sufficiently deeply artistic to contradict anxieties in that regard by what we say with the brush?' Conversation with Wong's artist friend and poet Nikil Inaya, 31 August 2022.
26 M. Wong 2013: 'My process begins in a very arbitrary fashion, I may just pick a few colors at hand and squeeze them onto the surface, blindly making marks, but at a certain point I will inexplicably get a very fleeting glimpse of what the image I may finally arrive at will be, sort of like a hallucination, and as I read in a Bill Jensen interview once, as long as one can paint in service of such a hallucination or vision, the image will eventually paint itself.'
27 Barger 2020, p. 3.
28 Matthew Wong, Facebook message to Peter Shear, 19 March 2014.
29 Friends of his recall that at certain moments when they were together Wong would suddenly decide to go and buy artist's materials and set to work in a public park, for instance. Conversation with Nikil Inaya, 31 August 2022.
30 Strictly speaking, later in his career the ritual entailed gouaches on paper, rather than ink on paper.
31 Matthew Wong, Facebook message to Peter Shear, 11 July 2015: 'You see there's no space in either our hk or china home. My increasing body of work takes up all the space.'
32 The arrangement was made via a friend of the family. The studio was part of a large government-run complex for creative professionals. Wong was allowed to work there free of charge in exchange for two paintings a year. Conversation with Monita Wong, 26 May 2023.
33 Brennan 2013: 'My studio space in Zhongshan is a larger, proper studio set up so I have more freedom of movement when working there, can work on bigger pieces, and also since it is purely a work space where I do not live, it gets pretty messy as my painting process is quite physical.'
34 Miss Wong 2014: 'I've been right-handed my whole life, but when I paint I actually use both hands. It isn't something I started doing consciously, but some time in 2014 I noticed that I was actually passing painting utensils back and forth between each hand while working.'
35 Vogel 2018.
36 Two of Wong's poems can be found in this catalogue, pp. 16, 160.
37 Miss Wong 2014: 'When I'm not working, I'm at the library doing research into the history of art, figuring out where I can fit into the greater dialogue between artists throughout time, or on the internet looking at art-related websites and engaging in dialogue on social media with artists and art-world figures around the world.'
38 All these names feature in Matthew Wong's Facebook correspondence with Peter Shear.
39 Matthew Wong, Facebook message to Peter Shear, 28 February 2014: 'I'm working through de Kooning ATM [at the moment] and have no idea when I will find myself out of that. De Kooning and Resnick.'
40 Conversation with Fedor Deichmann, 17 January 2023.
41 Audio recording of panel discussion with Matthew Wong and others during the presentation of the book *Landscape Painting Now* at the Whitney Museum of American Art, New York, 17 April 2019, courtesy of Barry Schwabsky.
42 Matthew Wong, Facebook message to Peter Shear, 18 April 2014: 'yeah i'm trying to see where i can fit into the Chinese painting equation, the scroll format, etc. while bringing something more personal to time worn tropes.' See also Chan 2021.
43 Matthew Wong, Facebook message to Peter Shear, 22 April 2014.
44 Conversation with Fedor Deichmann, 17 January 2023.
45 Ma 2022, pp. 37–38.
46 See Luijten 2003.
47 Vincent van Gogh, letter to Theo van Gogh, January 1881 [162]: 'Now without in any way daring to claim to rise as high as them, nevertheless, by continuing to draw these types of workmen &c., I'm confident of succeeding in becoming more or less capable of working in magazine or book illustration.'
48 Vincent van Gogh, letter to Theo van Gogh, between about 23 and about 25 July 1887 [572].
49 *Matthew Wong: Chapter One* ran from 30 August to 20 September 2014.
50 Matthew Wong, Facebook message to Peter Shear, 24 March 2015: 'i'm actually on the waiting list to show at two spaces in Hong Kong but god knows when they'll clear me if ever [...] if some miracle happens and by April they email me at the Hong Kong Visual Arts Center that I can show in October, then obviously that will put travel plans on hold until November if our show materializes for some time then.' *Pulse of the Land* ran from 19 to 23 October 2015.
51 Conversation with Fedor Deichmann, 17 January 2023.
52 With thanks to Philippe Buetner for making this comparison.
53 Matthew Wong, Facebook message to Peter Shear, 28 October 2014.
54 Matthew Wong, Facebook message to Peter Shear, 1 April 2016.
55 See Hartmann 2022.
56 The works in question were chiefly from Nuenen, Antwerp and Paris.
57 Matthew Wong, Facebook message to Peter Shear, 29 October 2014: 'I feel like with this kind of work most people can't really distinguish between good or bad, which is why I feel I have to move out of it.'
58 Wong frequently cited Goodman and Auerbach as examples in his Facebook correspondence with Peter Shear. Soutine and Van Gogh are mentioned in the introduction to the *Pulse of the Land* catalogue (M. Wong 2015, p. 42).
59 M. Wong 2015, p. 42
60 Matthew Wong, Facebook message to Peter Shear, 11 November 2015: 'Thx a lot P – going through a dark phase your words mean much.'
61 Matthew Wong, Facebook message to Peter Shear, 17 December 2015: 'trying to show somewhat abstract art here in Zhongshan is such a humbling and even demoralizing experience. Really gives one a center front seat to oblivion for four days. Grow thicker skin by the end of it but also spiritually defeated/ exhausted.'
62 Khatchadourian 2022, p. 41.
63 Conversation with Monita Wong, 9 October 2022.
64 Matthew Wong, Facebook message to his artist friend Sofia Silva, 25 June 2017.
65 Conversation with Peter Shear, 12 October 2022.
66 See Van Tilborgh 2018.
67 All these names crop up regularly in the Facebook correspondence between Matthew Wong and Peter Shear in the period in question.
68 See Yau 2022.
69 Conversation with Monita Wong, 8 October 2022.
70 Peter Shear, Facebook message to Matthew Wong, 10 June 2016: 'I had done an interview and was talking about materials and how I use crappy brushes. I said I like a good bad brush and that's where Brian [Cypher: the person who provided the exhibition space] took it. I'm fine with it, I sort of like the sound.' The same

was true of Wong: 'i buy dirt cheap house painters brushes throw em away after one use.' Matthew Wong, Facebook message to Peter Shear, 17 May 2015.
71 Matthew Wong, Facebook message to Peter Shear, 1 January 2016: 'I was just using these very small cheap brushes from the art supplies store ridiculously cheap i treated them as disposable after use.'
72 Higgs and Li 2022, p. 24.
73 Ibid. See also the interview with Sofia Silva in this catalogue, Ten Berge 2000 and Cardinal 1972.
74 Matthew Wong, Facebook message to Peter Shear, 29 March 2015.
75 Matthew Wong, Facebook message to Sofia Silva, 25 June 2017: 'Anyway I go to the opening at Karma in September and that night one of my paintings sold so it gave me license to start talking to the owner and I guess the rest is what has lead [*sic*] to now.'
76 Matthew Wong, Facebook message to Peter Shear, 22 October 2016: 'they [Karma] have like over 60 works of mine and apparently they shipped everything to Paris. i wonder if anything sold.'
77 Matthew Wong, Facebook message to Peter Shear, 18 October 2016: 'it [FIAC] opens like late tonight over here my time pretty pumped.'
78 Ibid. 'Strange now that am in a gallery situation as they seem to think everything is great – i've been destroying a lot of work lately so that it just doesn't get a chance to surface weird how at a certain point criticality just drops away.[...] I've actually been tougher on myself than ever much more than when i was just painting for the internet.'
79 Ibid.
80 Matthew Wong, Facebook message to Sofia Silva, 4 July 2017: 'A lot of aspects of my touch come more from my self initiated study of Chinese ink art so it's not really the kind of touch you see in western art.'
81 Wong referred to Schiele, Klimt, Bess, Wood and Doig in his Facebook correspondence with Peter Shear. He mentioned Kusama in Vogel 2018 and Milne came up during a conversation with Brad Phillips, 4 May 2023.
82 Matthew Wong, Facebook message to Peter Shear, 29 July 2017: 'I've been looking at Schiele sunflowers.'
83 Wong painted a tribute to Bess in August 2016, revealing the importance of this painter to him at the time. The work was simultaneously dedicated to Albert Pinkham Ryder. Matthew Wong, Facebook message to Peter Shear, 25 August 2016. 'On another note I just painted a landscape that is a dedication to Bess and Ryder. It came together surprisingly quickly like they were helping me out.'
84 Wong evidently thought that the network of dots with which he had covered the painted surface in *The West* was still not sufficiently dense, as he applied even more at the Karma stand at the fair to make the overall effect yet more intense. See Hartman 2022, p. 31.
85 Vogel 2018: 'Living a fairly reclusive life and finding the most stimulation and enjoyment from matters of the mind, be they following the natural path of my imagination or watching films in the dark of my living room, an activity which is a part of my routine I pursue every night without fail, it's inevitable that the solitary nature of this pattern seeps into and informs my work.'
86 Milbrath 2017. Millbrath was one of Wong's many online friends and had frequent contact with him in 2017. She writes in her article that 'Matthew's favourite word is the Portuguese "saudade," meaning the nostalgic or profound longing for something or someone that is no longer.'
87 Matthew Wong, Instagram message to his artist friend Benjamin Styer, 13 May 2019.
88 M. Wong 2015.
89 See note 85.
90 Matthew Wong, Facebook message to Sofia Silva, 4 July 2017.
91 Matthew Wong, Facebook messages to Peter Shear, between 9 and 12 May 2017.
92 Wong sent a photograph of the works, stating: 'Karma solo date TBA [to be announced]'. Matthew Wong, Facebook message to Peter Shear, 12 May 2017. On 24 June, however, he told Sofia Silva that one of the paintings in the series had been sold. A second work was sold on 29 June, as he informed Shear on the same date.
93 Matthew Wong, Facebook message to Peter Shear, 20 June 2017: 'Still not yet able to move into new studio restless as hell.'
94 In Van Gogh's case the trees were poplars rather than birches, but that does not alter the effect of the composition.
95 I am grateful to Josh Abraham for pointing out the association.
96 Wong told his friend Fedor Deichmann that Wayne Thiebaud's work was a source of inspiration. Conversation with Fedor Deichmann, 17 January 2023.
97 Matthew Wong, Facebook message to Peter Shear, 15 June 2017: 'I find large works easier to paint than small (by small I mean anything under 30 inches).'
98 Matthew Wong, WhatsApp message to Brendan Dugan, 19 February 2018.
99 Vincent van Gogh, letter to Emile Bernard, 12 April 1888 [596].
100 Vincent van Gogh, letter to Emile Bernard, around 26 November 1889 [822]: 'This dark giant — like a proud man brought low — contrasts, when seen as the character of a living being, with the pale smile of the last rose on the bush, which is fading in front of him.'
101 Ibid. 'You'll understand that this combination of red ochre, of green saddened with grey, of black lines that define the outlines, this gives rise a little to the feeling of anxiety from which some of my companions in misfortune often suffer, and which is called "seeing red".' See also Van Tilborgh 2016a, pp. 13–28.
102 Conversation with Monita Wong, 5 August 2022.
103 M. Wong 2018; Matthew Wong, Facebook message to Peter Shear, 2 March 2015: 'If the day ever comes I get into a gallery, I'd like to initiate a policy of no press releases, no interviews, just the work itself.'
104 Matthew Wong, Instagram message to Benjamin Styer, 13 May 2019.
105 Matthew Wong, Facebook message to Sofia Silva, 25 June 2017: 'And now it's weird because I'm on here and try to occasionally interact with the artists who I knew since I started and there's a weird distance. People now may come on with excessive praise the subtext being maybe I can help them for old times sake or something I don't really trust any of it. [...] Yeah a lot of envy.'
106 Matthew Wong, Facebook message to Peter Shear, 10 May 2017.
107 Matthew Wong, Facebook message to Peter Shear, 15 May 2017.
108 Matthew Wong, Facebook message to Sofia Silva, 28 June 2017.
109 Matthew Wong, Facebook message to Peter Shear, 25 June 2017: 'Man that must've sucked to be Van Gogh he kept trying tho.'
110 Matthew Wong, WhatsApp messages to Brendan Dugan, 21 November 2018: 'A Van Gogh movie impossible to make I think the legend is too familiar to the point of cliché. Best to just look at the work. That said I see myself in him. The impossibility of belonging in this world.'
111 There is no evidence that Wong ever read Van Gogh's letters.
112 Aurier 1890: 'un terrible et affolé génie, sublime souvent, grotesque quelquefois, toujours relevant presque de la pathologie'.
113 Vincent van Gogh, letter to Albert Aurier, 9 or 10 February 1890 [853].
114 Matthew Wong, Facebook message to Peter Shear, 23 August 2017: 'I find doing these detours into severe limits much more thrilling than making the crowd pleasers. The ones where you really risk embarrassment or misunderstanding.' Although the message dates from the summer of 2017, Wong did not really put this approach into practice until 2018.
115 Wong mentioned these names in Vogel 2018.
116 Vincent van Gogh, letter to Theo van Gogh, 16 October 1888 [705]: 'My eyes are still tired, but anyway I had a new idea in mind, and here's the croquis of it. No. 30 canvas once again. This time it's simply my bedroom, but the colour has to do the job here, and through its being simplified by giving a grander style to things, to be suggestive here *of rest* or *of sleep* in general. In short, looking at the painting should *rest* the mind, or rather, the imagination.' See also Van Tilborgh 2016b.
117 I am grateful to Peter Shear for the reference.
118 Titled *Day by Night*, the show ran from 11 January to 16 March 2019.
119 *Blue*, Karma, New York, 8 November 2019–5 January 2020.
120 See Spector 2021.
121 Conversation with Benjamin Styer, 9 May 2023.
122 Conversation with Monita Wong, 9 October 2022.
123 Vogel 2018: 'My process is not limited to the time spent in my studio painting, in fact I would say over the past year the making of my work has come to a rhythm where most of the work is done in idle moments when I am at home daydreaming, or watching movies and listening to music, drinking coffee or going out on walks that have no destination or purpose in mind. During these in-between moments I'll often have quick flashes of imagery appear in and out of my thoughts, they could be shaped or triggered by something I saw or heard out in the world, an artwork I have seen, and more and more the works I have done in the past. Going by intuition and my emotions I will then head to the studio and set out to elaborate in paint these vague glimpses I get.'
124 See Van Tilborgh 2022.
125 Conversation with Wong's artist friend Claire Colette, 5 May 2023.
126 Hertwig 2019.
127 Freeman 2019.

Rain Rising

Richard Shiff

1 Guzman 2012, p. 120. On 16 August 2015, in a Facebook message to fellow painter Peter Shear, Wong referred to 'operating on intuition rather than mastery' (Shear has generously shared this documentation). For essential aid in research, I thank Joost van der Hoeven, Peter Shear, Phoebe Zipper, John Semlitsch and Donato Loia.
2 Vogel 2018. Wong's reflection on the 'flow' of figuration recalls Pablo Picasso's similar understanding: 'To know what you want to draw, you have to begin [the process of] doing it'; Picasso (speaking in 1943), in Brassaï 1998, p. 113 ('Pour savoir ce qu'on veut dessiner, il faut commencer à le faire').
3 See, for example, Cox 2021, p. 11. Wong referred to many of the artists who concerned him in his electronic correspondence with Shear.
4 Matthew Wong, Facebook message to Peter Shear, 8 July 2015: Neither the Van Gogh nor the Wong can be identified today as the post was deleted.
5 Among similar works by Doig, *Rosedale* may have come to Wong's attention because of its well-publicized record-breaking auction price at Phillips, London, in May 2017. In his electronic correspondence with Shear, Wong turns characteristically abruptly from one reference to another – in late 2015, he went from discussing Doig's representational imagery to an appreciation of Martin Barré's non-referential abstractions.
6 See W. Wong 2021.
7 See Shiff 2015.
8 Vincent van Gogh, letter to Theo van Gogh,

Munch n.d.
Edvard Munch, 'By the Shore, Melancholy', handwritten note, n.d., N 664, folio 1r., in *eMunch: Edvard Munch's Writings, English Edition*, trans. Francesca M. Nichols: emunch.no/english

Roberts 2010
John Roberts, 'Art After Deskilling', *Historical Materialism* 18 (2010), pp. 77–96

Saltz 2018
Jerry Saltz, 'Losing Myself in the Paintings of Facebook-Educated Matthew Wong', *Vulture*, 19 April 2018: vulture.com/2018/04/losing-myself-in-the-art-of-facebook-educated-matthew-wong.html

Schachter 2020
Kenny Schachter, 'Remembering the Beautiful Melancholy of Matthew Wong', *The Art Newspaper*, 21 August 2020: theartnewspaper.com/2020/08/21/remembering-the-beautiful-melancholy-of-matthew-wong

Shiff 2001
Richard Shiff, 'Realism of Low Resolution: Digitisation and Modern Painting', in Terry Smith (ed.), *Impossible Presence: Surface and Screen in the Photogenic Era*, Chicago 2001, pp. 124–56

Shiff 2002
Richard Shiff, 'Puppet and Test Pattern: Mechanicity and Materiality in Modern Pictorial Representation', in Bruce Clarke and Linda Dalrymple Henderson (eds.), *From Energy to Information: Representation in Science and Technology, Art, and Literature*, Stanford 2002, pp. 327–50

Shiff 2010
Richard Shiff, 'Dream of Abstraction', in Terence Maloon (ed.), *Paths to Abstraction 1867–1917*, Munich 2010, pp. 52–69

Shiff 2015
Richard Shiff, 'Optiken [Optics]', in Christoph Schreier (ed.), *New York Painting*, Cologne 2015, pp. 28–52

Smith 2019
Roberta Smith, 'A Final Rhapsody in Blue from Matthew Wong', *The New York Times*, 24 December 2019

Spector 2021
Nancy Spector, 'The Blue in You', in Cox 2021, pp. 18-27

Taine 1875 [1870]
Hippolyte Taine, *On Intelligence*, trans. T.D. Haye, 2 vols., New York 1875 [1870]

Van Tilborgh 2016a
Louis van Tilborgh, 'An Introduction: Seeking Calm in the Storm', in *On the Verge of Insanity: Van Gogh and his Illness*, exh. cat., Amsterdam (Van Gogh Museum) 2016, pp. 13–28

Van Tilborgh 2016b
Louis van Tilborgh, 'Van Gogh's Quest for Affection and Peace of Mind', in Gloria Groom (ed.), *Van Gogh's Bedrooms*, exh. cat., Chicago (Art Institute of Chicago) 2016, pp. 50–67

Van Tilborgh 2018
Louis van Tilborgh, 'In the light of Japan: Van Gogh's quest for happiness and a modern identity', in Louis van Tilborgh et al., *Van Gogh and Japan*, exh. cat., Amsterdam (Van Gogh Museum) 2018, pp. 40–91

Van Tilborgh 2022
Louis van Tilborgh, 'Van Gogh, Gauguin and Rembrandt: On Chairs, Portraits and Poetry', *Simiolus: Netherlands Quarterly for the History of Art* 43 (2022), no. 4, pp. 331–52

Vellekoop and Zwikker 2007
Marije Vellekoop and Roelie Zwikker with the assistance of Monique Hageman, *Vincent van Gogh, Drawings 4: Arles, Saint-Rémy & Auvers-sur-Oise, 1888–1890* (2 vols.), Amsterdam / Zwolle 2007

Vogel 2018
Maria Vogel, 'Matthew Wong Reflects on the Melancholy of Life', *Art of Choice*, 15 November 2018: artofchoice.co/matthew-wong-reflects-on-the-melancholy-of-life

M. Wong 2012
Matthew Wong, *Thesis Project Interim Report*, 2012 (Matthew Wong Foundation Archive)

M. Wong 2013
Matthew Wong, 'Artist Statement', 2013, published in Paul Behnke, 'Artist Profile: Matthew Wong', *Structure and Imagery: A Contemporary Art Blog*, 4 November 2013: structureandimagery.blogspot.com

M. Wong 2015
Pulse of the Land, exh. cat., Hong Kong (Hong Kong Visual Arts Centre), 2015

M. Wong 2018
Matthew Wong, exh. cat., New York (Karma) 2018

Miss Wong 2014
Miss Wong, 'They Are Artists: Matthew Wong', *Altermodernists* (blog), 29 October 2014 (Matthew Wong Foundation Archive)

W. Wong 2021
Winnie Wong, 'The Colour of Colour', in Cox 2021, pp. 28-35

Yau 2018
John Yau, 'Matthew Wong's Hallucinatory Pilgrimages', *Hyperallergic*, 22 April 2018: hyperallergic.com/439090/matthew-wong-karma-2018

Yau 2022
John Yau, 'Matthew Wong in Los Angeles', in *Matthew Wong. The New World*, exh. cat., New York (Cheim & Read) 2022, unpaginated

List of Works in the Exhibition

Vincent van Gogh

Paintings by Vincent van Gogh

Trees and Undergrowth, 1887
Oil on canvas, 46.2 × 55.2 cm
Van Gogh Museum, Amsterdam
(Vincent van Gogh Foundation)

The Bedroom, 1888
Oil on canvas, 72.4 × 91.3 cm
Van Gogh Museum, Amsterdam
(Vincent van Gogh Foundation)

Wheatfield, 1888
Oil on canvas, 54 × 65 cm
Van Gogh Museum, Amsterdam
(Vincent van Gogh Foundation)

Garden of the Asylum, 1889
Oil on canvas, 72 × 91 cm
Van Gogh Museum, Amsterdam
(Vincent van Gogh Foundation,
gift of Paul Gachet jr.)

Wheatfield with a Reaper, 1889
Oil on canvas, 73.2 × 92.7 cm
Van Gogh Museum, Amsterdam
(Vincent van Gogh Foundation)

Works on paper by Vincent van Gogh

Landscape with Hut, 1888
Pencil, pen and reed pen and ink on paper,
34.8 × 25.7 cm
Van Gogh Museum, Amsterdam
(Vincent van Gogh Foundation)

Matthew Wong

Paintings by Matthew Wong

Valley, 2014
Oil on canvas, 100 × 157.5 cm
Private collection

Contemplating Infinity, 2015
Oil on canvas, 144 × 114 cm
Matthew Wong Foundation

Nostalgia, 2016
Acrylic on canvas, 50.8 × 40.6 cm
Private collection, Wilfram AG, St. Moritz

The Sun, 2016
Acrylic on canvas, 61 × 50.8 cm
Courtesy of Level & Co

Far Away Eyes, 2017
Oil on canvas, 66 × 147.5 cm
Private collection

Figure in a Landscape, 2017
Oil on canvas, 50.8 × 40.6 cm
Collection of John Cheim

Landscape with Mother and Child, 2017
Oil on canvas, 71.1 × 55.9 cm
Brooker-Pardee Family Collection

Morning Landscape, 2017
Oil on canvas, 91.4 × 121.9 cm
Cindy and Armond Schwartz

Old Town, 2017
Oil on canvas, 243.8 × 183.9 cm
Green Family Art Foundation; courtesy
Adam Green Art Advisory

So Much Depends..., 2017
Oil on canvas, 61 × 50.8 cm
Matthew Wong Foundation

The Journey Home, 2017
Oil on three panels, 50.5 × 40.5 cm
Private collection, courtesy of HomeArt

The Kingdom, 2017
Oil on canvas, 121.9 × 182.9 cm
Liz Lange and David Shapiro

The Other Side of the Moon, 2017
Acrylic on canvas, 91.4 × 61 cm
Private collection

The Realm of Appearances, 2017
Acrylic on canvas, 101.6 × 76.2 cm
Matthew Wong Foundation

The West, 2017
Oil on canvas, 99.1 × 78.7 cm
Dallas Museum of Art. Dallas Art Fair
Foundation Acquisition Fund

Untitled, 2017
Oil on canvas, 182.9 × 121.9 cm
Private collection, courtesy of HomeArt

Untitled, 2017
Oil on canvas, 182.9 × 121.9 cm
Private collection

A Walk Through Primordial Garden, 2018
Oil on canvas, 101.6 × 76.2 cm
Matthew Wong Foundation

Coming of Age Landscape, 2018
Oil on canvas, 152.4 × 177.8 cm
Private collection, courtesy of HomeArt

Day 4, 2018
Oil on canvas, 203.2 × 165.1 cm
Josh Abraham

Dark Reverie, 2018
Oil on canvas, 76.2 × 101.6 cm
THE EKARD COLLECTION

Dialogue, 2018
Oil on canvas, 76.2 × 101.6 cm
Collection of Lisa and Michael Cotton

Good Morning, 2018
Oil on canvas, 101.6 × 76.2 cm
Private European Collection

Night Crossing, 2018
Oil on canvas, 121.9 × 152.4 cm
Collection of Nancy and Sean Cotton

Night 4, 2018
Oil on canvas, 203.2 × 165.1 cm
Private collection

Night Moods, 2018
Oil on canvas, 91.4 × 121.9 cm
Matthew Wong Foundation

Ripple in the Night, 2018
Oil on canvas, 101.6 × 76.2 cm
Matthew Wong Foundation

Solitude, 2018
Oil on canvas, 121.9 × 91.4 cm
Matthew Wong Foundation

Acknowledgements

This exhibition and catalogue have come about with the help of many people to all of whom I am sincerely grateful. Among those who have assisted me, my thanks are due in the first place to Monita Wong – Matthew Wong's mother and chair of the Matthew Wong Foundation. We met in Basel, New York, Amsterdam, Edmonton, Dallas and London, and on each occasion she found the time to share her son's story with me in conversations lasting hours on end. Monita introduced me to his friends and made herself available to answer my many and varied questions. Moreover, she was also generous enough to lend thirty-one works to the exhibition. I would like to take this opportunity to express not only my gratitude to her, but also my admiration. With enviable drive and passion, Monita has given herself over entirely to her son's legacy, working tirelessly on this mission while still having to contend every day with her immense loss. I respect her hugely for that and am incredibly grateful to her for all her help. It has been a privilege to be allowed into her life and that of her son.

Monita is supported in all this by her husband Raymond Wong, who accompanies her on all the trips and assists in all her activities. I am very much indebted to him too. John Cheim is also intimately involved with the Matthew Wong Foundation: having been Matthew's mentor during his life, he has remained faithful to that role ever since. John has likewise been crucial to this project, for which I am very much in his debt. The team from Cheim & Read gallery – Maria Bueno, Sara Hutchins, Howard Read and Charlotte Dozier – were similarly indispensable. I am also grateful to Winnie Ip, Brian Wong and Elizabeth Donnelly of the Matthew Wong Foundation for their help.

In the course of my research for the exhibition and this catalogue, I interviewed many of Matthew Wong's friends, part of the online community Matthew forged throughout his artistic career. I spoke to several friends of the family too. Everyone I approached was not only willing to talk to me, but did so with considerable patience, attention and candour. This project would not have been possible without their generosity. Of this group, I would like to begin by thanking Peter Shear, Sofia Silva, Brendan Dugan and Benjamin Styer for their interviews and for sharing with me their online correspondence or extracts from it: these proved to be vital primary sources. I am additionally grateful to Ludovica Barbieri, Fedor Deichmann, Jerry Saltz, Kenny Schachter, Nicole Wittenberg and Jonas Wood for consenting not only to be interviewed for my research but also on camera for the exhibition video. My sincere thanks are also due to the following for their willingness to speak to me: Josh Abraham, Claudia Albertini, Paul Behnke, Claire Colette, Frank Elbaz, Shaun Ellison, Kate Feng, Louis Fratino, Xavier Fuller, Paul Galvez, Jennifer Guidi, Kristy Heroy, Nikil Inaya, Scott Kahn, Amy Lam, Siniša Mačković, Phillip Meyer, Soumya Netrabile, John Pardee, Nicolas Party, Brad Phillips, Andrew Pope, Rebecca Ryba, Barry Schwabsky, Clark Siu, Frank Tough, Stephen Truax, Cody Tumblin and Michelle Wong. It was my privilege to receive an especially beautiful and informative essay from John Wall Barger, while Darby Milbrath and Peter Kennedy also provided me with information. I am very grateful, moreover, to Vivian Li – curator of the first museum survey of Matthew Wong's work – for her advice, and also for that of Lesley Ma, Julian Cox, Raffi Khatchadourian and Matthew Higgs.

Besides all the help I have received from Matthew Wong's family, friends and admirers, my special thanks go to all those who have worked on this project with me. Beginning with Emilie Gordenker, Director of the Van Gogh Museum, for the trust she has given me in compiling what is an unusual exhibition for this museum and for her commitment, advice and support. I would also like to thank the following:

The co-authors of this publication – Kenny Schachter, Richard Shiff, Sofia Silva and John Yau – whose inspired and pertinent essays form a material contribution to the emerging discourse surrounding Matthew Wong's work. The coordinating editor Heleen Ruijg and the Head of Publications at the Van Gogh Museum, Anniek Meinders, oversaw the production of this magnificent catalogue with vigour and vision, working closely with Ronny Gobyn and Barbara Costermans of Tijdsbeeld publishers. The elegant design was provided by Janpieter Chielens with Monique den Ouden, Suzanne Krom and Roxanne van den Bosch as picture editors. Maite van Dijk, Sara Tas, Teio Meedendorp, Harma van Uffelen, Sofia Silva, John Cheim and Monita Wong were thorough and informative readers of the text, the English version of which was copy-edited by Kate Bell and the Dutch by Els Brinkman. The translations are the diligent work of Ted Alkins for the English and Betty Klaasse for the Dutch.

In addition to all those whose combined work made this catalogue possible, I would like to thank everyone involved in the realization of the exhibition. As the enthusiastic project manager, Sander Rutjens has been the hub of all activities, while educator Harma van Uffelen has taken the exhibition to a higher level with her vision and focus. The distinguished exhibition design is the work of Willemijn Somers and Julian Kleyn of Studio Berry Slok. Registrars Mechtild Beckers and Frederieke Melsen, and the head of the Registrar's Office Annemieke Bouma-Bouwmans arranged the many loans and ensured that the artworks were transported flawlessly. Each of the following colleagues contributed their expertise to the exhibition: Corinne Jongh, Eline van Beek, Josine Vermei, Edwin Kolster, Amber Honing, Marguerite van Poll, Sarah Sprenger, Celine Rusman, Margot van den Burg, Bénine Stuijt, Charlotte Kösters, Marloes Bakuwel, Nina Bos, Alise Akimova and Babette Meerdink-Schenau. My special thanks are also due to Anna Jordans of Mals Media for the wonderful video she and Else Siemerink made for the exhibition. Nikolai van Nunen was responsible for the outstanding camerawork and Tim Schijf for the editing. The audio tour created for the exhibition by Simon Heijmans, meanwhile, is a work of art in itself.

I am likewise grateful to Maria Ararat Cortès, Agustín Arteaga, Hilda Bakker, Nienke Bakker, Evan Beard, Aukje Beenhakker, Martine Blok, Ann Blokland, Jonathan Boos, Lisa van den Bos, Amy Cappellazzo, Melissa Carn, Alex Chapin, Jonathan Cheung, Paul van Dalsen, Chase Dougherty, Nadia Dougherty, Lucia Dunlap, Yonnie Fu, Bregje Gerritse, Lily Goldberg, Michiel Goosen, Rob Groot, Astrid Grootson, Sonia Gunning, Jen Hua, Martijn Jacobsen, Aida Jellinghaus, Andrew Kambel, GiGi Kisgen, Luuk van de Klundert, Emily Kodama, Eden Kösters, Alina Krotenko, Michelle Kwok, Sabrina Lovett, Courtney Lynch, Nicole di Mauro, Chloe McWhirt, Mike Morret, Maria Nonato, Emily Pantelias Garces, Aucke Paulusma, Steven Platzman, Clarissa Post, Henry Primmer-Pyke, Katie Province, Susan Reynolds, Robert Ritter, Fleur Roos Rosa de Carvalho, Kathryn Sawabini, Caroline Shields, Lukas Steffen, Michael Stines, Bailey Summers, Matthew Teitelbaum, Abigail Thomas, Ghyslaine Tromp, Marije Vellekoop, Jay Vince, Amanda Vollenweider, Rosaline Wong and HomeArt, Kels Xuan, Jennifer Yum, Aki Zhu and Ilias Zian.

Our museum partner for this exhibition, the Kunsthaus Zürich, has been a delightful and stimulating collaborator, to whom I am likewise indebted. I offer my sincere gratitude to Ann Demeester, Franziska Lentzsch, Philippe Buettner and Jonas Beyer from the Kunsthaus. This fine partnership means that it will be possible to see the exhibition in Europe for almost a year.

Joost van der Hoeven

Photo Credits

Every effort has been made to trace and credit all known copyright or reproduction right holders; the publishers apologize for any errors or omissions and welcome these being brought to their attention.

Copyright of works of visual artists affiliated to a CISAC organization has been arranged with Pictoright in Amsterdam, © c/o Pictoright Amsterdam 2024. Unless otherwise noted, photography of artworks in the collection of the Matthew Wong Foundation are by the Matthew Wong Foundation and are copyrighted by the Matthew Wong Foundation.

All images of work from the Matthew Wong Foundation © 2024 Matthew Wong Foundation, New York / c/o Pictoright Amsterdam 2024

Van Gogh Museum, Amsterdam (Vincent van Gogh Foundation): 36, 51, 56, 59, 67, 99, 112, 119

Adam Green Art Advisory: 52
© The estate of Etel Adnan, courtesy Galerie Lelong & Co., Paris, photo Primae/Louis Bourjac: 89
Album/Scala, Florence: 108
Alexandre Gallery, New York: 58
Brian Buckley: 54
Cheim & Read, New York, photo Alex Yudzon: 2, 87
Cincinnati Art Museum/Bridgeman Images: 49
Dallas Museum of Art: 39, 95
DeAgostini Picture Library/New Picture Library/ Scala, Florence: 48
DeAgostini Picture Library/Scala, Florence: 46
Jim Frank: 60
Frankie Rossi Art Projects, London/Bridgeman Images: 23
HomeArt: 5, 43, 66
Joan Mitchell Foundation, New York: 93
Kröller-Müller Museum, Otterlo, photo Rik Klein Gotink: 6
Kunstmuseum Bern: 19
Level & Co., New York: 31
The Metropolitan Museum of Art/Art Resource/ Scala, Florence: 7
Estate of David Milne, represented exclusively by Mira Godard Gallery, Toronto: 32
Minneapolis Institute of Art: 26
Museum of Contemporary Art, Chicago, photo Nathan Keay: 34
The Museum of Modern Art, New York: 125
The Museum of Modern Art, New York/Scala, Florence: 12
Peter Blum Gallery, New York: 104
Philadelphia Museum of Art/Art Resource/Scala, Florence: 103
Phillips Auctioneers LLC, London: 70, 82
Pierluigi Siena: 3
Saint Louis Art Museum / © 2024 Succession H. Matisse: 28
Scala, Florence: 64, 80
Jeffrey Sturges: 55
© 2024 Whitney Museum of American Art, New York/Scala, Florence: 16
Jonas Wood, photo Marten Elder: 33
© Christopher Wool. Courtesy of the artist: 4

Chronology
p. 162: Courtesy of Mingpao (A), the Matthew Wong Foundation (B, C) and Peter Shear (D)
p. 164: Courtesy of the Matthew Wong Foundation (E), MASSIMODECARLO (F), Karma (G) and Jonas Wood (H)
p. 176: Studio Matthew Wong, Edmonton, photo Nikolai van Nunen

Details and cover
Front cover: Matthew Wong, *Unknown Pleasures*, 2019 (fig. 125)
Back cover: Vincent van Gogh, *Wheatfield*, 1888 (fig. 51)
Contents (pp. 4–5): Matthew Wong, *Night Crossing*, 2018 (detail of fig. 61)

Colophon

This catalogue was published on the occasion of the exhibition:
Matthew Wong | Vincent van Gogh: Painting as a Last Resort

Van Gogh Museum, Amsterdam
1 March – 1 September 2024

Kunsthaus Zürich
20 September 2024 – 26 January 2025

The exhibition was co-organized by the Van Gogh Museum, Amsterdam and Kunsthaus Zürich.

Editor
Joost van der Hoeven

Authors
Joost van der Hoeven, Kenny Schachter, Richard Shiff, Sofia Silva and John Yau

Editorial board
John Cheim, Maite van Dijk, Teio Meedendorp, Sofia Silva, Sara Tas, Harma van Uffelen and Monita Wong

TIJDSBEELD PUBLISHING

Publisher
Ronny Gobyn

Project management
Barbara Costermans

Design
Janpieter Chielens

VAN GOGH MUSEUM

Publications management
Anniek Meinders

Coordination
Heleen Ruijg

Image editors
Roxanne van den Bosch and Monique den Ouden

Copy-editing
Kate Bell

Translation
Ted Alkins

Colour separations and printing
Graphius, Ghent

First published in the United Kingdom in 2024 by Thames & Hudson Ltd, 181A High Holborn, London WC1V 7QX

First published in the United States of America in 2024 by Thames & Hudson Inc., 500 Fifth Avenue, New York, New York 10110

British Library Cataloguing-in-Publication Data
A catalogue record for this book is available from the British Library

Library of Congress Catalog Card Number 2023951364

ISBN 978-0-500-29805-3

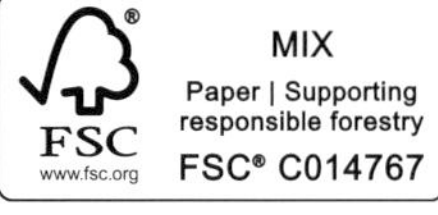

The exhibition at the Van Gogh Museum and this catalogue were made possible by the support of:

Matthew Wong Foundation;
Monita and Raymond Wong

Main partners Van Gogh Museum

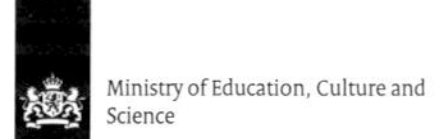

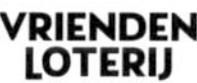

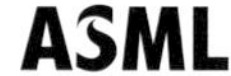

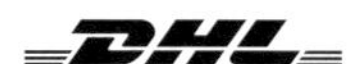

Exhibition partners Van Gogh Museum

FONDS 21

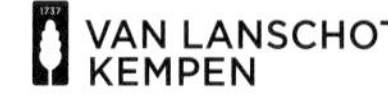

Sunflower Circle

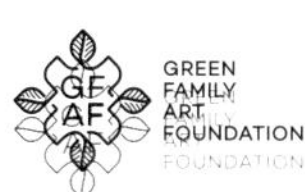

The exhibition was also made possible by the generous support of Rosaline Wong and HomeArt.

The exhibition has been supported by the Dutch government: an indemnity grant has been provided by the Cultural Heritage Agency of the Netherlands on behalf of the Minister of Education, Culture and Science.

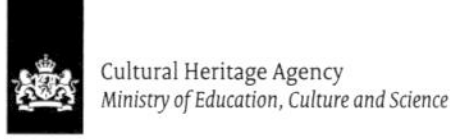

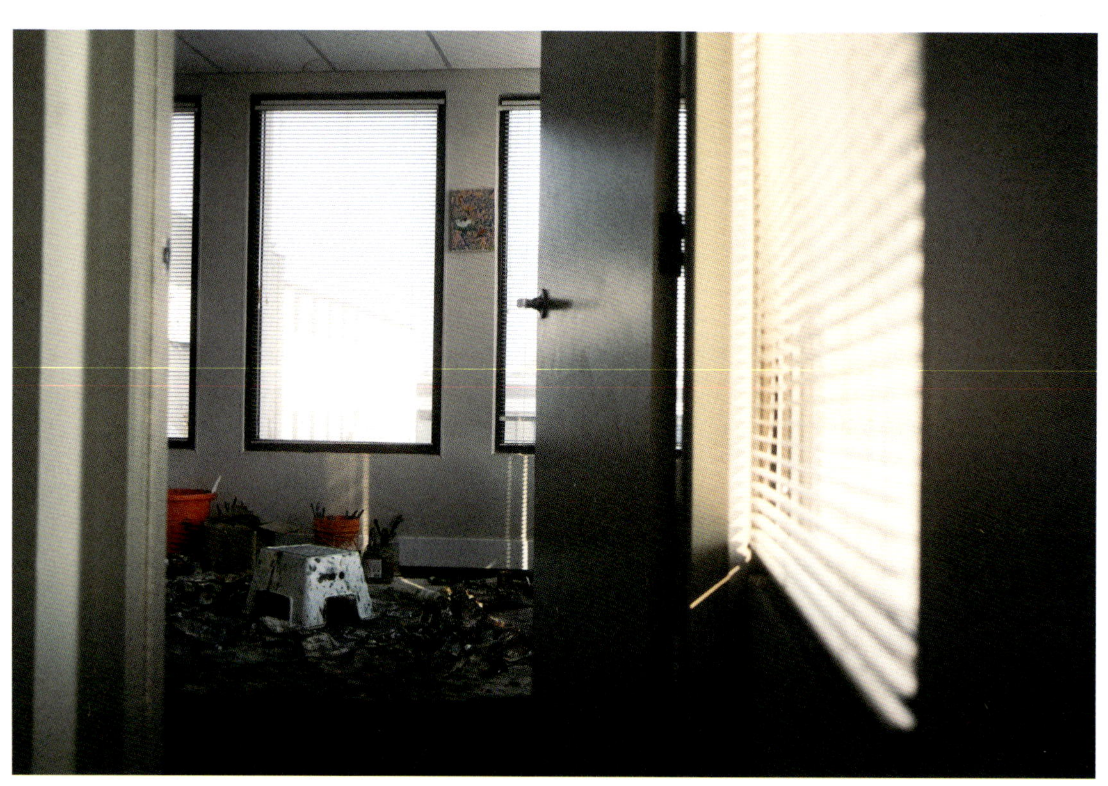